Model-Based Systems Engineering and Requirements Definition

Achieving a Uniform Management and Engineering System View

Dennis Hansen

Apress®

__Model-Based Systems Engineering and Requirements Definition: Achieving a Uniform Management and Engineering System View__

Dennis Hansen
Satellite Beach, FL, USA

ISBN-13 (pbk): 979-8-8688-2042-7   ISBN-13 (electronic): 979-8-8688-2043-4
https://doi.org/10.1007/979-8-8688-2043-4

Managing Director, Apress Media LLC: Welmoed Spahr
Acquisitions Editor: Melissa Duffy
Editorial Assistant: Gryffin Winkler

Cover designed by eStudioCalamar

Cover image designed by Pexels

Distributed to the book trade worldwide by Springer Science+Business Media New York, 1 New York Plaza, New York, NY 10004. Phone 1-800-SPRINGER, fax (201) 348-4505, e-mail orders-ny@springer-sbm.com, or visit www.springeronline.com. Apress Media, LLC is a Delaware LLC and the sole member (owner) is Springer Science + Business Media Finance Inc (SSBM Finance Inc). SSBM Finance Inc is a **Delaware** corporation.

For information on translations, please e-mail booktranslations@springernature.com; for reprint, paperback, or audio rights, please e-mail bookpermissions@springernature.com.

Apress titles may be purchased in bulk for academic, corporate, or promotional use. eBook versions and licenses are also available for most titles. For more information, reference our Print and eBook Bulk Sales web page at http://www.apress.com/bulk-sales.

Any source code or other supplementary material referenced by the author in this book is available to readers on GitHub. For more detailed information, please visit https://www.apress.com/gp/services/source-code.

If disposing of this product, please recycle the paper

I dedicate this book to my wife of 62 years, without whose love and support this book would not be possible.

Table of Contents

About the Author

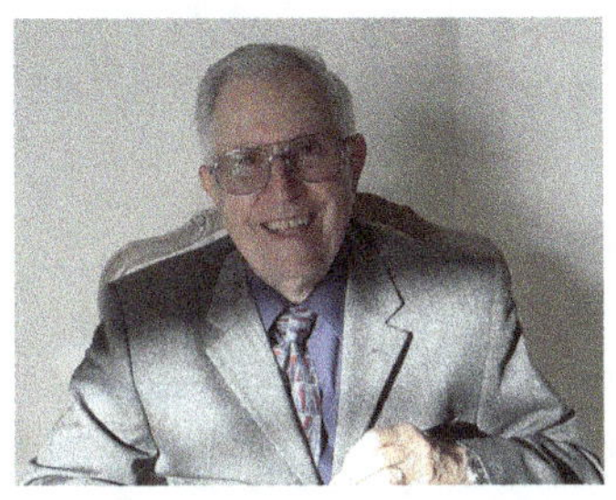 **Dennis Hansen**'s career spans more than 60 years, supporting programs such as the Defense Meteorological Satellite Program and the GOES-R weather satellite ground system development and sustainment programs in both systems engineering and management roles. Combined with his work providing support to other programs, he has observed problems and successes spanning a complete system life cycle. During his career, he has participated in the evolution of ground systems from analog to digital implementations and the incorporation of computer technology for command and control, telemetry analysis, and mission planning. Now retired from the corporate realm, Dennis continues to follow the evolution of programs and technology through membership in the Air & Space Forces Association, IEEE, AIAA, and the American Meteorological Society. In daily life, he keeps in touch with associates from his previous work life and occasionally has lunch with his previous program teams and with neighbors.

About the Technical Reviewer

 **Swapnil Shevate** is a Lead Senior Site Reliability Engineering professional and an expert with more than a decade of industry experience working in fast-paced production environments.

Throughout his career, he has launched hundreds of critical products working for renowned companies that define the standards for the rest of the information technology industry. He is a subject matter expert in the field of Site Reliability Engineering and DevOps with expertise in several domains like Cloud Computing, Architecture, System Design/ Engineering, Distributed Systems, Kubernetes, Amazon Web Services, Payment Systems (PCI Compliance), and more. He is an author and technical reviewer for several popular media publications which are among the top sellers today. He is an excellent speaker with a detail-oriented skill set when it comes to researching topics, deep diving, providing mentorship, and disseminating knowledge with engineers across the industry. Swapnil graduated from the Indiana University-Purdue University Indianapolis with a master's degree in Informatics.

Acknowledgments

I am indebted to the many colleagues who have guided my career progression and, consequently, the foundation of this book. Notably, I would like to thank Maj. General Stephen McElroy for encouraging me to work on both space and ground systems, Frank Misciasci for his guidance in collaborating with end users and acquisition organizations to define system requirements, Mike Singer for his support on the GOES-R program, and Macaulay Osaisai for our numerous discussions on the approaches and benefits of MBSE. There are many others, too numerous to mention, who have influenced my career over the past 60+ years.

Introduction

Materials in this section should be of use to both engineers and managers. For engineers, it addresses steps in the process. For managers, it highlights the basis in public law and areas of work that should be closely monitored to ensure that the system's definition has been covered and does not stray from the intent of the mission being accommodated.

This book has been structured to aid the end user (customer) program offices, development organization program managers, development engineering, and the engineering support team (i.e., Federally Funded Research and Development (FFRDC) team support). It deals with how Model-Based System Architecture (MBSA) and Model-Based System Engineering (MBSE) can be used to reliably define and track system development. It calls out specific MBSA/MBSE views but does not go into depth on all aspects of modeling languages, such as the DoD Architecture Framework (DoDAF) and SysML. The book uses a scenario-based approach, using the development of a satellite ground system as an example, to walk using MBSA/MBSA throughout the system's life cycle.

The satellite ground system scenario illustrates the use of MBSA and MBSE to properly define the system and system capabilities and requirements under consideration. Later in the system development, the model provides a roadmap to ensure that all system elements are correctly structured and aligned to the system requirements. After system deployment, the model can be used to assess potential upgrades/modifications. Note that references to government requirements do not limit the use of this book for government purposes alone.

The use of a modeling language for the definition of a system is not new and dates to the early 1980s. In terms of Government contracting, the concept was formalized in the Clinger-Cohen Act (Part of Public Law No. 104-106-Feb. 10, 1996) Division E; Subtitle C; SEC. 5125. (AGENCY CHIEF INFORMATION OFFICER); (b)(2)(3) (Refer to (d) for the definition of Information Technology Architecture) [1]. It is important to note that the law applies to all executive agencies of the federal government, including the Department of Defense (DoD), Department of Commerce (DoC), etc. Each agency has developed its own architecture framework to comply with the mandate. For example, the original DoDAF version 1.0 and version 1.5 Volume I: Definitions and Guidelines Section

Table 3-1 [2] refers to Clinger-Cohen and the general definition as a basis for DoDAF. An often-overlooked point is that this act emphasized preparation for system procurement and the use/support of systems and the associated budgeting. In other words, the use of an architecture framework was to ensure the proposed/supported system is defined as a basis for the budget.

The expanded use of Information Technology (IT) was a primary driver for adding specific provisions into public law to control the proliferation and management of IT systems. Within the DoD, the use of DoDAF was prudently extended to non-IT systems. For example, an aircraft may be the focus in an Operations View-1 (OV-1) diagram to define the mission application. Additional views from DoDAF may be used to define aircraft activities and interfaces. Note that the OV-1 view is the graphical view containing the proposed item or items and how they operationally relate to perform a mission. This Operations View-1 (OV-1) pictorial is most often seen in briefings and potential news releases.

Note that the DoD Architecture Framework is used in this book for initial capability and activity definition; however, other agencies have their own frameworks, for example, the Federal Enterprise Architecture Framework (FEAF). In terms of methodologies, there were earlier attempts to develop an approach to model and define systems. Examples include Integration Definition (IDEF), Object-Oriented Modeling and Design, and the currently used Unified Modeling Language (UML) which was extended for SysML. There are current moves to use the Unified Architecture Framework (UAF) in place of DoDAF; however, regardless of the framework used, there are always initial architectural views that can function as aids in defining system requirements.

An example of model and specification development for a satellite ground system is used to illustrate techniques that can be used. This includes an example of how the model can be updated to accommodate changes when the allocations between capabilities, activities, and supporting actions are determined necessary. The key is the progression of the thought process in defining the system, as illustrated below.

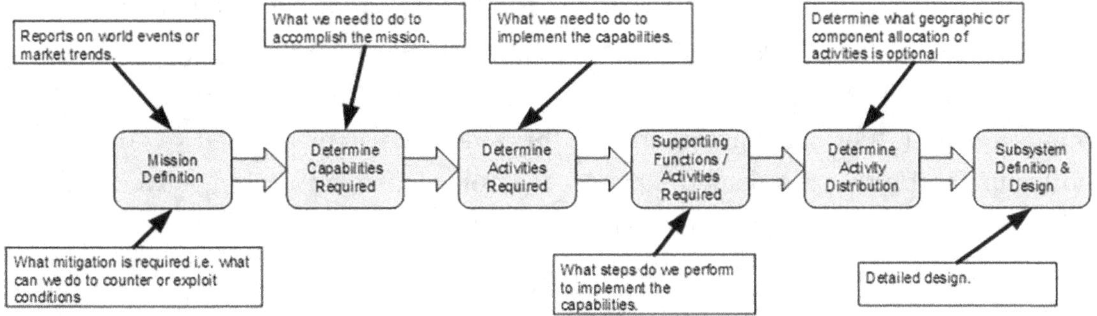

Key point. We are not considering commercial or off-the shelf items during the process until we reach detailed definition and design.

Progression of the thought process

The key point is that the engineering thought process used in generating these architectural views should be extended to system/subsystem/component requirement development. The architectural and engineering views are not products intended (in the case of a government program) to only meet CDRL (Contract Data Requirement List) requirements. Modeling aids in developing the system definition and providing a basis for specifications called for by the CDRL. Properly maintained, the models developed can be used in managing maintenance and upgrading of systems later in the life cycle. For long-term missions where market trends or world events are evolving, a copy of the model can be made using the original mission and capabilities as the starting point. The analysis and evolution of conditions can be continually updated during operation of the original system until it becomes clear that a new system is required. The remainder of the model will use this as the starting point.

Guide for Managers and Engineers

Materials in this section should be of use to both engineers and managers. For managers, it highlights the steps in the engineering process that will affect both cost and schedule. For the specific system being developed, each step could point to technical risks leading to cost and schedule risk.

We will look at the use of DoDAF and SysML as an aid for development and crosscheck of requirements throughout this book. Not all possible DoDAF views are used in this book. The views shown are the minimum set needed to develop requirements for the Capability Development Document (CDD), Technical Requirements Document (TRD), System and Subsystem Specifications. The focus of these views is not to perform the detailed design. As a result, not every possible DoDAF view is presented.

INTRODUCTION

The interplay between DoDAF and SysML is seldom mentioned in publications. There is no direct official linkage of DoDAF and SysML; however, there have been presentations given by personnel from agencies such as the Defence Information Systems Agency (DISA) that have addressed the issue. Keep in mind that DoDAF is architecture and SysML is system design. An example of the relationship between the DoDAF (white boxes) and SysML views is shown below.

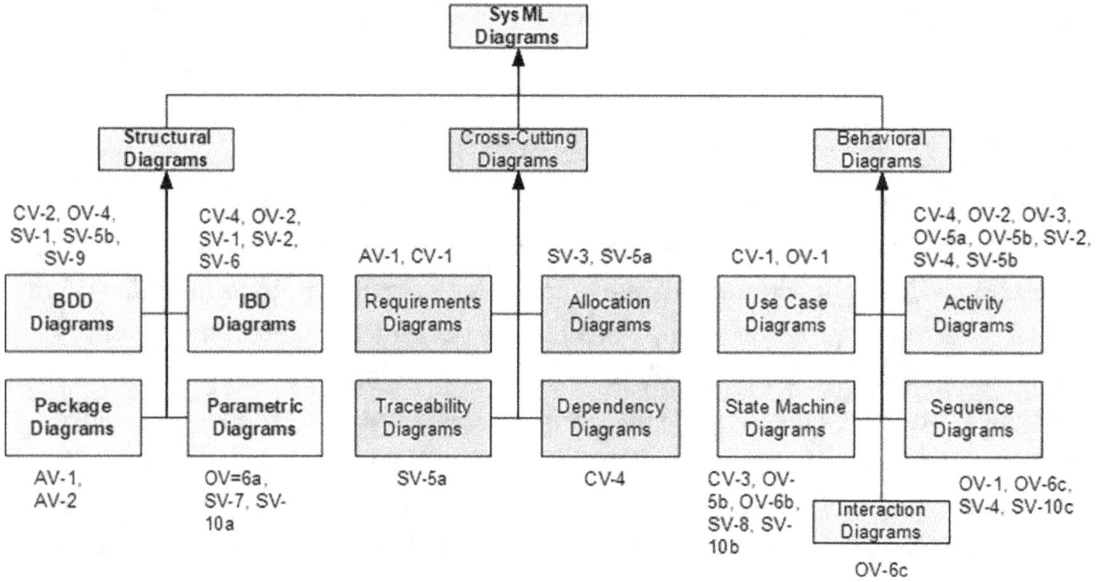

DoDAF vs. SysML equivalence

Graphical representations may look similar or the same in some cases; however, the background information gathered for each model element and the interfaces will, in many cases, be more detailed in the case of SysML to support design vs. architecture definition. The Modeling tools available are built upon a database and a toolset to develop graphical views and document associated requirements and constraints. Building upon a database makes it easy to keep all the information for each element and interface in one place. If the engineer only draws graphics with the tools and skips the documentation step, they are NOT performing MBSE or MBSA (Model-Based System Architecture)!

References

[1]   Clinger-Cohen Act (Part of Public Law No. 104-106-Feb. 10, 1996) Division E; Subtitle C; SEC. 5125. (AGENCY CHIEF INFORMATION OFFICER); (b)(2)(3) (Refer to (d) for the definition of Information Technology Architecture), `https://www.congress.gov/STATUTE-110-Pg186.pdf`

[2]   DoDAF version 1.0 and version 1.5 Volume I: Definitions and Guidelines Section Table 3-1

Acronym List

Acronym	Definition
CDD	Capability Development Document
CDRL	Contract Data Requirements List
DISA	Defense Information Systems Agency
DoC	Department of Commerce
DoD	Department of Defense
DoDAF	Department of Defense Architecture Framework
FEAF	Federal Enterprise Architecture Framework
FFRDC	Federally Funded Research and Development
IT	Information Technology
MBSA	Model-Based Systems Architecture
MBSE	Model-Based Systems Engineering
OV	Operations View
SySML	Systems Modeling Language
UML	Unified Modeling Language

CHAPTER 1

Project Initiation

Methodologies for Project Initiation and Management

System development and methodology are often described in terms of the Life Cycle V model (Figure 1-1). Simple and straightforward, this view covers the development of most systems. In terms of methodological execution, there has been a move toward Agile Systems Engineering, generally described by Figure 1-2. Note that the phases in the circular portion of the figure are essentially the left leg of the System Engineering V model. The primary difference between them is that the Agile version shows Stakeholder Needs vs. Stakeholder Requirements. For the purposes of modeling, consider these as equivalent statements since the needs are normally stated (by the acquisition agency) as capability requirements.

© Dennis Hansen 2025
D. Hansen, *Model-Based Systems Engineering and Requirements Definition*,
https://doi.org/10.1007/979-8-8688-2043-4_1

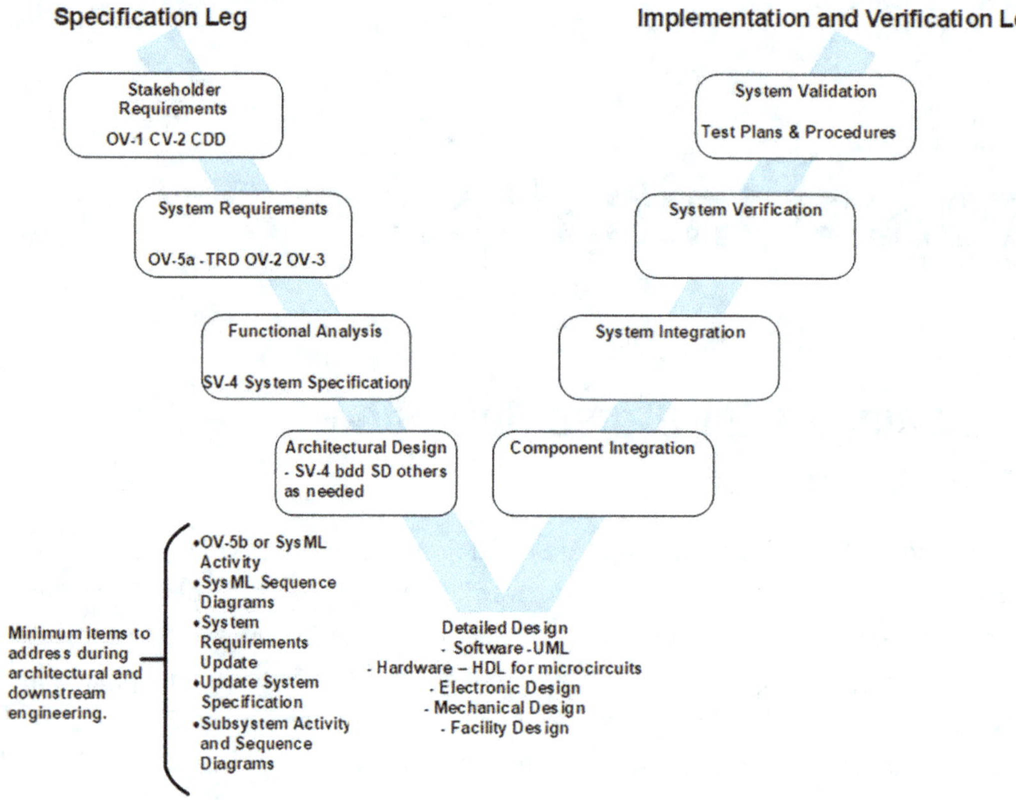

Figure 1-1. *Systems engineering V model*[1]

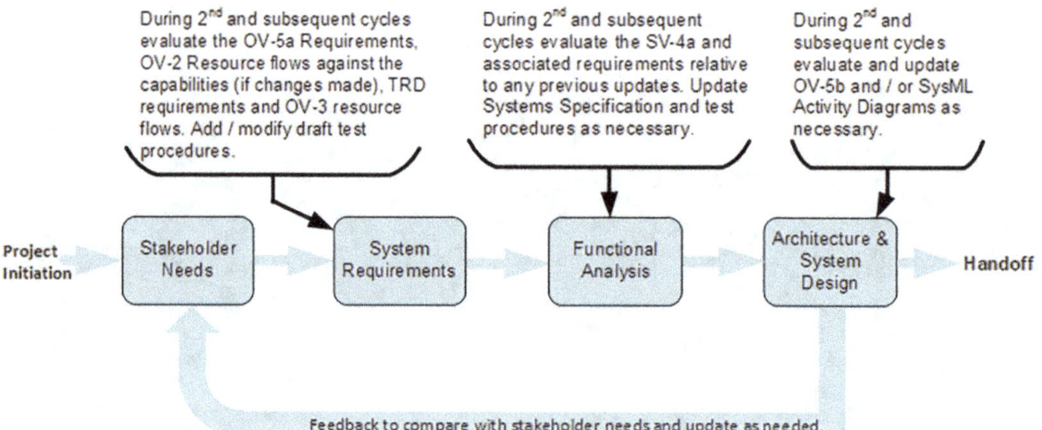

Figure 1-2. *Agile systems engineering workflow*[2]

---

[1] Author-created image

[2] Author-created image

The advent of Agile Systems Engineering has resulted in many programs, especially those with a tight schedule, defining and managing small to moderate-sized elements of work. Table 1-1 shows the relationship between the Systems Engineering V, Agile Systems Engineering Workflow, Recommended Model Views, and finally the Document involved.

Table 1-1. *Relationship between approaches and documents*

Systems engineering V model	Agile systems engineering workflow	Recommended model view	Document
Stakeholder requirements	Stakeholder needs	CV-2 capabilities taxonomy OV-1 high level operational concept[1]	Capability development document (CDD)
System requirements	System requirements	OV-5a activity taxonomy OV-2 operational resource flow and nodes[2] OV-3 operational resource flows matrix	Technical requirements document (TRD) Initial interface documents
Functional analysis	Functional analysis	SV-4 system functionality taxonomy	Systems specification
Architectural design	Architectural design	OV-5b operational activity model and/or SysML activity diagrams[3]	Subsystem and interface specifications

Notes:

1. The OV-1 is often drawn as a high-level graphic for presentations. It can also be constructed using a SysML Use Case diagram. For larger hardware/software systems, the SysML Block Definition Diagram approach can be used for transition to low-level design in the same model.
2. OV-2 can also be the basis for a high-level SysML Block Definition Diagram (BDD).
3. When considering the OV-5b development, consideration should be given to transitioning to SysML Activity Views since the OV-5b is based upon UML/SysML Activity Diagram. Refer to Chapter 4 coverage of the transition subject.

At each level of requirement definition—for example, stakeholder-level tasks—it is recommended to develop a capability taxonomy and a simple OV-1 graphic that clearly articulates the project's objective. Comparable model views should be created at each subsequent level of requirements development, tailored to the granularity and scope appropriate to that level.

The type of model used depends on the specific requirements being addressed. The model views referenced represent the minimum expected for the requirements level indicated in column 1.

Tasks at each level should be scheduled and broken down into short, measurable units. This structured approach helps maintain project focus and mitigates the risk of derailment due to ad hoc "new ideas" that fall outside the defined scope.

A way to avoid schedule issues using Agile methods [1] is shown in Figure 1-3. Note how the Project Backlog item Capability Document relates to an activity iteration. This iteration shows several actions to be accomplished. The iteration actions can be broken down into separate iterations to break up the work if necessary. Each of the other items in the backlog will also have one or more iterations. These backlog items and associated iterations can be used as a basis for the engineering portion of the program schedule. If the program level schedule is kept to just the backlog items, it is recommended that an engineering schedule be developed to cover the lower-level activities of the iterations.

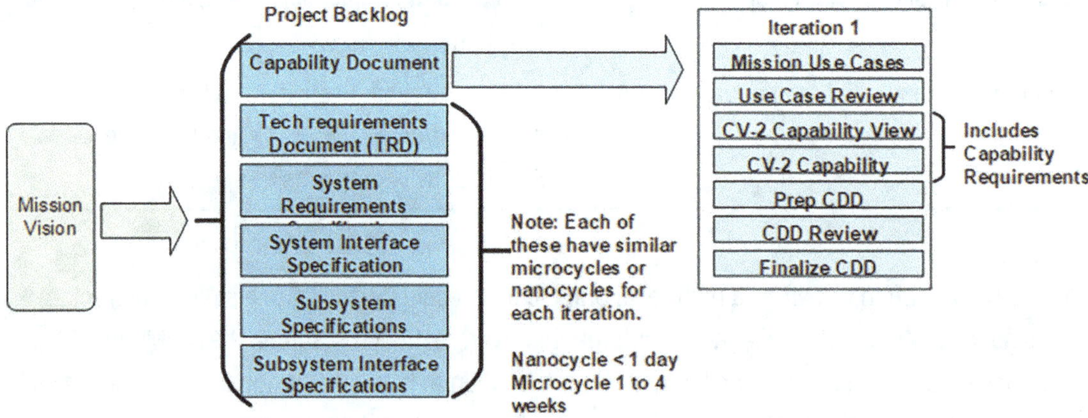

Figure 1-3. *Example of agile backlog*[3]

____

[3] Author-created image

Note that Iteration 1 in the graphic shows a capability view (CV-2) task. It is imperative that the applicable model views be included within each iteration for each level of the project backlog. Previously developed model views and requirements may need to be modified based on discoveries made during the progression of the project. In any case, it is important to continue to mature the model and requirements. This will ensure consistency throughout the modeling and requirements. Strong management and configuration control are recommended during the maturation process to ensure that the baseline does not drift.

Note that Downstream Engineering, shown at the bottom of the Engineering V, will most likely make use of UML for software and SysML for more detailed system design if required. This software UML and additional SysML definition provides the basis for lower-level product specifications. It also provides a roadmap for detailed design. As such, the model should be maintained throughout the right half of the engineering V. Upon completion of the final testing, the model should have a complete description of the entire system/subsystem.

Keep in mind that Figure 1-5 is only an example of one part of a system. Depending on the organization and project, the backlog and iteration details will be different and may include additional details.

System Definition

The definition of a system should begin with the mission and involve decomposition of the mission in successive layers. Note that the term mission is used within this book to address the result that contains the lower-level activities and actions. For the military, the mission could be to provide air cover for a particular area of interest. A civilian mission could be to provide banking services. For an appliance, the mission could be to wash clothes. The danger in defining a mission is that the individual or working group can easily dive too deeply into details involving what needs to be done rather than just defining the overall mission objective.

The best way to visualize system definition is the "onion." The onion illustrates system definition because of its layered structure, as seen in Figure 1-4.

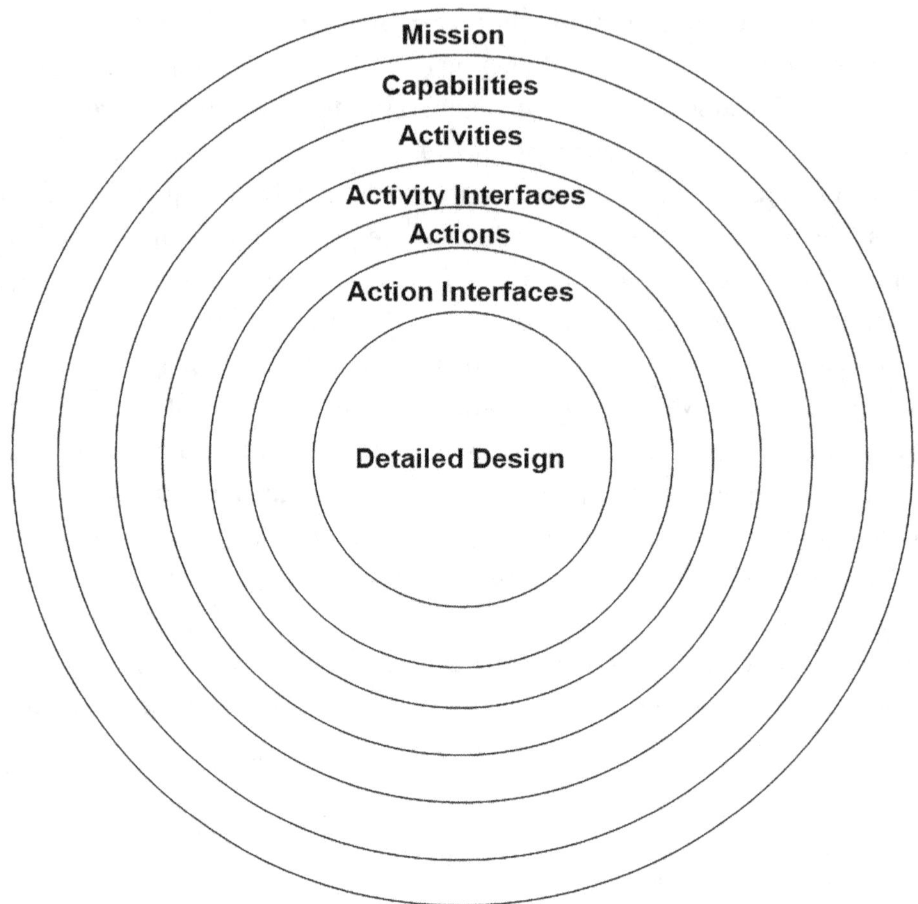

Figure 1-4. *System onion model*[4]

In the top layer of the "onion," the mission is often described using a DoDAF
OV-1, which provides an executive overview of the proposed system in the context
of the intended mission. The OV-1 illustrates the highest-level system elements and
signal/information interchanges. An example of a high-level mission view is shown
in Figure 1-5. This OV-1 view was produced using an MBSE Modeling tool. For formal
presentations, especially to executive-level individuals within the organization or to
potential customers, an artist/illustrator rendered view will normally be used. Regardless
of the graphical approach taken, i;e. Professional graphics or developed from the model,
the OV-1 view of the mission is very important. It establishes the project intent and the
relationship of the major elements necessary to meet mission objectives.

---

[4] Author-created image

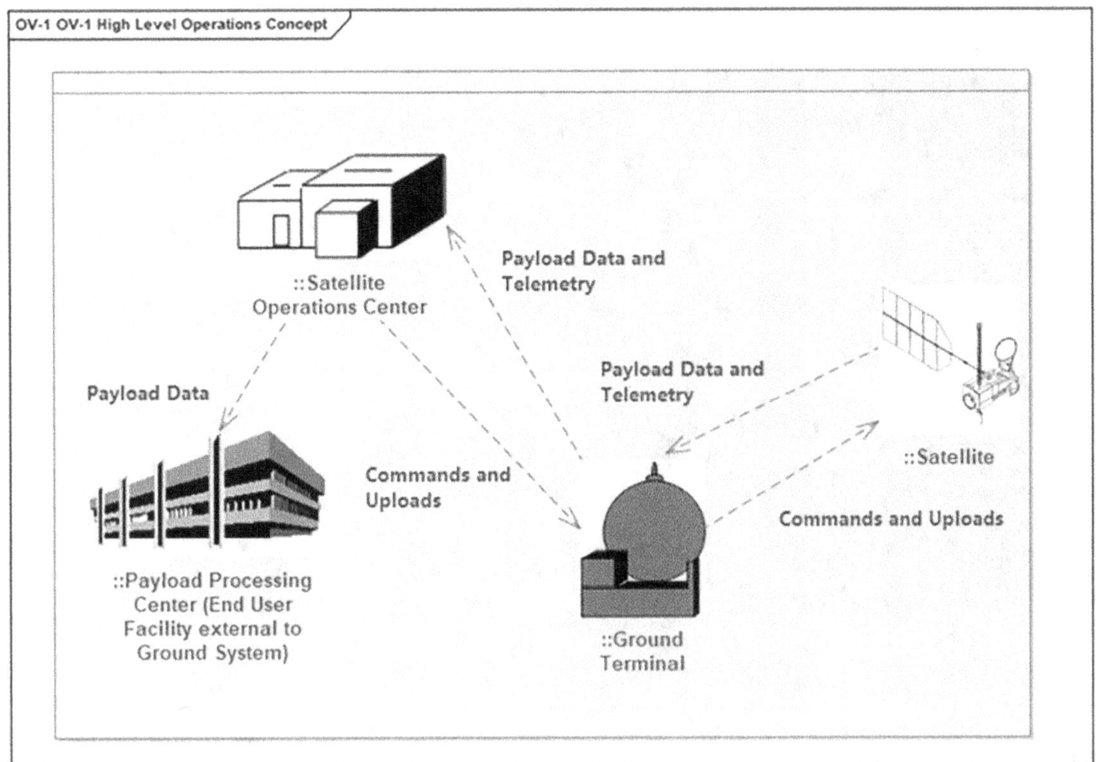

Figure 1-5. *OV-1 mission view*[5]

Several versions of the OV-1 may be produced during the system development. For example, Figure 1-6 shows an engineering level version of the OV-1, which may be of better use to the team. In contrast to Figure 1-5, this view concentrates on mission functions and interactions rather than the physical distribution of major subsystems – i.e. the view is often overlaid on a map.

---

[5] Author-created image

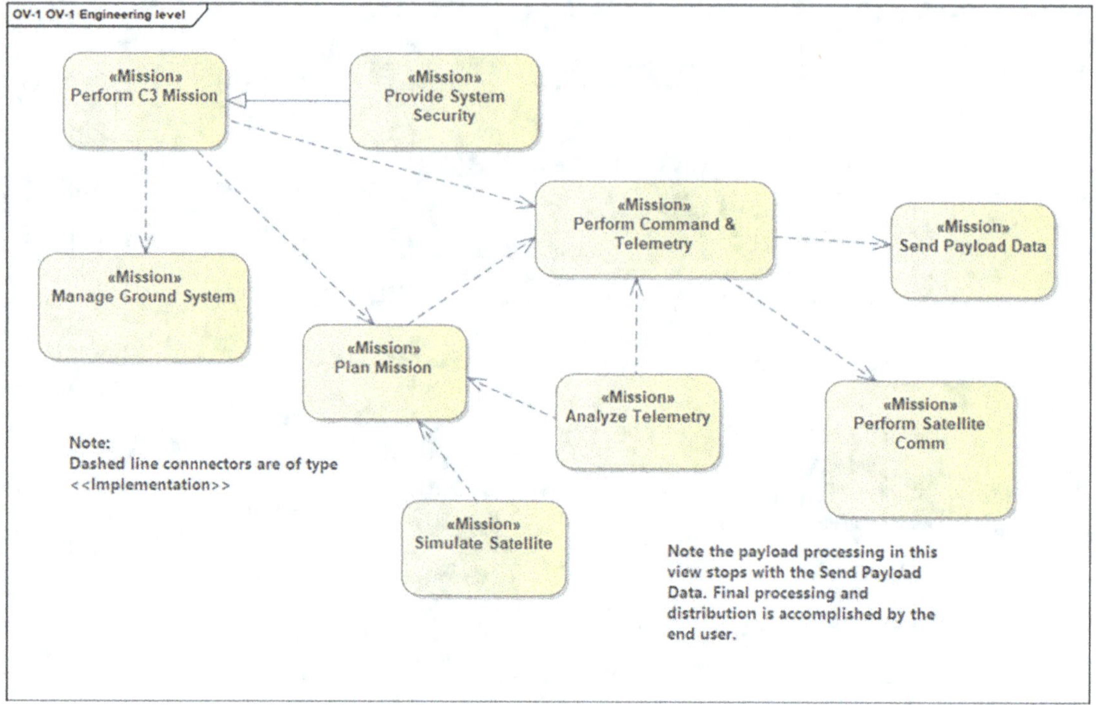

Figure 1-6. *Engineering level OV-1<Original to Author>*

In instances where an early transition to SysML is anticipated, a use case view is used as the OV-1. Each use case is shown as an oval and represents a system transaction, as shown in Figure 1-7. In this case, the Use Case view provides the mission as the primary use case and Provide System Security as the child (by convention, the child is always shown at the base of the arrow). The Provide System Security provides details of the security steps that must be taken, while the Provide Mission inherits the steps applicable to "included" Use Cases. This is an especially helpful approach to defining architecture at one level lower than the original OV-1 views if the intent is to transition from DoDAF to SysML later in the design process.

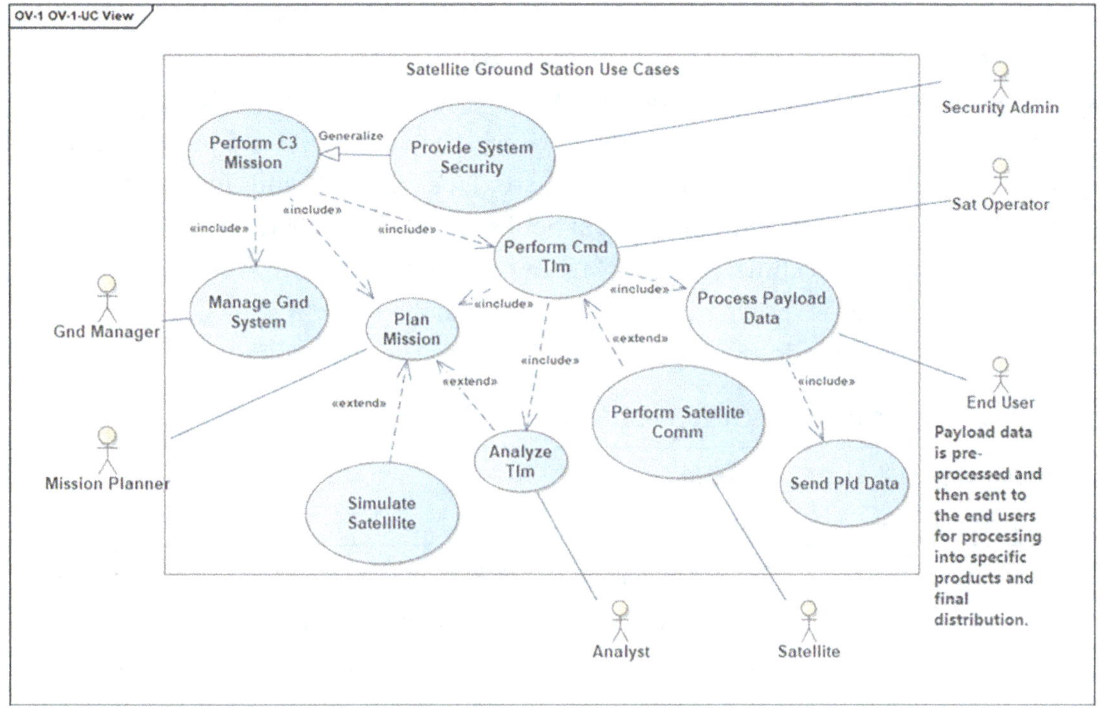

Figure 1-7. *OV-1 use case version*

When working with the Use Case OV-1 (and SysML) views, it is important to recognize that the Use Case elements in the diagram are not physical pieces of the system. They represent a grouping of activities and not a representation of specific subsystems. For example, Perform Satellite Comm encompasses several components and subsystems. The antenna subsystem may be a complete operational subsystem located at a physically different location than the components performing demodulation and initial processing for distribution to the command and telemetry system.

Another key point is that the interchanges shown are not physical communication between the use cases. For example, the interchange between Provide System Security is shown as a generalization, which means that the Perform C3 Mission inherits all the security requirements from Provide System Security. The <<include>> relationships shown indicate that the use case at the base of the arrow is included within the use case at the arrow end. In other words, the use cases could be contained in the same software or hardware package or reside separately. The key point is that the functionality is provided by the combination of the use cases. The <<extend>> relationships differ from <<include>> in that they are only inserted into the activities of the use case at the head of the arrow when called.

The Use Case view is especially useful for starting the requirements process when time is taken to provide a detailed definition of each Use Case. Remember, these are requirements for the activities and functions, not physical attributes (i.e., steel cabinetry, shielded cables, etc.). Required data, which will be used as a basis for detailed requirements, are often in the form of a use case specification. Details for development of this specification can be found in several books, one of which is *Writing Effective Use Cases* by Alistair Cockburn (chapter 11.1 in particular) [2]. An example of the specification contents is shown in Table 1-2. Note that the content shown in the table for each specification item addresses data that will govern the operations.

Table 1-2. *Use case specification content*

Specification item	Content
Use case name	**A verb phrase**
Scope	The entity that owns (provides) the use case (for example, the name of an organization, system, subsystem, or component).
Primary actor	The actor that invokes the use case (the actor whose goal the use case represents).
Supporting (secondary) actors	Actors that provide a service to the system (participate in the use case by performing actions).
Stakeholder	Someone or something with a vested interest in the behavior of the system.
Preconditions	The conditions that must be true for this use case to begin.
Guarantees	The conditions must be true at the end of the use case.
Trigger	The event that gets the use case started.
Main success scenario	The scenario (the sequence of steps) in which nothing goes wrong.
Extensions (alternative branches)	Alternative sequences of steps branching off the main success scenario.
Related information	Whatever your project needs for additional information.

Note that from a SysML standpoint, a block definition diagram (bdd) can be used in place of the normal OV-1. It is not as pleasing for formal presentations as OV-1; however, it can be developed to provide greater detail. Block definition diagrams and internal block diagrams (ibd), as opposed to the OV-1, can be produced throughout the system model. They are not limited to the first phase of modeling. An advantage of the bdd and ibd is the incorporation of constraints (such as speed, movement limits, etc.) and system values (such as required memory capacity) within the block.

Coordination with Executive Management

Throughout the life of the project, there will be a need to keep executive and senior management advised as to the status of the project. Obviously, briefing on model details and requirements development may be beyond what management expects or desires.

Though not required for the development of the model, a package diagram is a form of graphics that can be used throughout the project life. It provides a structural view of the overall model packages and can provide a view for briefing executive management and the acquisition agencies. In general, there is no one right way to structure this view. In conjunction with the normal project Gannt schedule, a more complete view of the elements contained in the project schedule can be presented as shown in Figure 1-8.

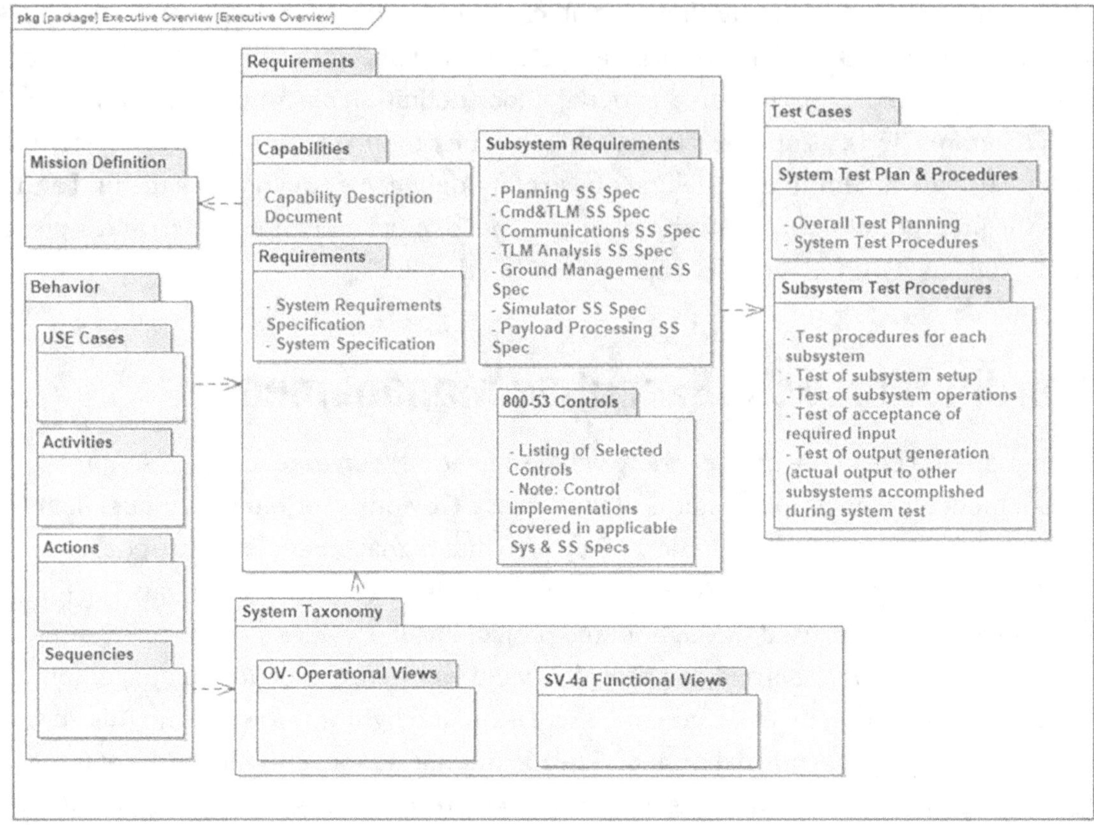

Figure 1-8. *Package diagram of modeling activities*[6]

The ability to illustrate the size and complexity of the system model and requirements development in a simple form will help to:

- Show that the modeling is not just a few diagrams.

- Provide a simple way to illustrate progress during the program by color-coding blocks as they progress from initial, in-work, and completed status. This can be expanded to show (by color coding) the status of specifications as shown in the Package Diagram nested packages in Figure 1-9. Note the addition of "TRD Completed" and the highlighting of the package in green.

---

[6] Author-created image

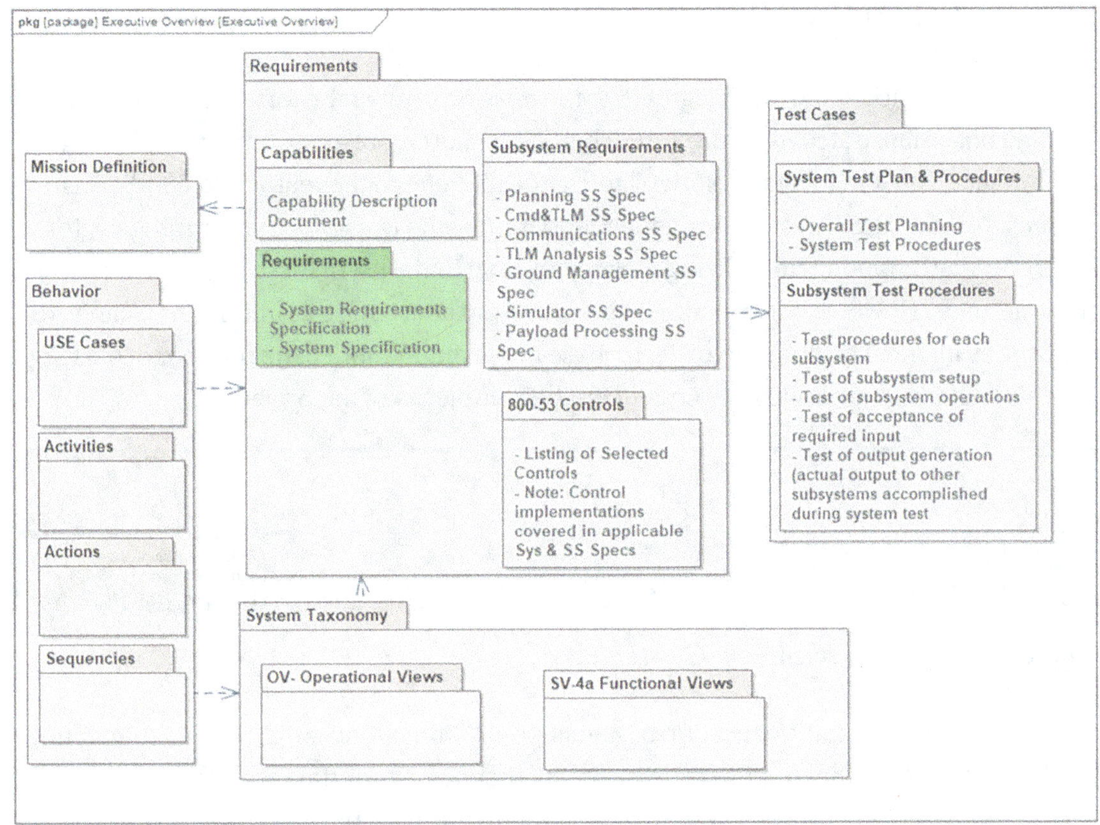

Figure 1-9. *Updated package diagram example*[7]

- Maintain the management view of developing the requirements as we are developing the model to ensure a complete system definition while avoiding over-specification. The package diagram depicts model elements and associated requirements. The package interconnections shown are dependencies between the elements of work represented by each package. You can read the diagram as: Requirements are dependent on the Mission Definition, Test Cases are dependent on Requirements, etc.

---

[7] Author-created image

Initial Planning

Using the onion model shown in Figure 1-4, the mission layer at the top aligns with the initial planning phase illustrated in Figure 1-10. This Gantt chart represents the very beginning of the project. The "circumstances" depicted at the top refer to the real-world conditions that must be addressed and that form the foundation of the mission. The planning begins with a one-day duration, symbolizing the receipt of an initial list of these circumstances and conditions. However, the process of collecting and analyzing this information can take significantly longer. The duration of each phase in the onion model, the number of backlog tasks, and iterations are highly dependent on the complexity of the project.

ID	Task Name	Start	Finish	Duration	Q2 25	Q3 25			Q4 25		
					Jun	Jul	Aug	Sep	Oct	Nov	Dec
1	Receive report of circumstances	6/2/2025	6/2/2025	1d							
2	Formulate Statement of Need	6/2/2025	6/12/2025	9d							

This is the starting point and is determined by the using agency/organization.

Figure 1-10. *Initial planning Gantt chart[8]*

For instance, in a national security scenario, circumstances might involve detecting an adversary's capability to penetrate national airspace. Potential responses could include increased airborne surveillance or satellite monitoring. In a different context, such as an automobile factory, the need might be to produce smaller, lighter vehicles - requiring redesigns of the assembly line, new materials for car bodies, and specialized tools for installation. The circumstances and conditions received from the organization that will use the system will be jointly formulated into a statement of need by the using organization and the acquisition organization.

Throughout this book, we will focus on a case study involving a ground system designed to support a satellite constellation.

Chapter Lessons Learned

Key for Executive and Management Briefings and Planning

- Modeling provides a foundation for program development.

- Modeling applies to all phases of a program.

---

[8] Author-created image

Important for Engineering and Mangement

- There are several architecture frameworks (depending on the end user/acquisition organization) available. Use the one that is required by the organization and supplement with more systems definition views from DoDAF, UAF, and SysML to thoroughly define the proposed system.

- Modeling can begin with the system's end user/acquisition organization to define the mission and required capabilities.

- Modeling aids the engineer's thought process in defining a system.

- Modeling and requirements development should be conducted concurrently.

- High-level model views can be used for briefing executive management and customers.

Management Planning with Engineering Support

- Modeling activities can be broken down into cycles for an agile approach to systems engineering and program planning.

- Agile cycles can be assigned to tasks in a conventional Gantt schedule.

System and Development Test

- Start test planning early to ensure the capabilities and requirements can be tested.

Importance for Government Projects and Programs

- For Government programs, remember that the need to define a system before acquisition is established in law and is not a suggestion. The means to provide the definition is established in each Government department—that is, Defense, Commerce, etc., in the form of DoDAF, FEAF, or other framework.

References

[1]   Douglass, Dr. Bruce Powell. Agile Model-Based Systems Engineering Cookbook. Agile Model-Based Systems Engineering Cookbook. Birmingham: Packt, 2022

[2]   Cockburn, Alistair. *Writing Effective Use Cases.* Boston, New York : Addison-Wesley, 2001

Acronym List

Acronym	Definition
BDD/bdd	Block Definition Diagram
C3	Command Control Communications
CDD	Capability Development Document
CV	Capability View
DoDAF	Department of Defense Architecture Framework
FEAF	Federal Enterprise Architecture Framework
IBD/ibd	Internal Block Diagram
MBSE	Model-Based Systems Engineering
OV	Operations View
SV	System View
SysML	Systems Modeling Language
TRD	Technical Requirements Document
UAF	Unified Architecture Framework
UML	Unified Modeling Language

CHAPTER 2

System Capabilities Development

The process of defining and refining the initial system capabilities is discussed in terms of how the capabilities support the mission/organizational needs. Use of an architectural model and a modeling language such as DoDAF/UPDM or Unified Architecture Framework (UAF) aids in developing the initial technical requirements and refining capability descriptions and potentially promoting capabilities to technical requirements. The development and use of operational views CV-2, OV-1, OV-2, and OV-3 aid in visualizing the relationship between capabilities and requirements. The modeling tool provides a means to document requirements, constraints, and notes for use in preserving the original thought process used to define a capability or operational activity. A critical feature for supporting future peer review.

Background

Guide for Managers and Engineers

The concepts in this chapter apply to both engineering and management. The Acquisition Organization manager, Development Chief System Engineer and Program Manager should concentrate on the steps required before moving to activity development.

Capability development should be based upon the original Statement of Need (SON) generated by the organization that will be using the system. The SON is based upon the mission description previously described in the OV-1 diagram and contains a description of the problem being addressed. For this book, satellite ground system modeling is being used for specific examples at each stage of requirements development.

© Dennis Hansen 2025
D. Hansen, *Model-Based Systems Engineering and Requirements Definition*,
https://doi.org/10.1007/979-8-8688-2043-4_2

Consider that there is a need for Earth observation satellites. The SON should define the mission while avoiding "how to perform" descriptions. The focus should be on what is needed and not on how to implement the project. For example, "There is a need for whole earth observation, including polar." This need will establish that the satellite constellation being supported requires that the ground system support polar orbiting satellites and thus the need for the ability of antennas to perform azimuth and elevation movements. Next, there should be some bounding of the problem, for example, "Coverage of every area of regard must be reported 14 times per day." This need will drive the number of satellites, which in turn will drive the number of ground stations (for data download at least once per orbit) and the loading (i.e., number of contacts per day). Another bounding "need" could be "observations shall be available to the using organization within 1 hour of observation." This bounding statement impacts the number of stations and the communications network. Note that an Operational View (OV-1) graphic may be provided with the SON to illustrate the need. Overall, the SON needs should be phrased in terms of "what" operational capabilities the system should provide and not how the system should be built. Do not presume the "need" for specific hardware or software products or lower-level features that would drive design decisions.

Capability Development

Capability development is an extension of the "needs" with details of what needs to be accomplished to satisfy the needs, as shown in Figure 2-1.

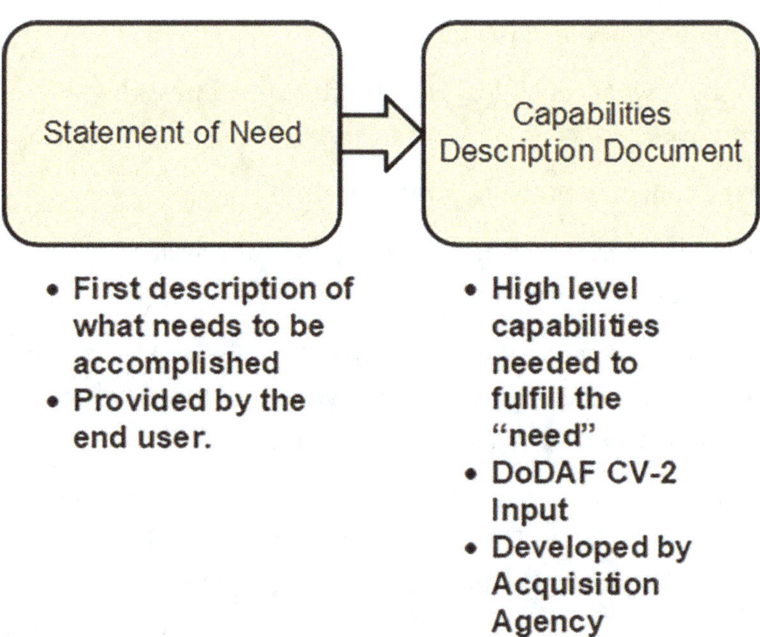

Figure 2-1. *Flow of needs to CDD*[1]

When developing capabilities, keep in mind what capabilities are. The DoD Architecture Framework documentation contains a definition of capability as follows: "The ability to achieve a Desired Effect under specified [performance] standards and conditions through combinations of ways and means [activities and resources] to perform a set of activities." In simple terms, for this example, the capability is what the system needs to accomplish the mission.

Within government organizations, development of capabilities is normally performed by the acquisition agency, possibly with Federally Funded Research and Development (FFRDC) organization assistance. One or more members of the organization/FFRDC will work as a team to develop the capabilities, potentially using a brainstorming approach. The brainstorming sessions should be a free flow of ideas. Don't worry about wording at this point since the capability candidates will be organized and filtered during follow-on activities. In general, when gathering candidate capabilities:

____

[1] Author-created image

- Evaluate the mission at the top level.

- Think about what capabilities are required to address the mission needs.

- Keep the capabilities at a very high level.

  - There is a danger of specifying activities or physical characteristics as a capability.

  - A large set of capabilities (relative to the mission) is a danger sign that you have moved into activities and the lower-level requirements that support the activities.

  - Identify Key System Attributes (KSA) and Key Performance Parameters (KPP). These are the measurable anchors for the capabilities. For example, an attribute could be to support polar orbiting spacecraft operations, which later would correspond to antenna movement activities, and a performance parameter could be to specify low earth orbit, which corresponds to the rate of movement—that is, the tracking rate for azimuth and elevation which would be addressed as a specification requirement attached to specific activities in the model.

  - Continuous development of notes, requirement statements, and constraints with each model artifact will substantially aid in keeping the number of capabilities at the correct level of specificity. The development of this material forces the team to consider each item and possibly redesignate a capability as an activity needed to provide the capability.

Initial Operations Views

The following discussion is patterned after a typical government program. For commercial programs, substitute the organization's name for a need statement.

Before generating capabilities, the end user and acquisition organization team should develop the SON and the supporting OV-1 (Figure 2-1). At this point, for the ground system example, we have only a rough idea of the system structure. The three ground elements in the OV-1 provide a clear foundation for supporting the mission.

After the SON and OV-1 have been developed, the requesting operations organization should begin working with the acquisition organization to develop OV-2 and OV-3 views. The OV-1 can be redrawn as an OV-2 node diagram to further enhance the description of communication between the elements, as shown in Figure 2-3. In this case, we have identified only the system facility locations and the messaging between the locations. The interchanges between nodes are annotated with a triangle symbol indicating that they are a Needline. Needlines represent a conduit for one or more resource exchanges. For example, the Configuration Needline in the figure (the rightmost Needline) can contain one or more instructions. Having individual Needlines reduces ambiguity in information interchange between the nodes. Each Needline represents a specific interchange. For example, Payload Data would be a specific file or data stream, while Configuration represents a class of directives sent to manage the ground station. A key point is that the needlines prevent ambiguity in the resource exchanges.

Keep in mind that the OV-1, OV-2, OV-3, or Unified Architecture equivalents and Mission bdd views are generally the first things developed by the system users and acquisition organization. This is due to the need to define the mission at a high level. The details of the mission and the capabilities supporting each element, as well as the interaction capabilities, should be developed. The capabilities should be developed using a Modeling tool rather than a spreadsheet or drawings. Inclusion of the capability statements and notes as the capability items are added to the diagram will ensure that the diagram and capabilities are kept together throughout the development process. More importantly, it aids in seeing the capabilities in context with the other capabilities that have been added to the model and helps to avoid replicating or missing capabilities, that is, the graphics make these errors easier to recognize and correct. Keeping the diagram and capabilities together in the modeling tool is an essential process that pays dividends later in the development process and, most importantly, avoids issues during acceptance testing when a different team may be involved. Having all of the data together in context can help to avoid disagreements as to the meaning of individual test steps and the interpretation of test results.

Details of the interchanges between nodes within the ground station are shown in Ground Station OV-2, Figure 2-4. Note that in this case, the nodes represent the major subsystems rather than the facility relationship.

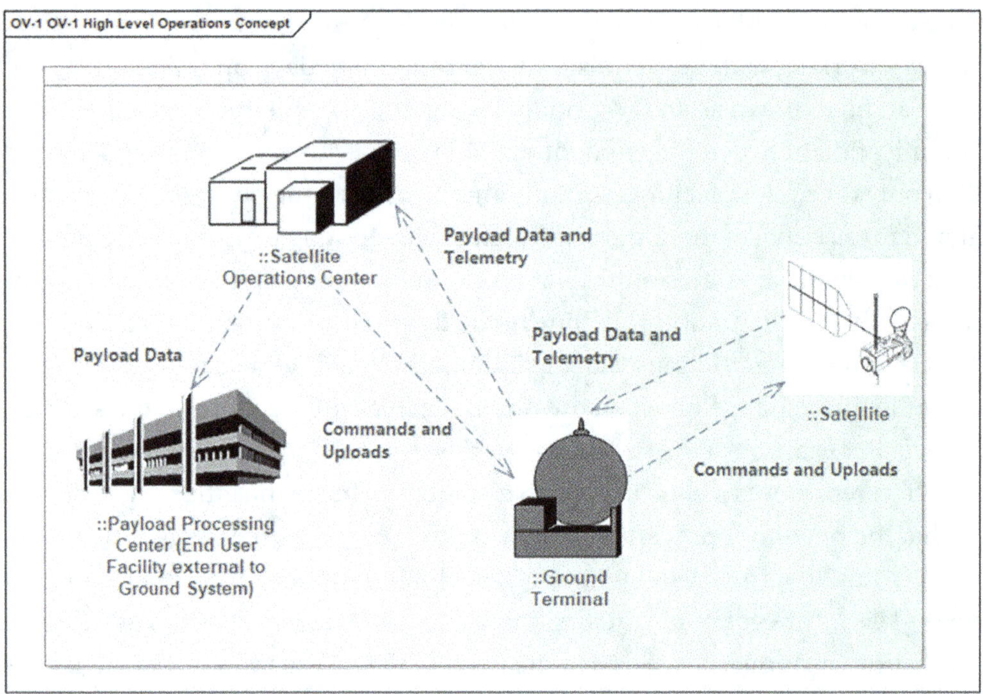

Figure 2-2. *OV-1 mission view*[2]

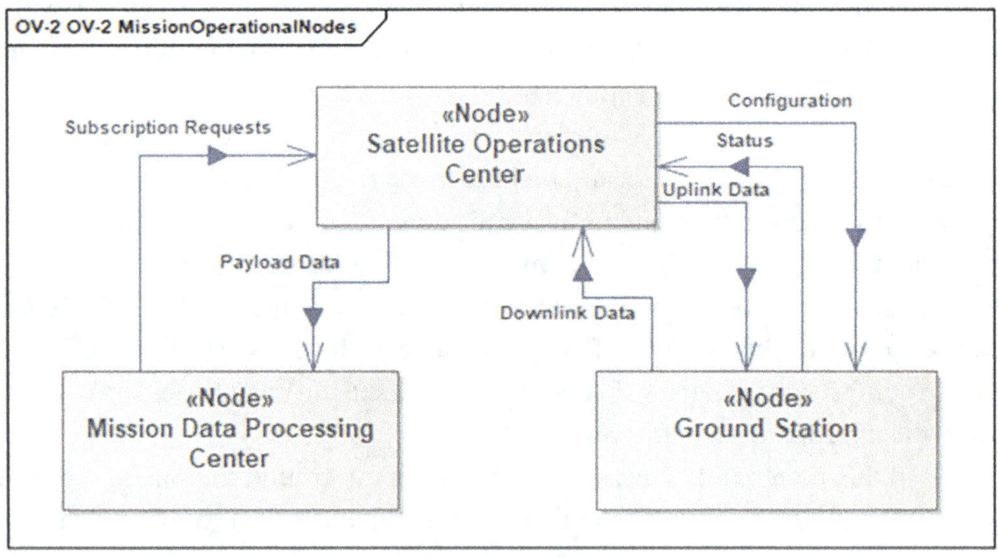

Figure 2-3. *OV-2 mission operations node diagram*[3]

---

[2] Author-created image

[3] Author-created image

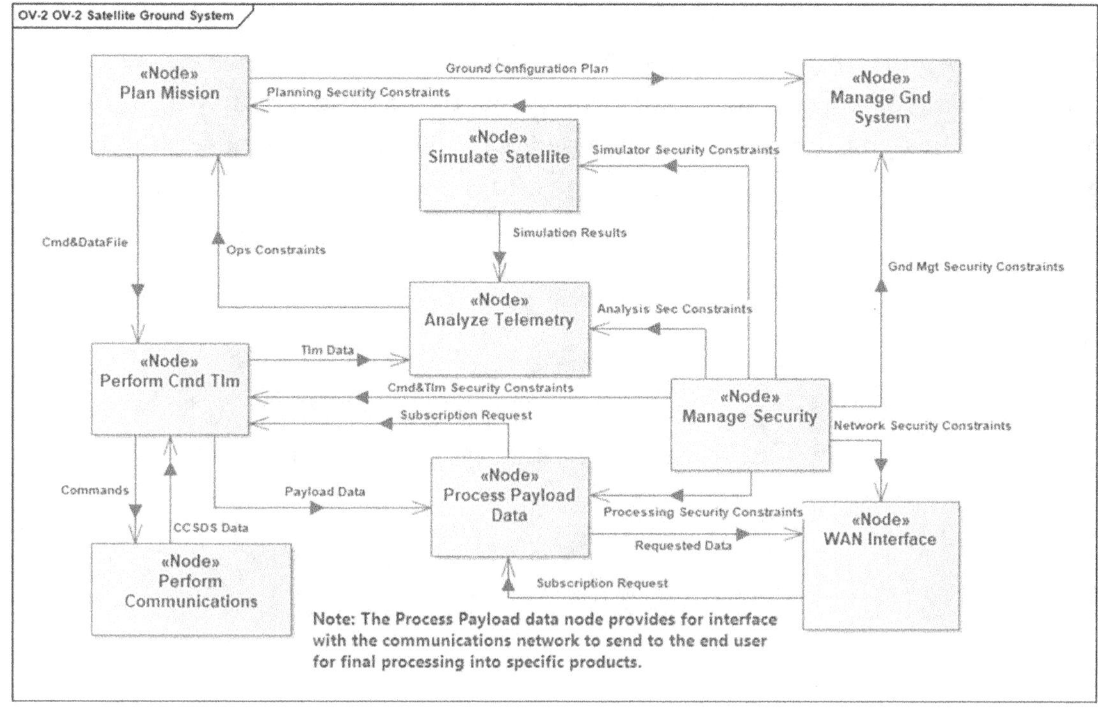

Figure 2-4. *OV-2 satellite ground station node view*[4]

The OV-3 view provides a listing of operational flows between nodes. Figure 2-5 contains a matrix of the resource interchanges shown in Figure 2-3. In this case, the listing is of the information items being interchanged between ground station nodes. For both program managers and engineers, the content provides a form of a dictionary for the information interchange. An extract of the resource flow matrix in Figure 2-5 can be expanded to start an analysis of data perishability and vulnerability. The vulnerability analysis can help in planning for design efforts supporting mission and system security beyond what may be called for in documents such as NIST SP 800-53. The view can be extracted and expanded as necessary as part of a detailed examination of potential security vulnerability points in the ground station. For those organizations that start with SysML at the beginning of the effort or are anticipating a move to SysML later in the program, Figure 2-7 illustrates the mission using a Block Definition Diagram (bdd) model.

---

[4] Author-created image

Depending on the Modeling tool, the expanded view may have to be generated external to the Modeling tool—that is, copy and paste into a spreadsheet and expand as desired with additional columns. Keep in mind that the controls within NIST SP 800-53 primarily address the administrative and operational aspects of system security. This expansion of the ground system OV-3 (Figure 2-6) can serve as a basis for addressing the technical details, that is, the hardware and software design security constraints.

List of Operational Exchanges

Connector_Name	Connector...	Flow_Type	Conveyed...	Conveyed_Name
Ground Configuratio...	Needline	OperationalE...	ExchangeE...	Ground Configurati...
Ground Configuratio...	Needline	OperationalE...	ExchangeE...	Ground Configurati...
Planning Security Co...	Needline	OperationalE...	ExchangeE...	Planning Security Co...
Planning Security Co...	Needline	OperationalE...	ExchangeE...	Planning Security Co...
Simulator Security C...	Needline	OperationalE...	ExchangeE...	Simulator Security C...
Simulator Security C...	Needline	OperationalE...	ExchangeE...	Simulator Security C...

Rows Continued

Conveyed_Name	Producer...	Producer_Name	Consumer...	Consumer_Name
Ground Configurati...	Node	Plan Mission	Node	Manage Gnd System
Ground Configurati...	Node	Plan Mission	Node	Manage Gnd System
Planning Security Co...	Node	Manage Security	Node	Plan Mission
Planning Security Co...	Node	Manage Security	Node	Plan Mission
Simulator Security C...	Node	Manage Security	Node	Simulate Satellite
Simulator Security C...	Node	Manage Security	Node	Simulate Satellite

Figure 2-5. *Mission operational resource flow OV-3*[5]

---

[5] Author-created image

List of Operational Exchanges

Connector_Name	Connect...	Flow_Type	Convey...	Conveyed_Name	Produc...	Producer_Name	Consum...	Consumer_Name
Ground Configurat...	Needline	Operational...	Exchang...	Ground Configura...	Node	Plan Mission	Node	Manage Gnd Syst...
Ground Configurat...	Needline	Operational...	Exchang...	Ground Configura...	Node	Plan Mission	Node	Manage Gnd Syst...
Planning Security ...	Needline	Operational...	Exchang...	Planning Security...	Node	Manage Security	Node	Plan Mission
Planning Security ...	Needline	Operational...	Exchang...	Planning Security...	Node	Manage Security	Node	Plan Mission
Simulator Security...	Needline	Operational...	Exchang...	Simulator Securit...	Node	Manage Security	Node	Simulate Satellite
Simulator Security...	Needline	Operational...	Exchang...	Simulator Securit...	Node	Manage Security	Node	Simulate Satellite

Rows Continued

Conveyed_Name	Producer_T...	Producer_Name	Consumer_...	Consumer_Name
Ground Configuration Plan	Node	Plan Mission	Node	Manage Gnd System
Ground Configuration Plan	Node	Plan Mission	Node	Manage Gnd System
Planning Security Constr...	Node	Manage Security	Node	Plan Mission
Planning Security Constr...	Node	Manage Security	Node	Plan Mission
Simulator Security Cons...	Node	Manage Security	Node	Simulate Satellite

Figure 2-6. *Ground station OV-3*[6]

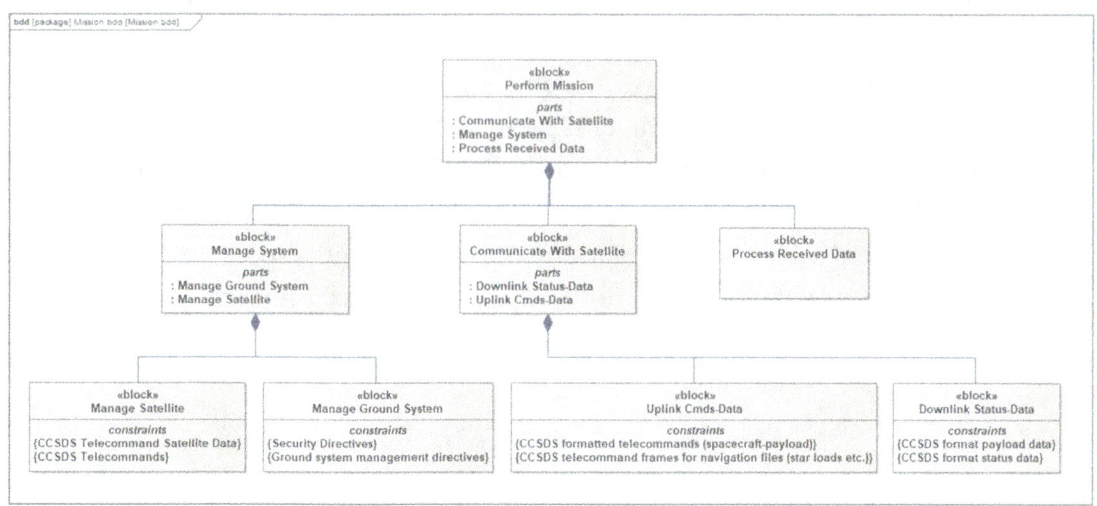

Figure 2-7. *Mission bdd example*[7]

---

[6] Author-created image

[7] Author-created image

Development of Capability Statements

Thinking in terms of capability requirement statements when working with the SON sounds easy. In practice, working with the capability statements outside of a model can be the start of issues with extraneous or ill-defined requirements later in the development process. The Modeling activity, including the projection of the model on a screen, provides a means for soliciting and incorporating team mission experience for documenting each capability item.

Figure 2-8 shows a taxonomical view of our ground system capabilities. Use of a taxonomy view provides a quick and easy way to gather and categorize the capabilities. As mentioned in the earlier notes, relative to operational experience, capability requirements are added for each capability as shown in Figures 2-8 and 2-9.

This is an ideal time to evaluate each item and determine whether it represents a capability or an activity performed to support that capability. Review the CV-2 view and clearly document what each capability provides—both during its formulation and after it is finalized. To support this evaluation, it is considered good practice to make use of the notes feature within the Modeling tool. Figure 2-9 provides an example of this. These notes should contain sufficient detail to remind the architect or systems engineer of the rationale behind the capability definition. Referencing applicable standards is also recommended where relevant.

Capability statements should be written and entered in the "requirements" section of each capability element, as illustrated in Figure 2-10. During this evaluation, you may also identify constraints associated with a capability. For example, the "Transmit Cmds & Data" capability in Figure 2-8 may be subject to radiation limits based on International Telecommunications Union (ITU) regulations. Such constraints should be documented in the Modeling tool's "constraints" section, as shown in the example in Figure 2-11.

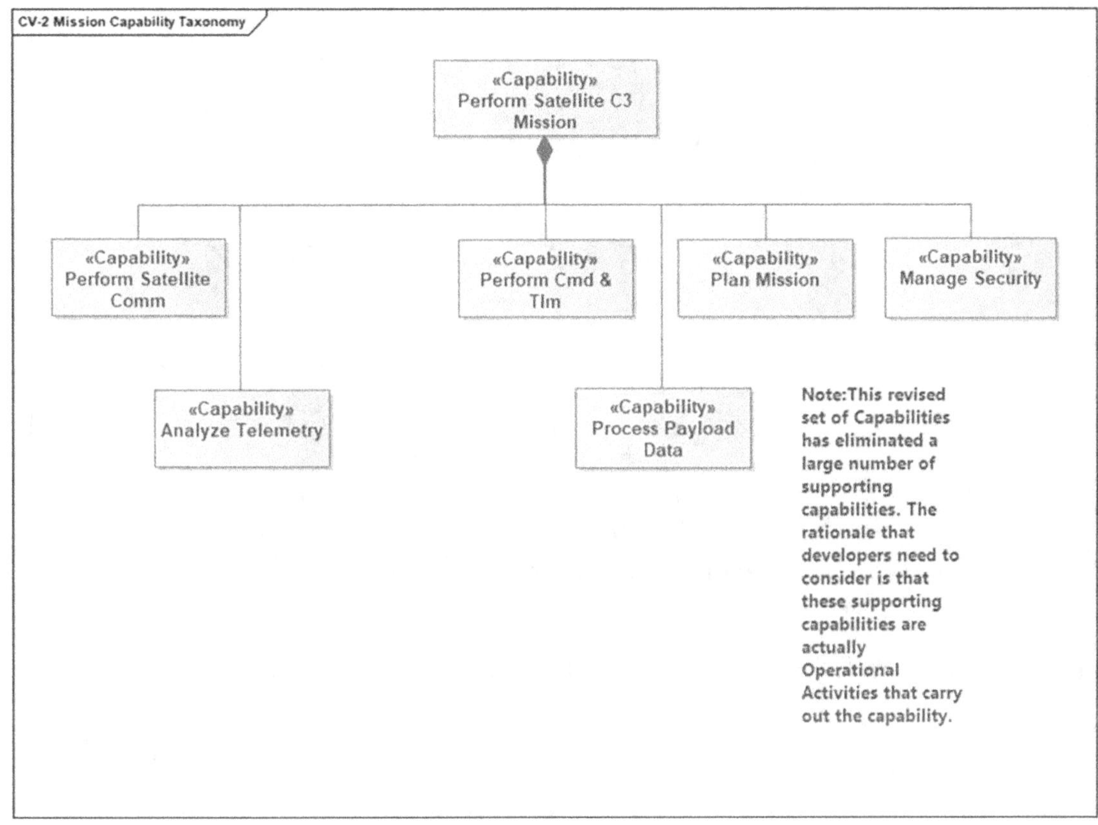

Figure 2-8. *Mission capability CV-2 view[8]*

---

[8] Author-created image

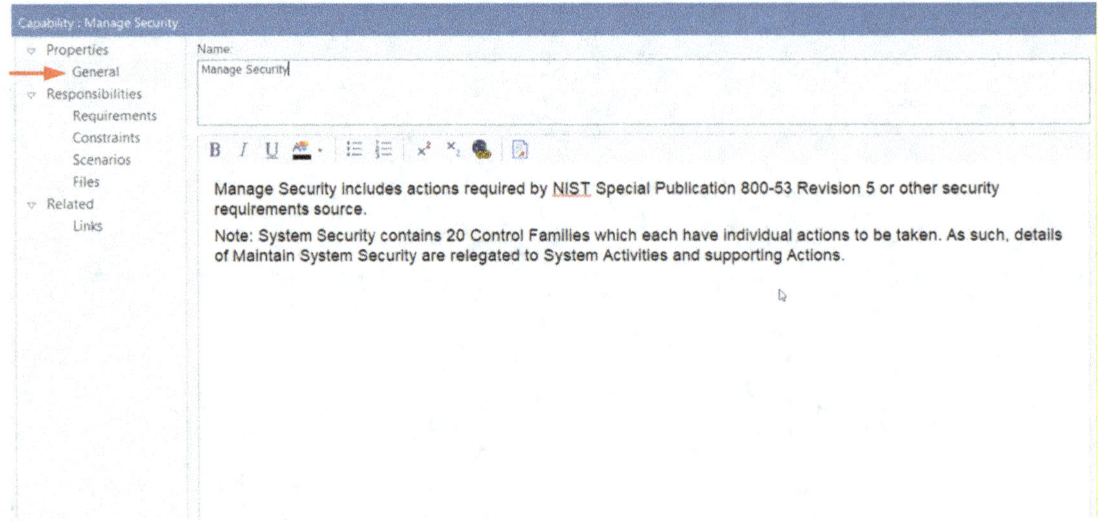

Figure 2-9. *General section of model element*[9]

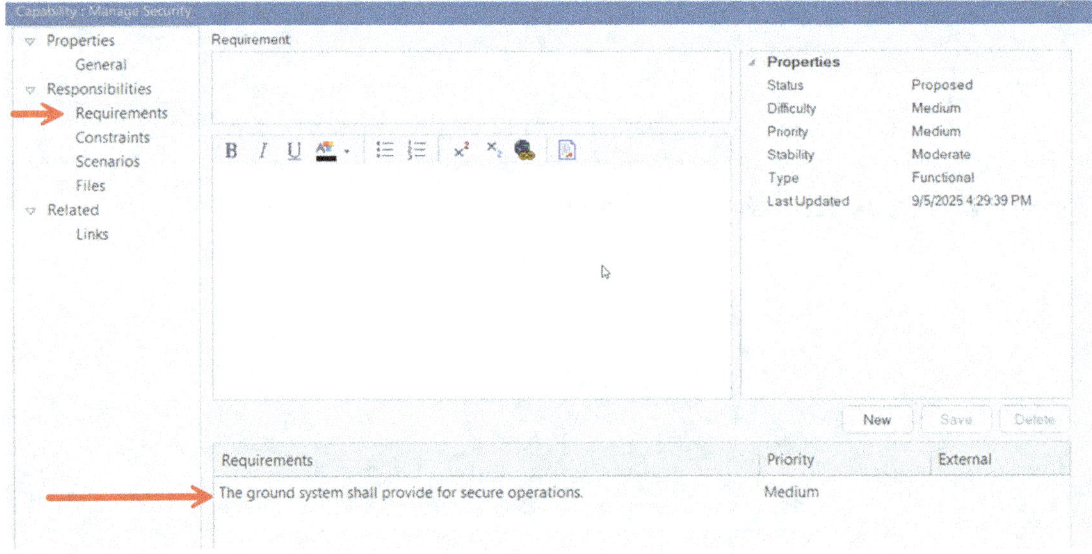

Figure 2-10. *Requirements section of model element*[10]

---

[9] Author-created image

[10] Author-created image

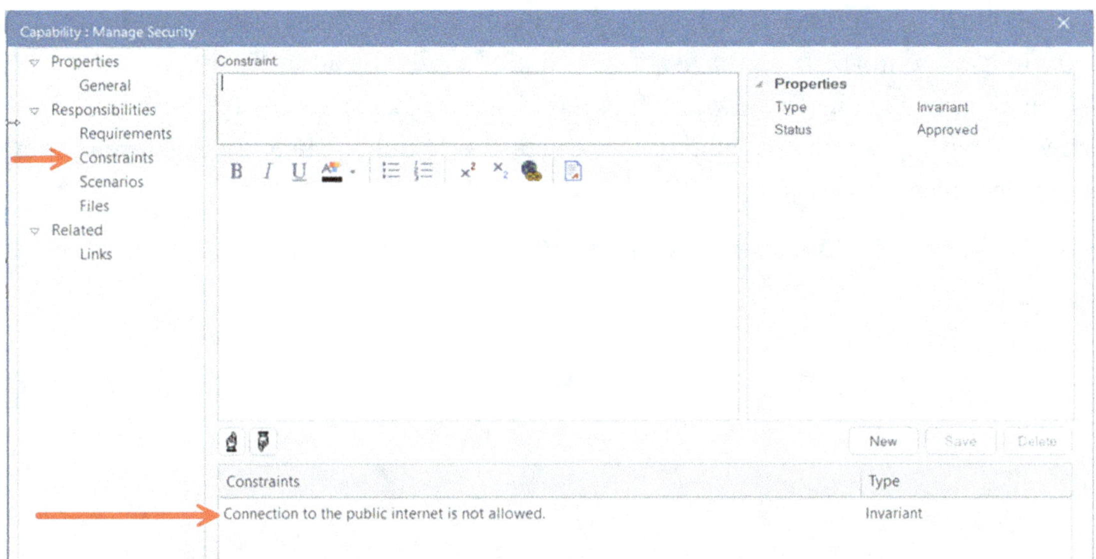

Figure 2-11. *Constraint section of model element[11]*

After constraints have been added, additional capabilities may be added as shown in Figure 2-12. Note how the constraint was worded as a "do not" type of statement. This is inadequate for the capability requirement. Always reword constraints (e.g., "Connection to the public internet is not allowed.") into a positive statement, in this case "Dedicated non-public communications links shall be used." If capabilities are added, be sure to update the requirements database (DoDAF and the Modeling tool) and the relationship between the requirements and CV-2 as shown in Figure 2-13.

---

[11] Author-created image

This evaluation process will help to close in on what items are really capabilities. Items that are removed from the list of capabilities should be added to an initial list of activities. It will help if the list is organized in terms of a capability, followed by the activities that support the capability. These activities should be held for the development of Activity Views and the Technical Requirements Document (TRD).

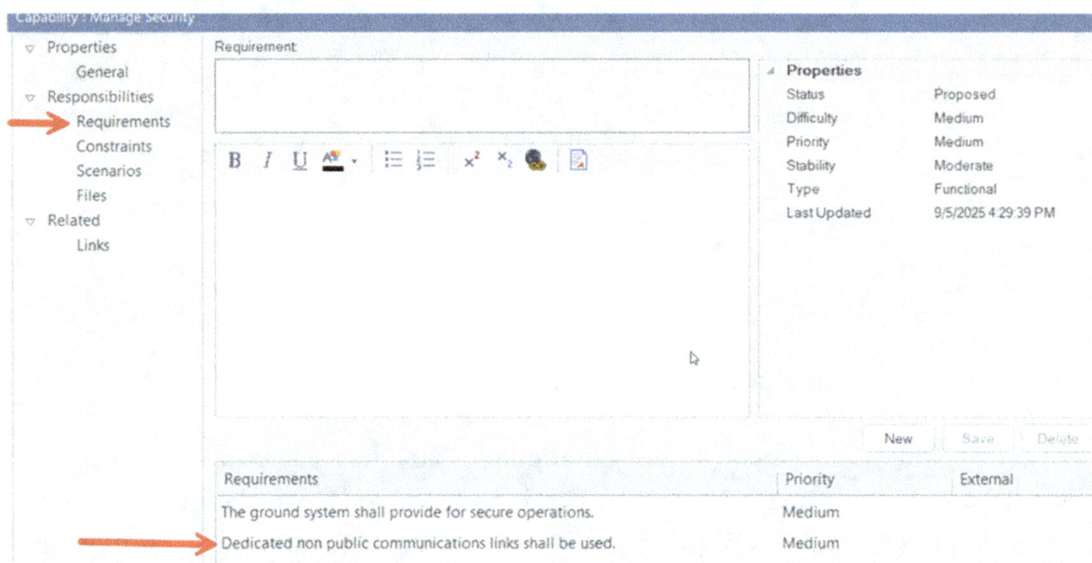

Figure 2-12. *Capability update*[12]

Figure 2-13. *Capability relationship update*[13]

---

[12] Author-created image

[13] Author-created image

The DoDAF CV-2 nomenclature was used in this discussion; however, DoDAF is an architecture framework as discussed in the introduction. The Modeling language used to document DoDAF is the Unified Profile for DoDAF / MODAF (UPDM). DoDAF is often made a contractual requirement; however, thought should be given to a hybrid approach. UPDM CV-2 and OV-5a views provide an easy means to gather capabilities and activities. In comparison, the SysML views used in industry are formalized and require additional time and effort to complete. This could interfere with the free flow of ideas during the initial stages of a project.

Capability development should be based upon the original Statement of Need (SON) generated by the organization that will be using the system. The SON contains a description of the problem being addressed. The model being used is for a satellite ground system.

Consider that there is a need for Earth observation satellites. The SON should define the mission and avoid "how to perform" descriptions. For example, "There is a need for whole earth observation, including polar," which would imply that the ground system will be supporting polar orbiting satellites. Next, there should be some bounding of the problem, for example: "Coverage of every area of regard must be reported 14 times per day." This need will drive the number of satellites, which in turn will drive the number of ground stations and the loading (i.e., number of contacts per day). Another bounding "need" could be "observations shall be available to the using organization within 1 hour of observation." This bounding statement impacts the number of stations and the communications network. Note that an Operational View (OV-1) graphic may be provided with the SON to illustrate the need.

It is always good practice to perform a peer review at each stage of model development. This review will potentially remove or add capabilities. If Agile methods are used, the review should be scheduled as a part of the (in this case) Capability Document "iteration" and not as an item in the "project backlog." When the review is complete, the Capability Development Document can be generated using the notes, requirements, and constraints reworded into positive statements, documented with each capability. Figure 2-14 provides an Onion Model for the project's documentation. The lack of an interface layer between capabilities and activities is a reminder that the activities are building blocks to implement the capability. Interaction between the activities is covered by the activity interface layer. Note that activities are most often grouped to provide physical subsystems. Interface specifications are used to address this physical interface. The key is to get the level of detail within each document correct.

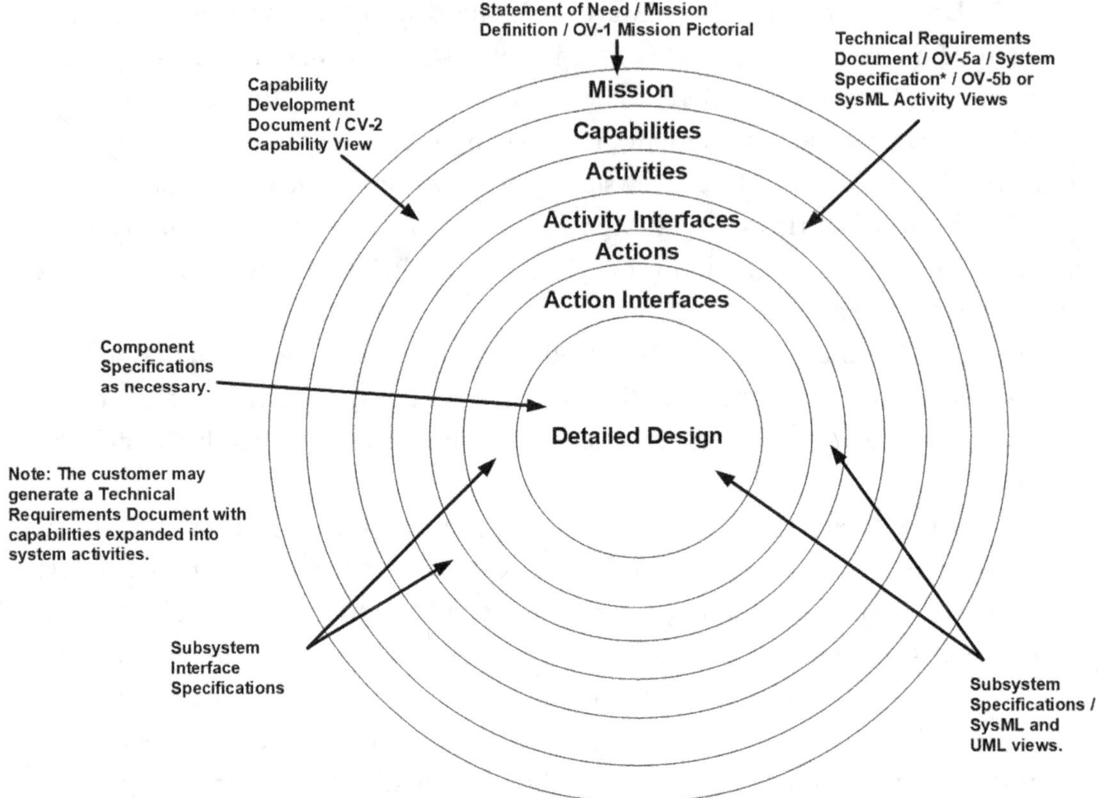

Figure 2-14. *Model layers to documentation*[14]

Test Planning

The activities in this chapter are accomplished in the very early stages of planning and preparation for acquisition or assignment to an in-house development team. Often, the end users and acquisition agencies do not think about system tests during this phase of development. As a result, the development team must generate the initial test planning and test procedures (with expected results). Both parties should remember that this is a collaborative effort. The development team does the initial planning and test procedures, and the end user/acquisition organization reviews the documentation to ensure that their end goals will be met.

---

[14] Author-created image

For capabilities, it is best to just add a linked Word or other document to the Capability view. The capabilities will generally act as headings for the more detailed system test procedures document. These headings should also match the capabilities that are documented in the Technical Requirements Document. These linked documents should be updated as the model matures. Depending on the tool, the linked document may need to be relinked. In most cases, the update of the linked document retains the same link as before. By doing this, the capabilities and the test procedure headings will remain consistent. This will serve as a cross-check as the activity views mature, and procedures are added to each heading area. This may seem a minor point, but it helps to maintain focus on the headings (capabilities) are "what is to be done" while the activities and related test steps are covering "how the capabilities are being provided."

System Capabilities and Technical Requirements Document

The following Gantt Chart is an example of planning that should be performed once the statement of need is received. It begins with developing the capability views and requirements associated with each capability. It progresses with the Modeling and requirement tool usage to format the capability requirements into a document and finally review and update for publication and release. Keep in mind that this is a simplified generic example of the planning schedule and that individual organizations may need additional time for some tasks and have additional steps that are required. The results of this phase of activity will be the production of the CDD and Technical Requirements Document (TRD), which contains details as to what the system must do to provide the required capabilities. Note that the System Specification detailed requirements and documentation will be conducted during the following phase of activity by the development organization or a technical group within the acquisition organization.

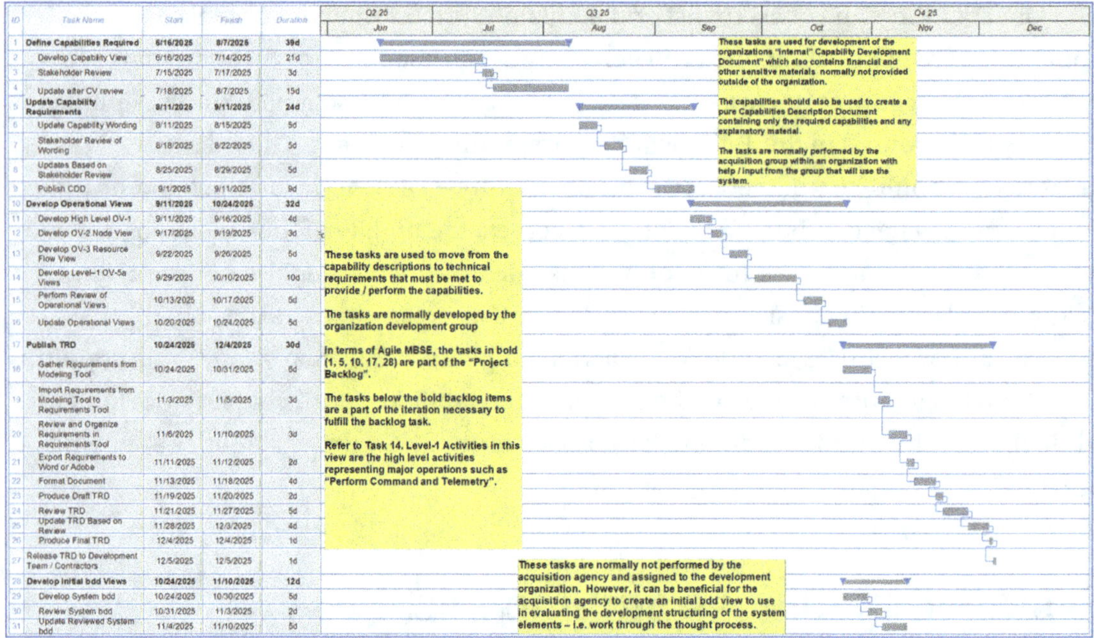

Figure 2-15. *Example schedule for acquisition planning and management*[15]

Chapter Lessons Learned

- An organization needs a clear and concise statement of need describing the mission and operational needs.

- Use a modeling tool to develop and track capability and operational views and their associated data. As requirements and constraints are identified, they may be linked to a requirements tool separate from the modeling tool if the development organization requires the use of a requirements tool such as IBM DOORS. Note that modeling tools often provide for linkage between tools, which will ensure consistency.

---

[15] Author-created image

- A high-level OV-1 diagram with explanations for each element and interface in the diagram is essential for documenting the mission and providing materials to responsible management to ensure that the mission is properly described and is approved for further development of preparatory materials for program approval and funding.

- A capability view CV-2 is used to define the capabilities required to meet mission needs. It supports the OV-1 and statement of need/mission description for preparation of acquisition (contractual or assignment to in-house development team) documentation.

- Capability statements/requirements should be documented in the Modeling tool as the capabilities are being defined and entered in the CV-2.

- Interfaces between systems/subsystems are essential and should be documented in the Modeling tool as OV-2 and OV-3 views.

- A mission-level bdd should be developed in the modeling tool and used to begin structuring the system.

- Establish initial test planning to act as a basis for test procedure development by the developer test engineer as the program/project proceeds.

- An initial Gannt schedule should be prepared. The details, such as an Agile description of lower-level cycles, can be delayed if the project is contracted or passed to the in-house development team, if applicable.

Acronym list

Acronym	Definition
Bdd	Block Definition Diagram
CDD	Capability Development Document
cmds	Commands
CV	Capability View
DoDAF	Department of Defense Architecture Framework
FFRDC	Federally Funded Research and Development
ITU	International Telecommunications Union
KPP	Key Performance Parameters
KSA	Key System Attributes
MODAF	British Ministry of Defence Architecture Framework
NIST	National Institute of Standards and Technology
OV	Operations View
SON	Statement of Need
SP	Special Publication
SysML	Systems Modeling Language
TLM	Telemetry
TRD	Technical Requirements Document
UPDM	UML Profile for DoDAF/MODAF

CHAPTER 3

Level 1 Operational Activity Views

This chapter discusses how operational activity views, used in combination with system node views, support the development of requirement statements for the Technical Requirements Document (TRD). It highlights the importance of utilizing the *requirements, constraints*, and *notes* sections within the modeling tool to ensure that requirement statements are clearly linked to the corresponding modeling elements. The chapter also describes how these efforts transition into a System Specification, emphasizing the need for thorough documentation of system activities.

A frequent challenge in new system development is properly addressing *security*. This chapter demonstrates the value of incorporating security requirements at all relevant activity levels early in the modeling and requirements development process. Doing so helps prevent issues during system security accreditation and ensures better protection during operations.

The chapter also examines the use of commercial and other off-the-shelf components. It stresses that the model should serve as the foundation for selecting these components. Evaluating off-the-shelf items within the modeling context helps ensure that required capabilities are not overlooked, while also avoiding the inclusion of unnecessary features that can lead to system bloat and increased support costs.

The integration of activity views in TRD development, combined with early consideration of security, establishes a foundational framework for the project. When a modeling tool is used to derive TRD requirements from these activities, it creates a baseline that supports ongoing tracking of modeling progress, requirements evolution, and final testing. This end-to-end traceability throughout the system lifecycle not only enhances development effectiveness but also promotes efficient and cost-effective sustainment.

© Dennis Hansen 2025
D. Hansen, *Model-Based Systems Engineering and Requirements Definition*,
https://doi.org/10.1007/979-8-8688-2043-4_3

Guide for Managers and Engineers

For managers, the examples in this section illustrate how the definitions of capabilities and requirements can shift or be refined throughout the process. There's no need to delve deeply into the logic behind each view—simply focus on understanding what the engineer is responsible for producing.

For engineers, it's important to stay alert to cases where a "capability" may be an activity that enables another capability, and vice versa.

For both managers and engineers, the views developed are integral to the thought process of defining both activity and capability requirements.

The next step in system definition is to continue the behavior analysis by developing activity views, as previously shown using the "onion" layered approach (see Figure 3-2). This step ultimately supports the development of the Technical Requirements Document (TRD), as shown in Figure 3-1. As with capabilities, the most effective way to identify and organize the required activities is using a taxonomy diagram.

The proposed taxonomy approach provides a simple approach that provides for grouping activities to support the capabilities previously developed. The team's attention remains focused on what activities may be needed rather than the details of how they relate within a more complex diagram. It also helps to evaluate the capabilities related to activities to ensure that they are correctly classed—that is, a capability may be worded at a depth that makes it an activity or vice versa. In total, the process allows the team to rapidly develop the technical requirements without getting bogged down in design detail.

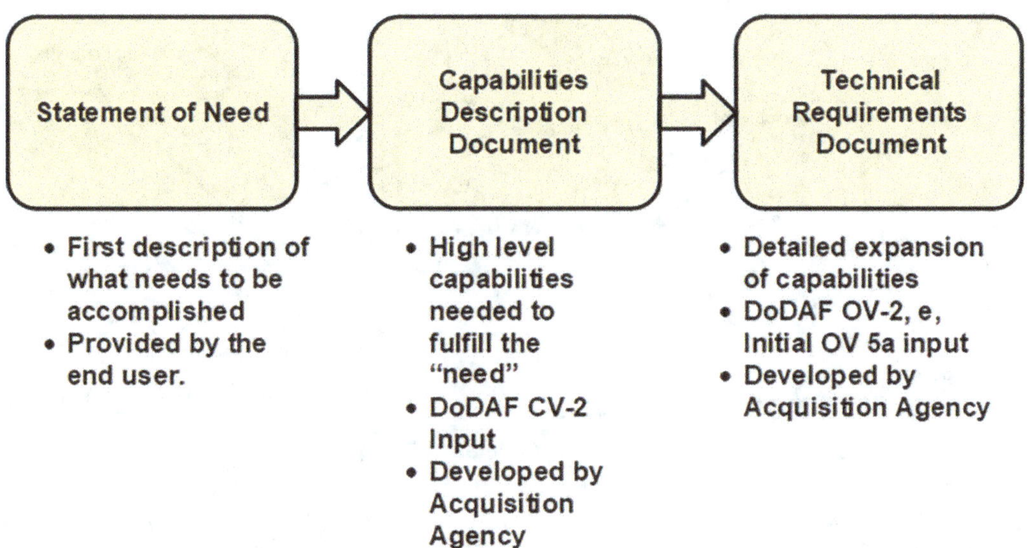

Figure 3-1. *Progression to technical requirements document (TRD)[1]*

---

[1] Author-created image

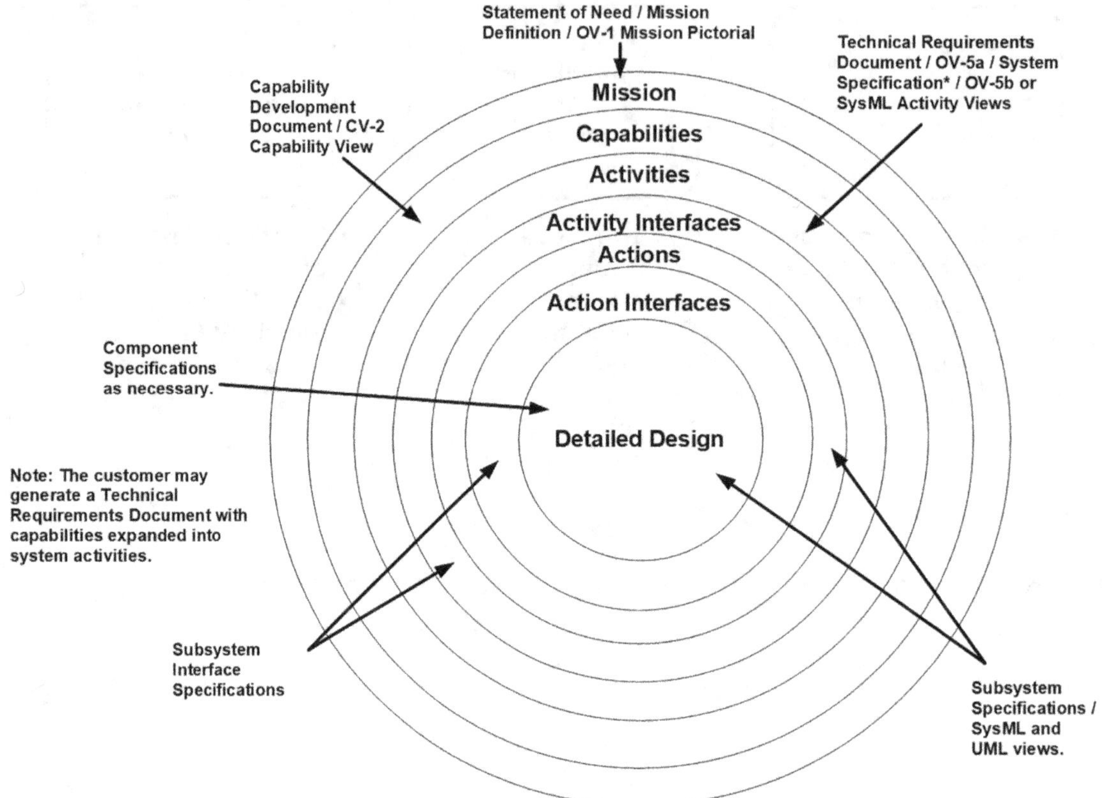

Figure 3-2. *Model layers to documentation[2]*

Operational View and System Nodes

A basic operational view is shown in Figure 3-3. This simplified representation highlights the relationships between the system's major components. Such a high-level overview is often sufficient for presentations to management and end users. In some cases, however, a more detailed depiction may be necessary. This can be accomplished using an alternative Use Case—style view, as illustrated in Figure 3-4.

In most cases, the view presented in Figure 3-3 is required for meetings with senior management and end users during program reviews. The use case diagram, however, serves as the starting point for documenting fundamental interactions within system operations. When developed using a modeling tool, it can be linked to capability and

---

[2] Author-created image

40

activity diagrams, enabling traceability throughout system evolution. Each use case, when properly constructed, includes a specification that defines its function. As part of the modeling tool's linking capability, this specification supports continued traceability of both activities and requirements across the system lifecycle.

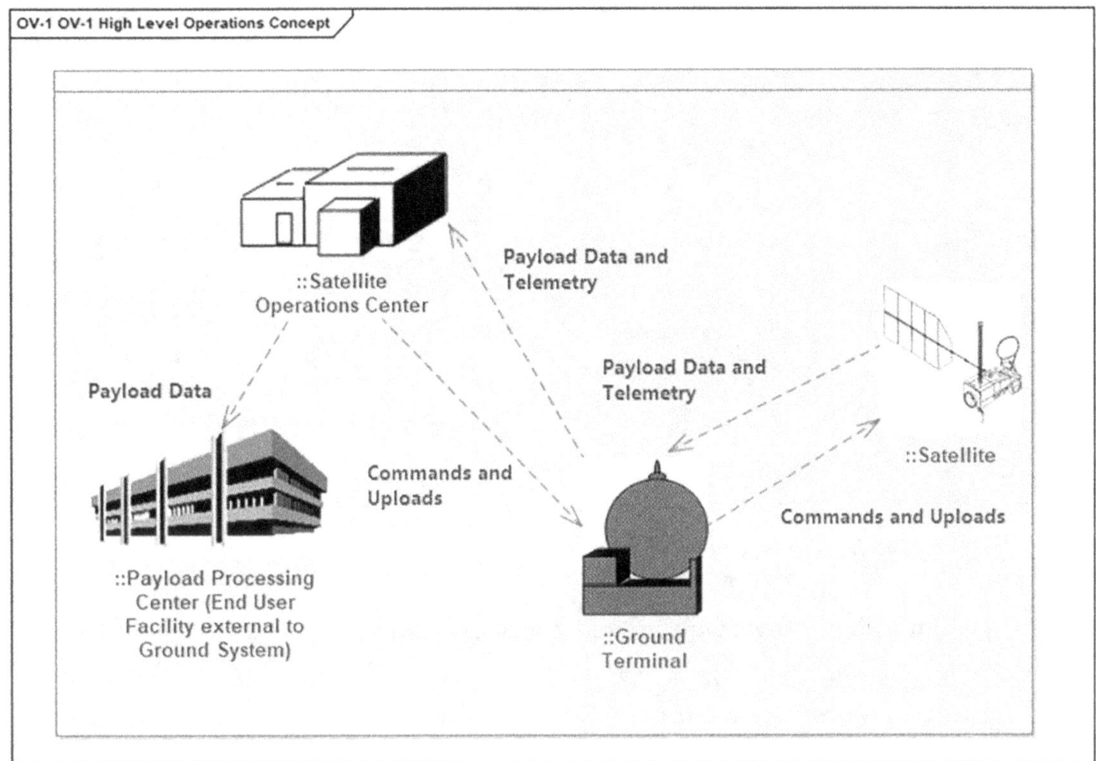

Figure 3-3. *System mission view[3]*

---

[3] Author-created image

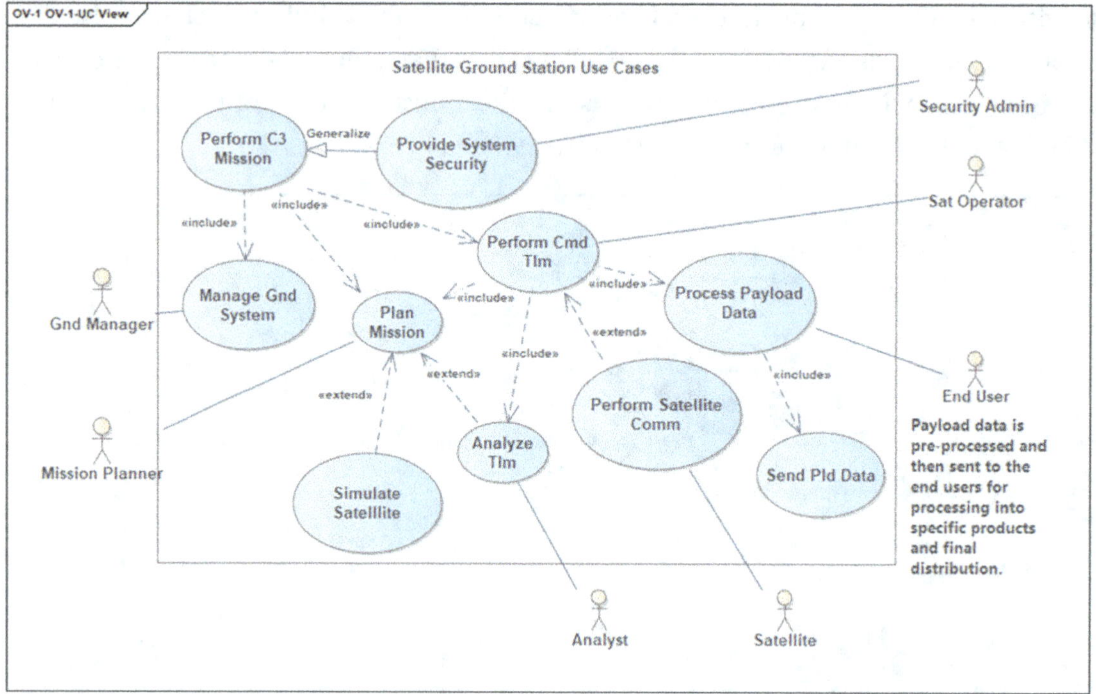

Figure 3-4. *OV-1 in use case view*[4]

Often, when a higher-level view is used, the acquisition support team will utilize an OV-1 node view (as shown in Figure 3-5) or an OV-2 node view (as shown in Figure 3-6). The OV-1 node view provides the functional nodes for the entire ground system, while the node view OV-2 (Figure 3-7) illustrates the distribution among operational centers and the ground station. Additional information can be included in an OV-2 node view by leveraging the model's notes, requirements, and constraint sections of the model for each component.

It's important to recognize that these views are not merely illustrations—they are distinct modeling approaches used to visualize system behavior. Collectively, they bridge system-level understanding with detailed operational responsibilities. Select the view that best supports the team's efforts to refine the mission description and requirements beyond the executive-level OV-1 briefing. The purpose of modeling here is to facilitate the thought process that leads to well-defined requirements and specifications.

---

[4] Author-created image

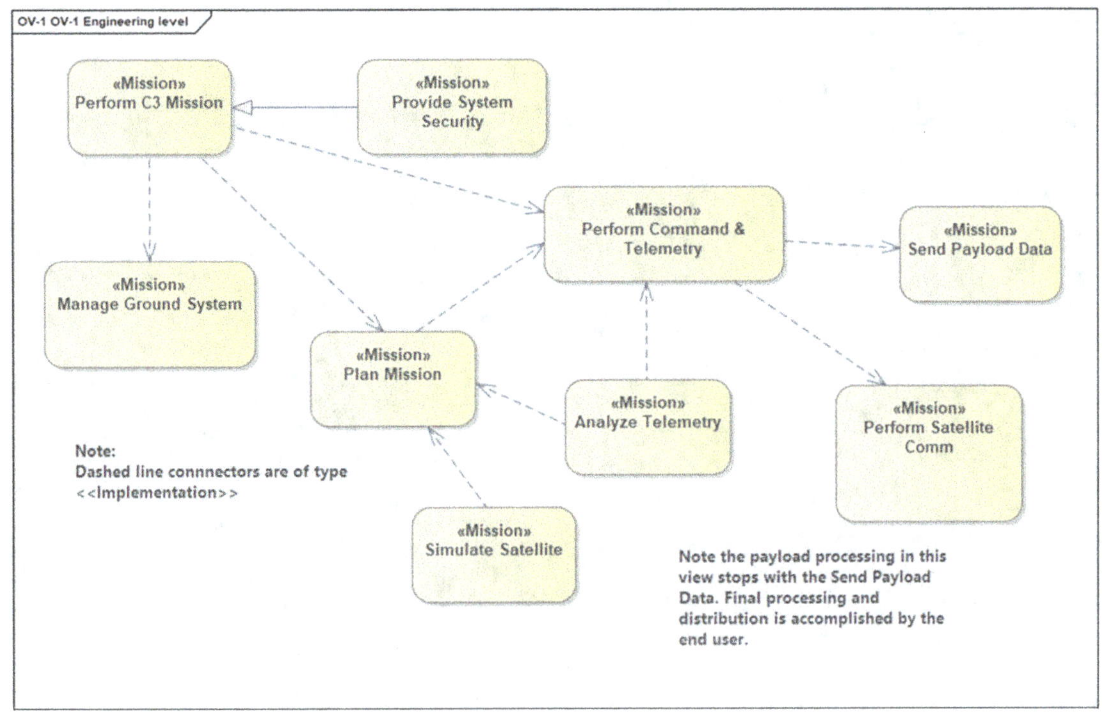

Figure 3-5. *Engineering level OV-1*[5]

---

[5] Author-created image

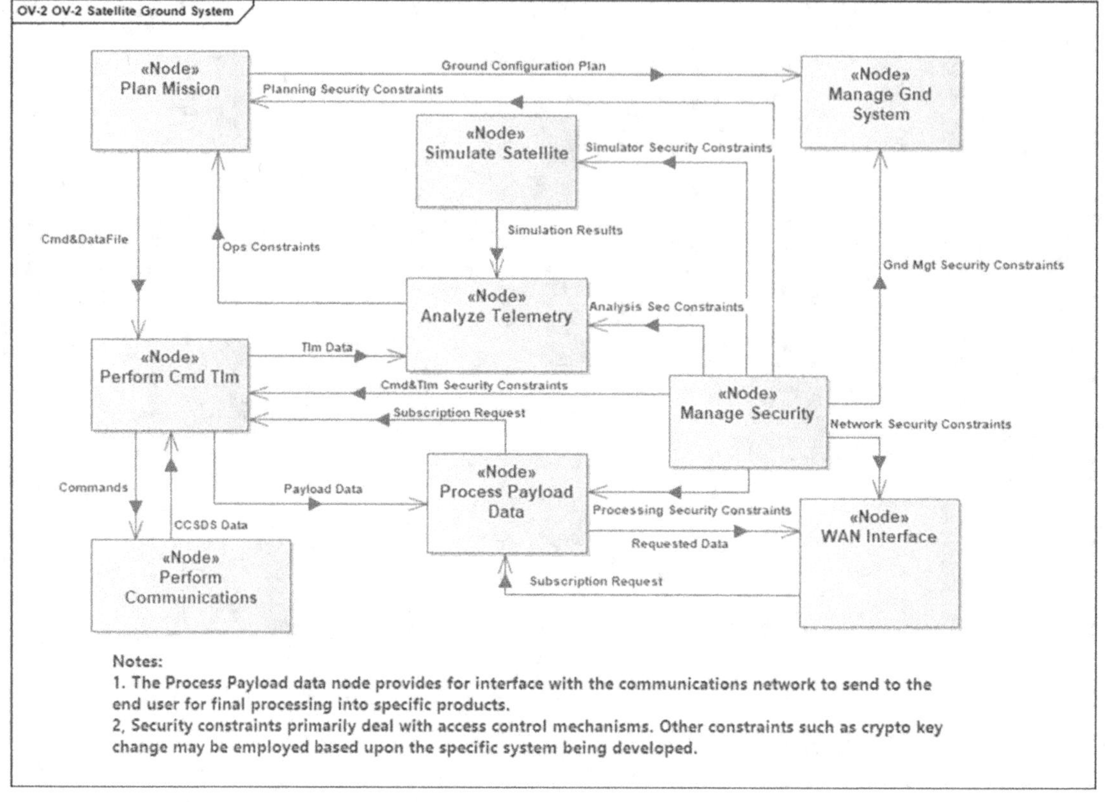

Figure 3-6. *OV-2 satellite ground system node view*[6]

[6] Author-created image

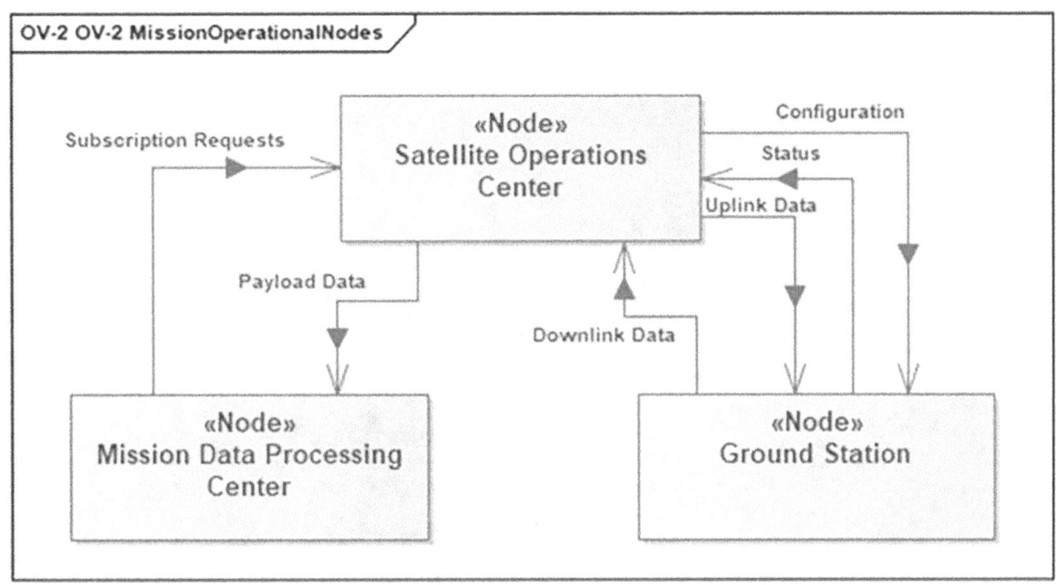

Figure 3-7. *OV-2 mission operational nodes[7]*

Proceeding to TRD development, the OV-1 and OV-2 views provide a system perspective. The OV-5a taxonomy view (Figure 3-8) offers a good starting point for categorizing the TRD system-level requirements. For the OV-2 diagrams (Figures 3-6 and 3-7), we focused on nodes within the system. The Manage Security node accounts for the administrative aspects of security, primarily the access control aspects of NIST SP 800-53, from a central point. This Manage Security node is carried forward in the model and shown as an activity in the OV-5a Perform Mission activity (Figure 3-8). In this view, maintaining Manage Security as an operational activity within Perform Mission operational activities keeps security applicable across the system. As the Modeling continues, it ultimately includes activities performed in multiple nodes. In contrast, the Provide System Security OV-5a (Figures 3-9a and 3-9b) provides a breakout of system security activities that will address System Specification requirements and constraints. Note that a convention of adding the NIST-800-53 references has been included. This is not required by NIST or DoDAF; however, it will help to begin tracking security to required system activities and eventually how it is provided for in the design, test, and security certification. The inclusion of these references will also aid in performing future reviews of the model.

---

[7] Author-created image

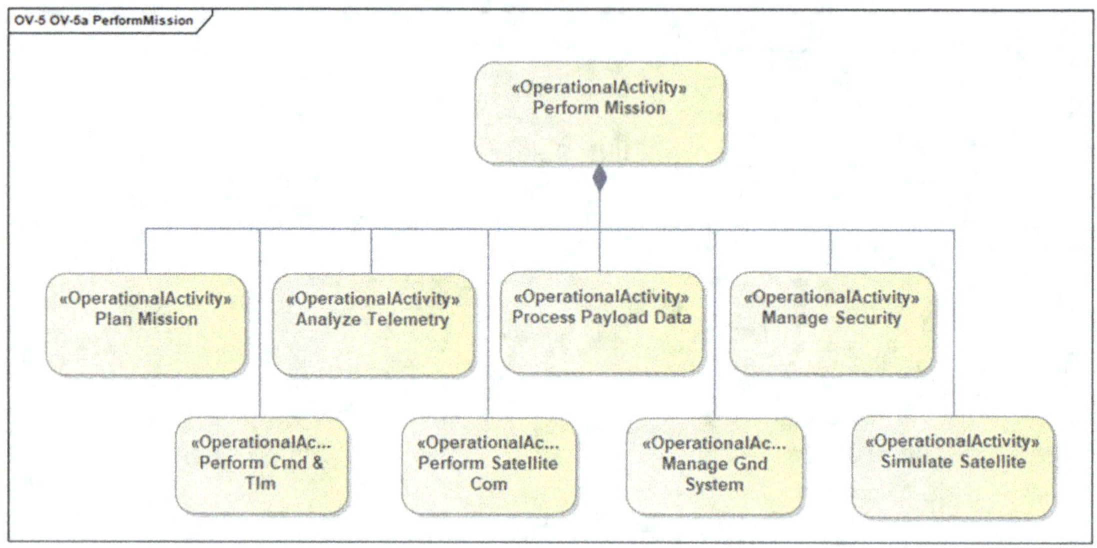

Figure 3-8. *OV-5a perform mission taxonomy view*[8]

---

[8] Author-created image

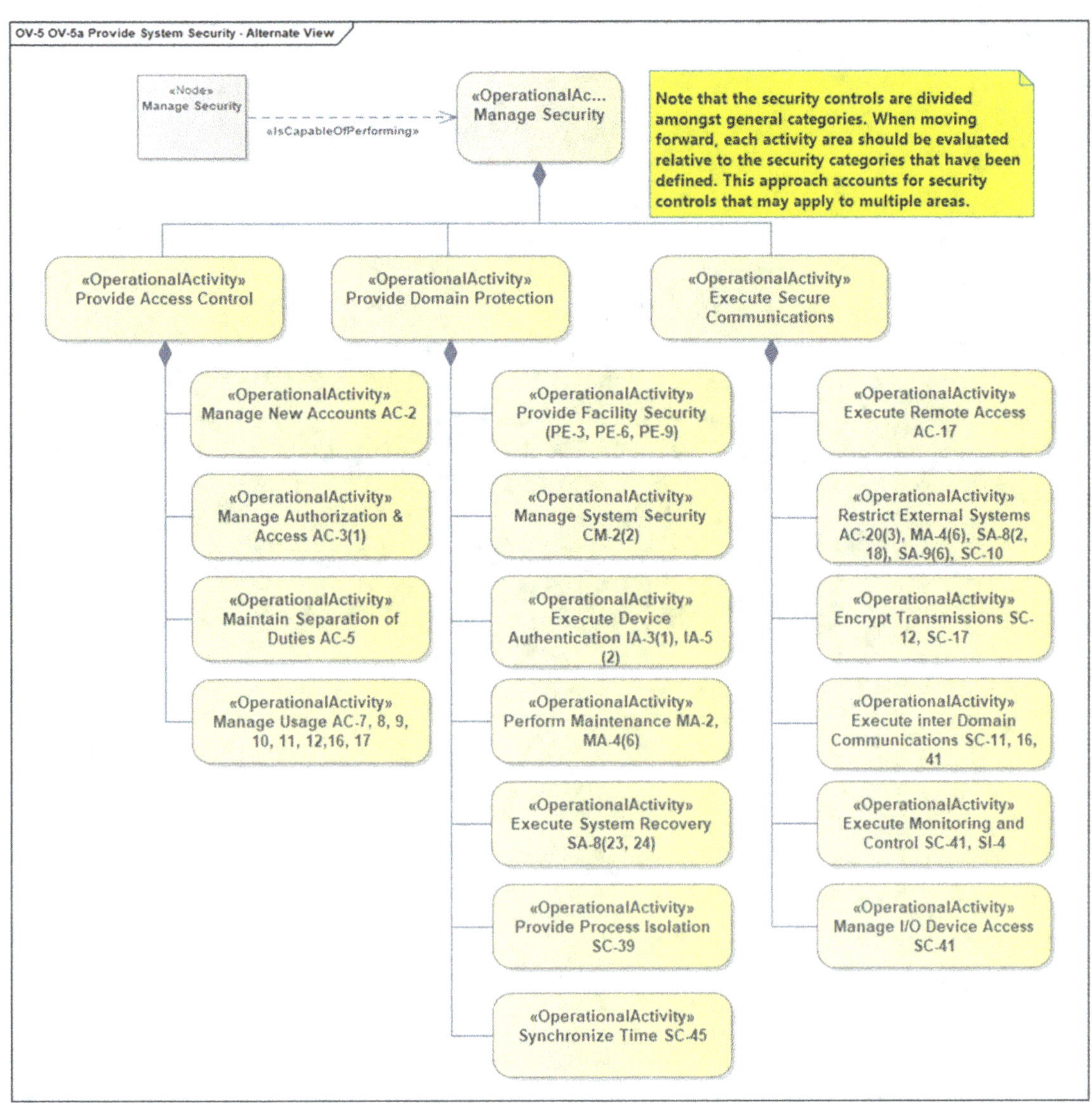

Figure 3-9a. *Provide system security OV-5a*[9]

---

[9] Author-created image

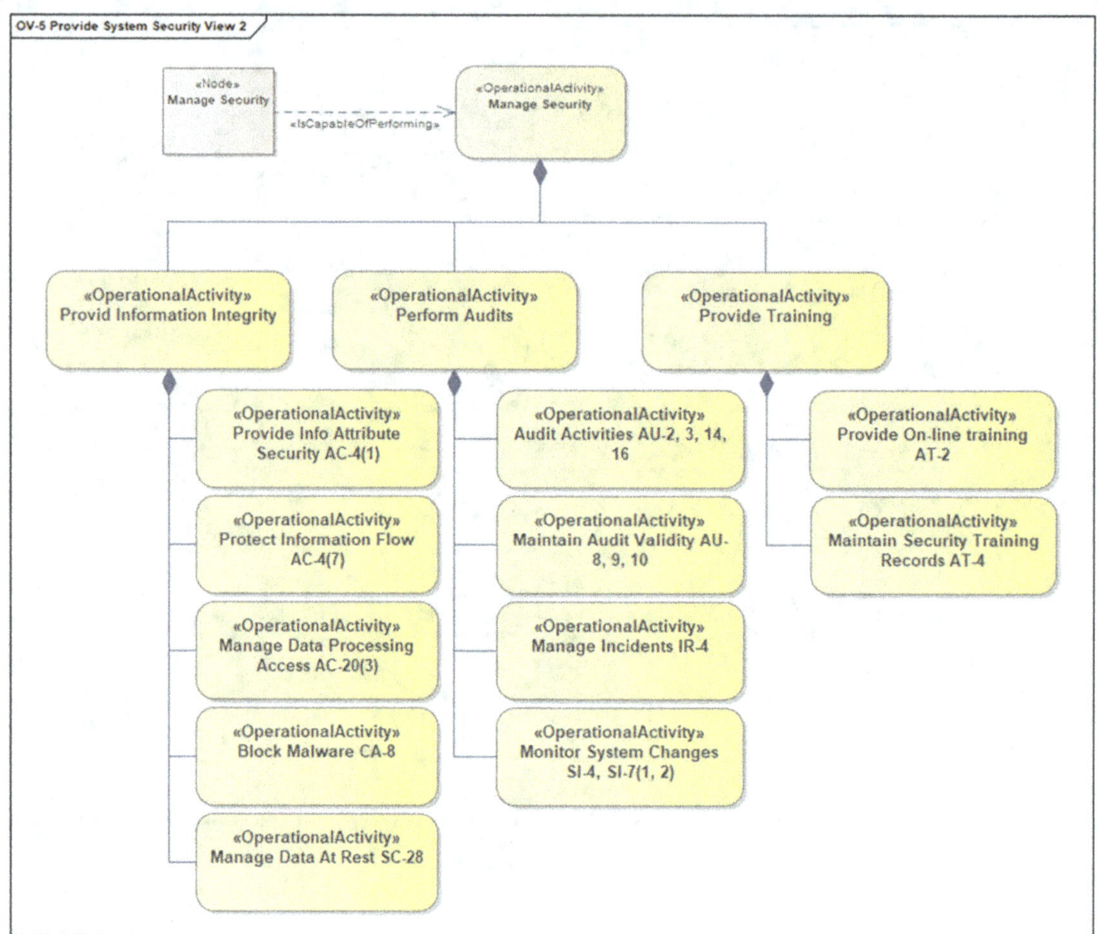

Figure 3-9b. *(continued)*

TRD Requirements and Constraints

OV-1, OV-2, and OV-5a provide more than just graphical high-level views of the system. When properly developed, they outline and provide context for developing the TRD requirements (or system requirements if a TRD is not used). This simultaneous development of the requirements and constraints, particularly while developing the OV-5a models, helps avoid extraneous requirements or the omission of needed ones. It forces concentration on what each OV-5a element provides. Good modeling tools offer a means to document the requirements and constraints as part of the element contained in the graphical view.

When developing an element, first consider if there are any constraints. For example, a constraint might be that the transmission system should operate in the S band. Specifying a particular transmit frequency or frequency range would be classified as a requirement. Constraints may be included in the specification as explanatory text or a "for example" statement. Remember that a constraint is often an overarching general restriction, while a requirement is very specific in terms of values/parameters or system/ subsystem actions. An example of adding a constraint to the model element "Perform Satellite Comm" is shown in Figure 3-10. The requirements associated with this model element, and its constraints, are shown in Figure 3-11.

Documenting the requirements in the tool as you develop the view helps in the thought process needed to provide a rationale for each functional TRD requirement. If the modeling tool is linked to a requirements tool such as DOORS, the requirements added to the model should be added to the requirements database. In most cases, both the requirements tool and the modeling tool have a publishing capability that can output a nearly completed specification. The key point is to keep the requirements consistent between the tools. Make use of the export and import capabilities of the tools. Develop a template for documents to be produced (TRD, System Requirements Document, System Specification, etc.). The modeling tools often provide externally developed templates that can be imported into the tool and applied as needed. For requirements database tools such as DOORS, the formatting and static text (headings, introductory text, etc.) are embedded within the requirements.

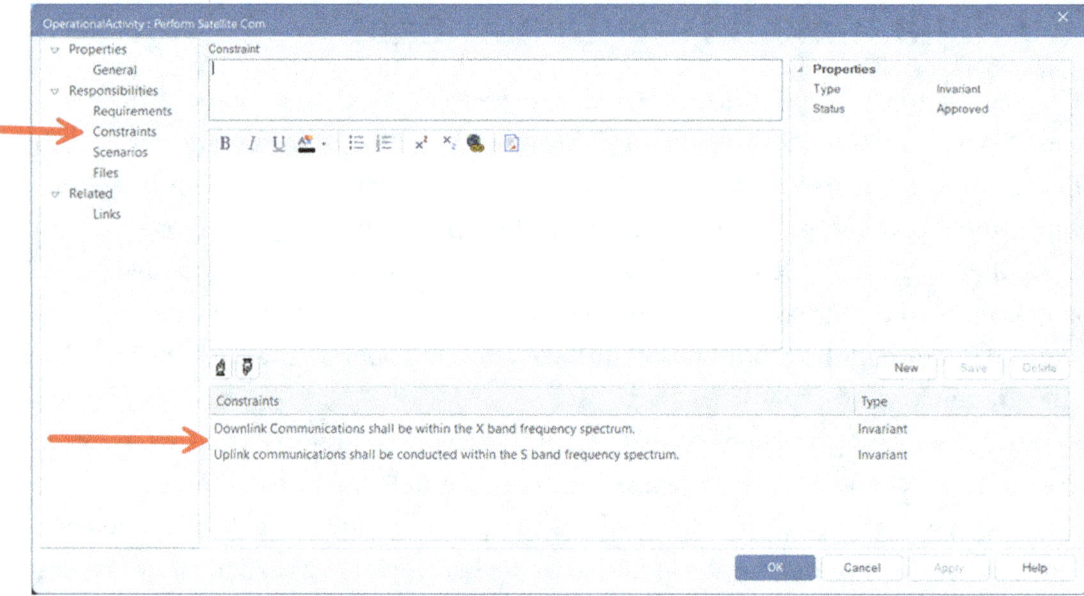

Figure 3-10. *Model element constraints[10]*

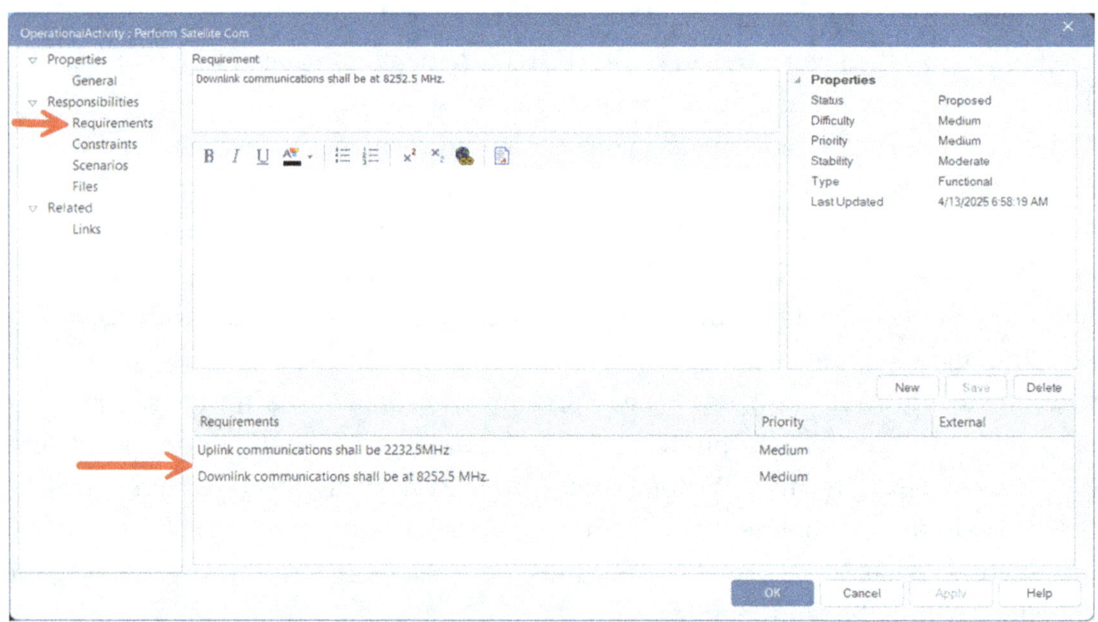

Figure 3-11. *Model element requirements[11]*

---

[10] Author-created image

[11] Author-created image

Regardless of the approach, it is recommended to develop the specification template early so that interim specifications can be produced as soon as the model for the applicable document (TRD, System Specification, Subsystem Specification, etc.) is completed. Early development of the templates, incorporated into the Modeling tool, aids in conducting a peer review of the documents as soon as possible after the completion of the applicable model views. This is essential if an agile systems engineering approach is used for the project to avoid delays between iteration steps. When requirements tools such as IBM DOORS are used, it is a good practice to link the modeling tool and the requirements tool. For example, tools such as SPARX EA and Magic Draw have an add-in available to establish this linkage. In this case, a template can be created within the requirements tool. Note that this template is normally a module with the format headings and other text inserted in a form that the tool recognizes as added text rather than requirements. Refer to the instructions provided with the requirements tool for details on how to accomplish this linkage and template creation.

Even if agile systems engineering is not employed, the rapid development of the applicable documents will provide for good reviews while the details are still fresh in the minds of the team members. Engineers who have worked on several programs can attest to the fact that many of the comments received are non-technical and grammatical when there is a significant delay between model completion and document review. The objective of reviewing is to ensure that the technical content is complete, accurate, and understandable.

If the acquisition agency plans to provide a TRD with a Request for Proposal (RFP), it is still a good idea to generate an OV-5a and initial requirements/constraints. Having your own view of the requirements in advance to compare with the customer's TRD requirements provides a resource for evaluating and analysing how the customer and potentially the system user view the system. Differences in system viewpoints can potentially affect the cost estimates and the required project schedule.

Just a reminder, moving forward, DoDAF and SysML system-level views do not reflect physical design but rather provide a relationship between system behavioral activities and the actions necessary to perform those activities. The lower-level SysML and UML views will provide for the detailed design as shown in the System Engineering V (Figure 3-12). System design based on what off-the-shelf elements are available without regard for the required behavior and supporting activities results in significantly higher costs and program delays for changes to update detailed design, specifications, test plans, hardware, and software.

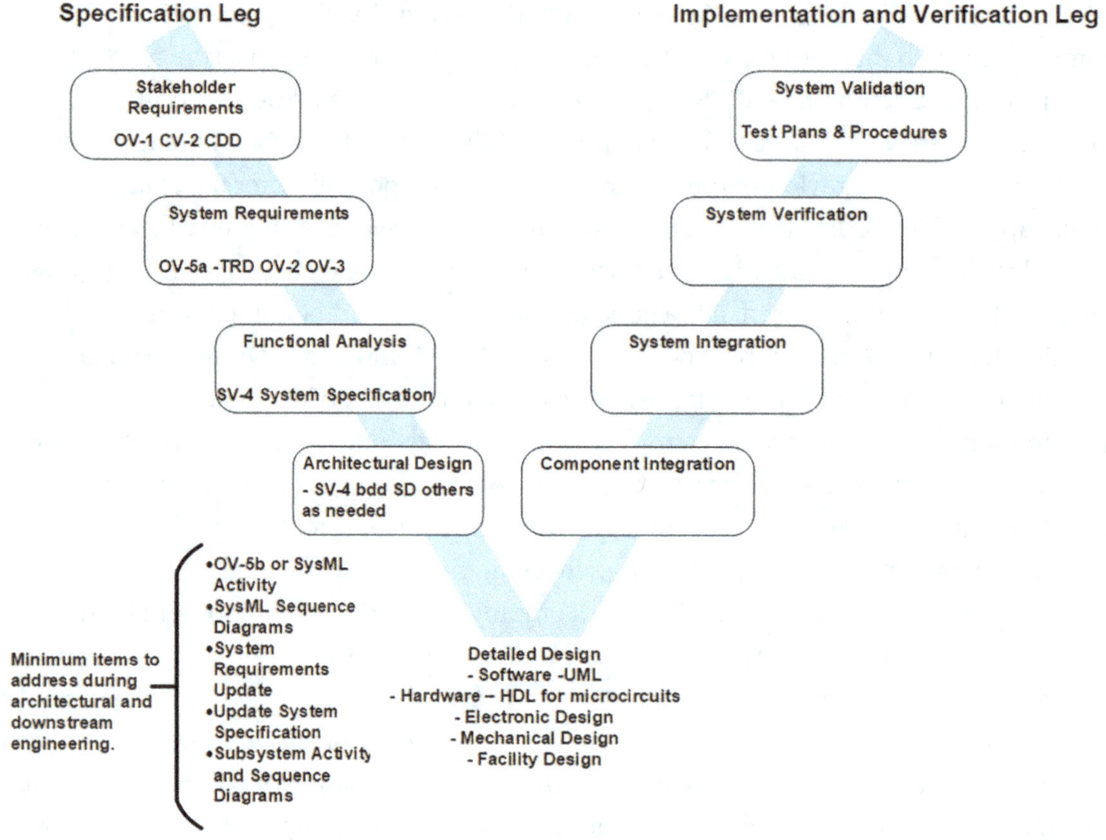

Figure 3-12. *System engineering V[12]*

Moving ahead, using our example model as the basis, revisions of the Perform Mission OV-5a and associated requirements should be made if there are differences between the original artifacts and the acquisition organization TRD. These revisions may affect the CV-2 (Figure 3-13), OV-2 (Figure 3-6), and OV-5a (Figure 3-8). The advantages of this approach become clear when working with the next level of model (and requirement) definition. Conducting peer reviews at the completion of each step further enhances the advantages of this approach. It can prevent delays later in the schedule due to rework of the development by catching errors early. Consider what would happen in terms of these issues cascading into hardware, software, and test planning if these changes were made later in the program. The result would be

---

[12] Author-created image

- Specification changes/additions.

- Changes to hardware/software.

- Potential changes to the test planning (if delayed too late in the program).

- Schedule delay, including missing required completion dates.

- Cost increases.

- When combined, these results create customer dissatisfaction.

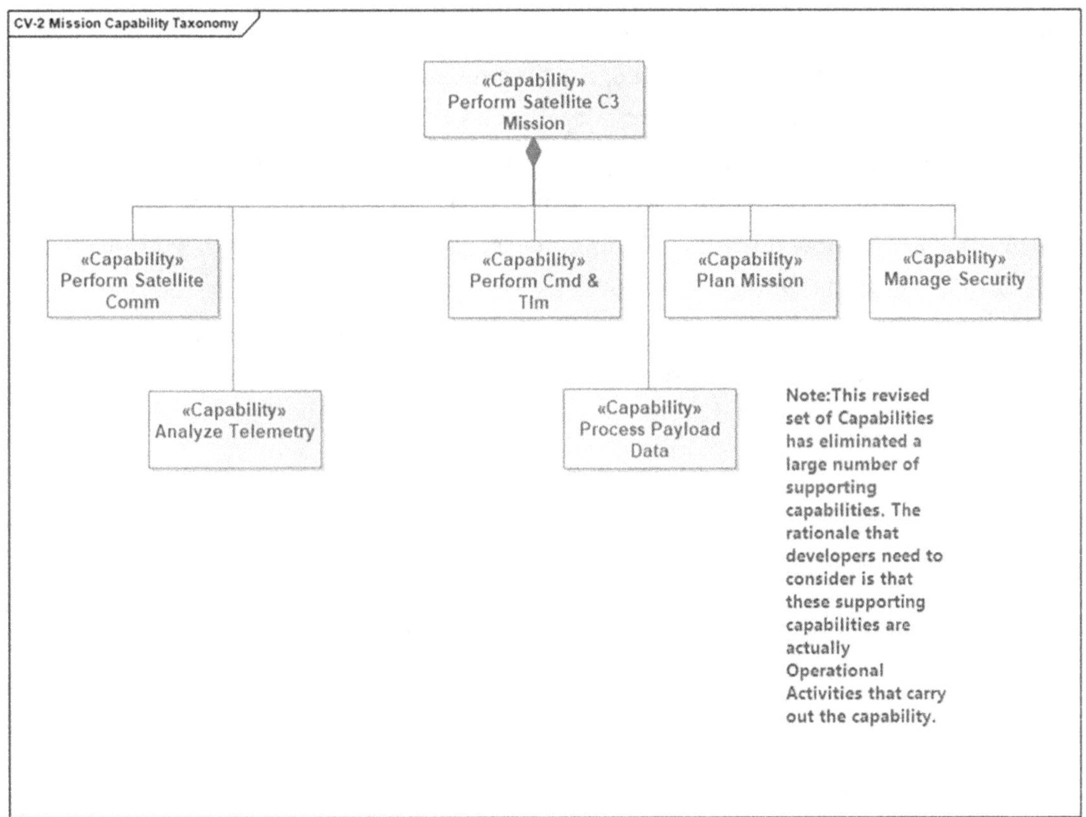

Figure 3-13. *Capability CV-2 view[13]*

---

[13] Author-created image

Earlier in this book, we emphasized using taxonomy views to rapidly develop the model and requirements. Now that we are progressing to greater detail for the TRD, we should look at the activity interactions. For larger systems, such as a satellite ground system, it is important to maintain consistency in the relationship between major activities throughout the model. To achieve this, generating a supplement to the OV-2 node diagram in the form of an OV-5b is a good idea. This is especially crucial if multiple engineers are working on the model and requirements. An example of the OV-5b is shown in Figure 3-14. The relationship of the CV-2 and OV-5b is shown in matrix form in Figure 3-15. The OV-5b and associated relationship matrix provide an initial step in the generation of a high-level sequence diagram to examine system interactions necessary to provide the required operational capabilities. This process can help to catch missed requirements if accomplished as part of the engineering thought process. An additional OV-5b view can be created for each activity shown in the Perform Mission OV-5a. The process also aids in finding any missing or extraneous connections between activities, including requirements and descriptions—notice the red arrows in Figure 3-15. It is a means of showing how the system would operate—i.e. how the activities interact to perform the required operation/mission. Keep in mind that when rigorously applied, this layered process strengthens consistency in the model and reduces or even eliminates overlooked requirements and misleading requirements that require rewording.

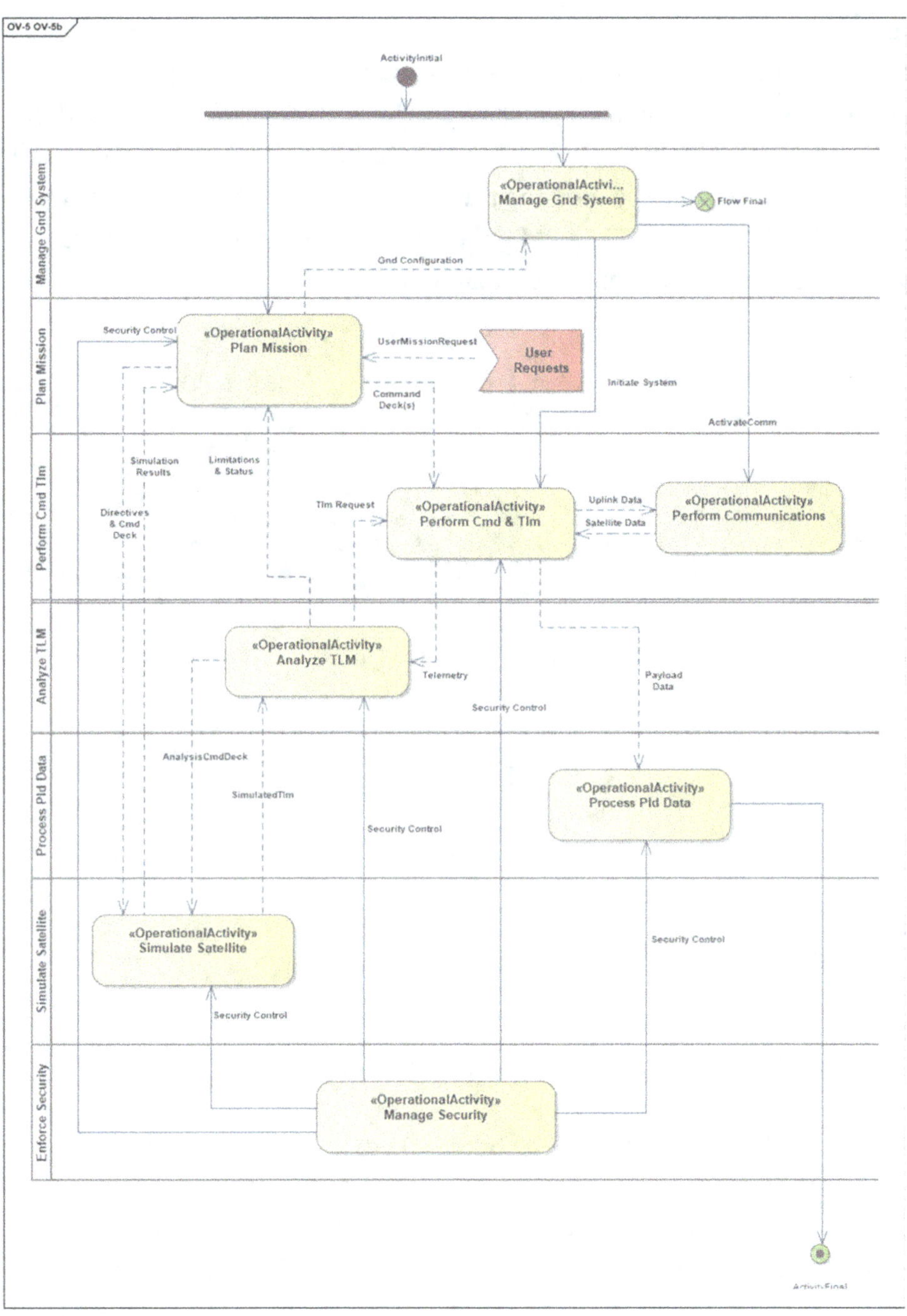

Figure 3-14. *Satellite ground system OV-5b*[14]

---

[14] Author-created image

It is good practice to compare each OV-5a activity with the associated capability. This acts as a second check to verify that each capability is not actually an activity. For example, during the development of the OV-5b Figure 3-14, it was discovered that a capability to Manage the Ground System and to Simulate the Satellite was missing. This discovery was accomplished by thinking through the process of satellite command and control while developing the OV-5b. When a comparison is made in the matrix view, Figure 3-15, we readily see the missing capabilities as highlighted by the empty columns.

Source \ Target	OV-5b::Analyze TLM	OV-5b::Manage Gnd System	OV-5b::Manage Security	OV-5b::Perform Cmd & Tlm	OV-5b::Perform Communication	OV-5b::Plan Mission	OV-5b::Process Pld Data	OV-5b::Simulate Satellite
CV-2 Initial Capabilities::Analyze Telemetry	⇑							
CV-2 Initial Capabilities::Manage Security			⇑					
CV-2 Initial Capabilities::Perform Cmd & Tlm				⇑				
CV-2 Initial Capabilities::Perform Satellite C3 Mission	⇑		⇑	⇑	⇑	⇑	⇑	
CV-2 Initial Capabilities::Perform Satellite Comm					⇑			
CV-2 Initial Capabilities::Plan Mission						⇑		
CV-2 Initial Capabilities::Process Payload Data							⇑	

Figure 3-15. *CV-2 to OV-5b perform mission matrix*[15]

Iteratively updating CV-2 and OV-5a helps ensure that all required capabilities are captured early, reducing the risk of missed requirements, costly rework, and delays during later program phases. Using the OV-5a to ensure that the CV-2 contains all required capabilities eliminates a cause of confusion later in the program, especially during test planning and procedure development. Some of the available Modeling tools, such as SPARX EA, provide a matrix view that can be used to cross-check capabilities against activities.

---

[15] Author-created image

When there is a mismatch between the capabilities of the CV-2, OV-5a and OV-5b activities, there is a good chance that either a capability is missing or that a capability is not valid or the OV-5a is not complete. Don't force a match! Forcing a match only increases the probability of problems ahead. Examine both the OV-5a logic and the capabilities. Keep in mind that a correct CV-2 adds to the validity of a CDD that may have been provided by the acquisition agency.

In this example, we have updated the CV-2 as shown in Figure 3-16 and the OV-5a as shown in Figure 3-17. The resultant CV-2 to OV-5a profile view matrix updates to the matrix shown in Figure 3-18.

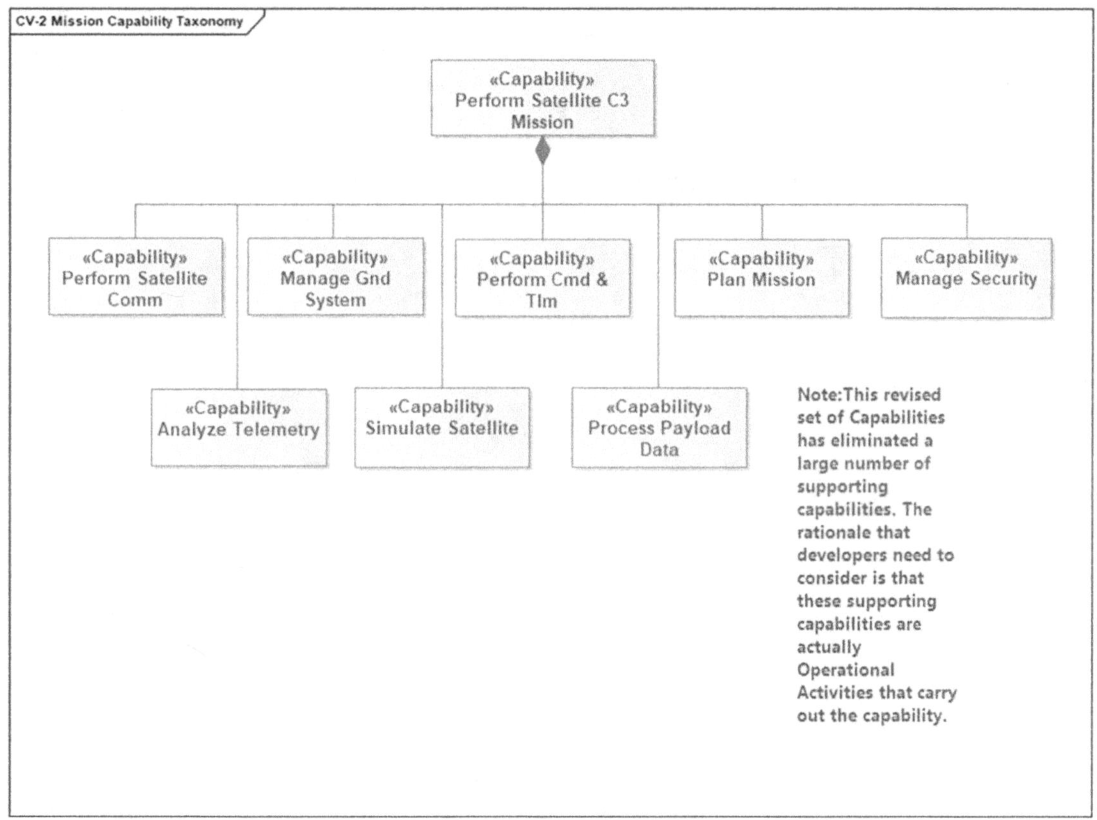

Figure 3-16. *Updated CV-2[16]*

---

[16] Author-created image

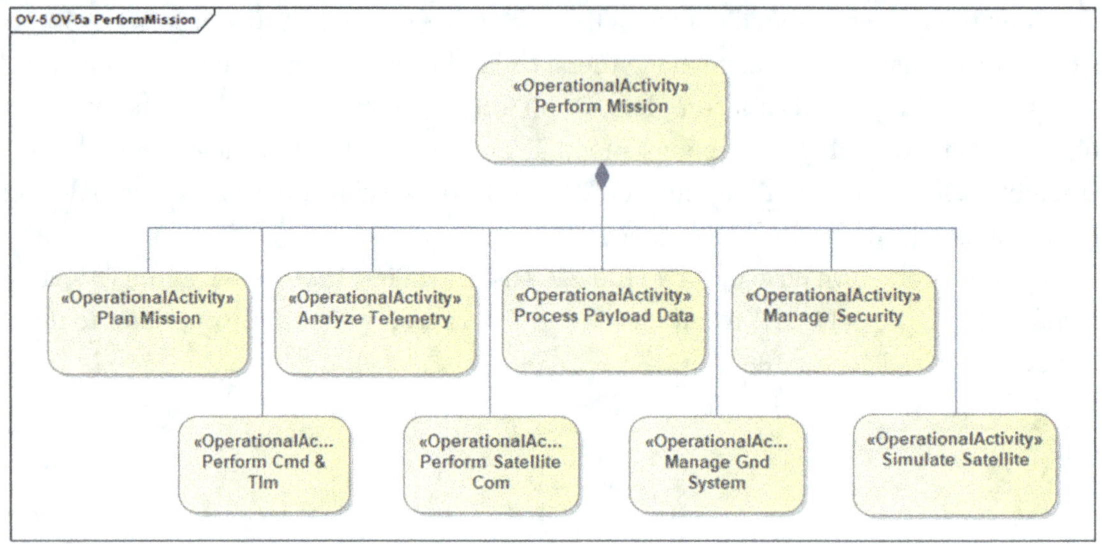

Figure 3-17. *Updated OV-5a perform mission diagram*[17]

---

[17] Author-created image

Source \ Target (+)	OV-5a PerformMission::Analyze Telemetry	OV-5a PerformMission::Manage Gnd System	OV-5a PerformMission::Manage Security	OV-5a PerformMission::Perform Cmd & Tlm	OV-5a PerformMission::Perform Mission	OV-5a PerformMission::Perform Satellite Con	OV-5a PerformMission::Plan Mission	OV-5a PerformMission::Process Payload Data	OV-5a PerformMission::Simulate Satellite
CV-2 Base Model::Analyze Telemetry	↑								
CV-2 Base Model::Manage Gnd System		↑							
CV-2 Base Model::Manage Security			↑						
CV-2 Base Model::Perform Cmd & Tlm				↑					
CV-2 Base Model::Perform Satellite C3 Mission					↑				
CV-2 Base Model::Perform Satellite Comm						↑			
CV-2 Base Model::Plan Mission							↑		
CV-2 Base Model::Process Payload Data								↑	
CV-2 Base Model::Simulate Satellite									↑

Figure 3-18. *Updated CV-2 to OV5a perform mission matrix example*[18]

Finally, in this review, the engineer may come up with additional features that are required. One example is the effort to extract data from the CCSDS Telemetry frame. Before adding this type of capability to the OV-5a view, consider if the extraction is part of an overarching capability, a supporting activity, or a function that is performed to implement the activity. In this case, an OV-5a expansion of the Perform Cmd & Tlm activity in Figure 3-8 was created as shown in Figure 3-19. Note the reference to the OV-2 node Perform Cmd & Tlm as well as the repetition of the Perform Cmd & Tlm at the head of the activities. This approach, though not called out by DoDAF standards, helps the engineering group when investigating a potential issue. Knowing the predecessor for the activities in review without having to physically trace back to the source can help to reduce the time required to perform the investigation.

---

[18] Author-created image

Use of OV-5b, shown in Figure 3-14, provides a good cross-check on the OV-5a activities as mentioned earlier.

Returning to the discussion of the CCSDS extraction process, note the Display Tlm Operational Activity. For this example, Display Tlm was used to house the extraction process since this operational activity is involved with the CCSDS content. Further explanations are provided as shown in Figure 3-20.

In this example, the extraction was moved down to the SysML Activity view that supports the OV-5a Display-Tlm view. The detailed expansion of Perform Cmd & Tlm resulted in a clarification of activity scope and supported requirement traceability and strengthened alignment with the TRD. Reminder, an initial decision should be made and documented in the notes section of the higher-level activity as shown in the bold text within Figure 3-20. Overall, this is a good example of how thinking through the model results in refinement of the requirements that will be documented in the specification.

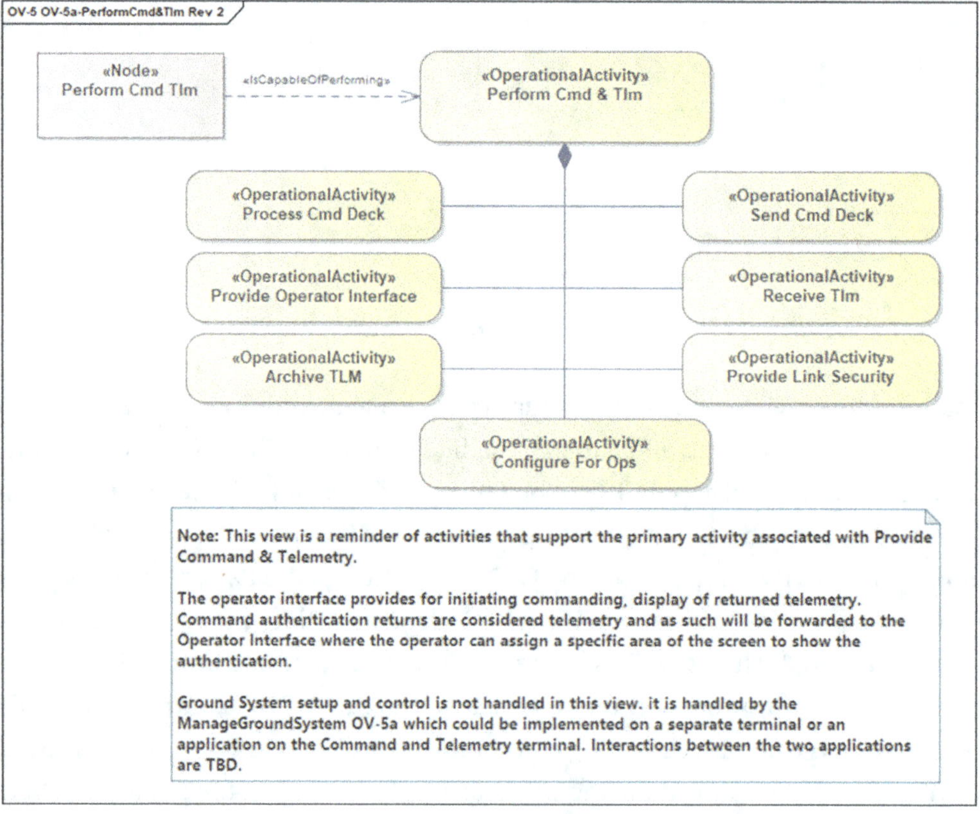

Figure 3-19. Updated perform Cmd & Tlm OV-5a[19]

---

[19] Author-created image

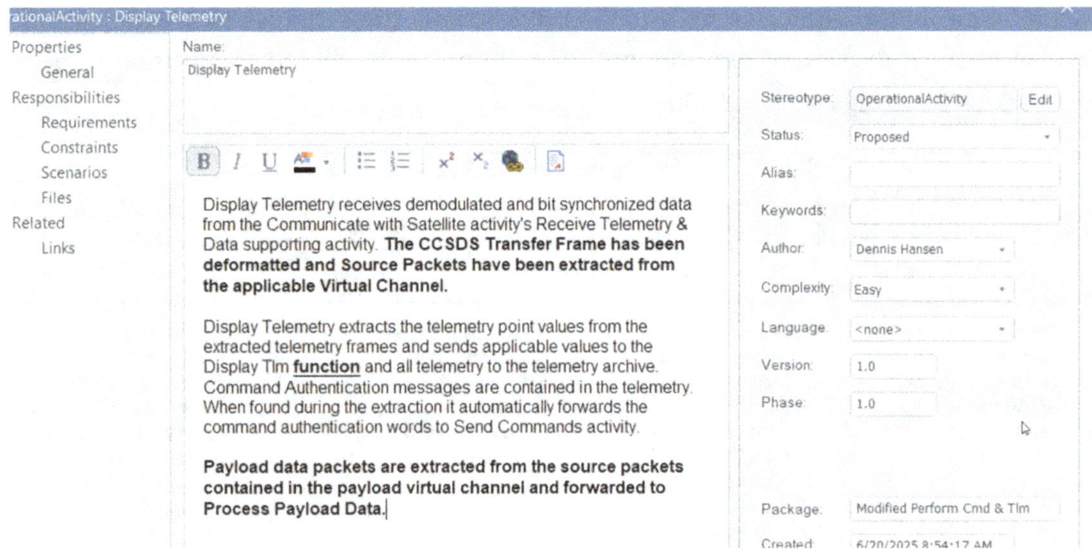

Figure 3-20. *Reminder of data frame processing decision*[20]

In combination, Figures 3-16 through 3-20 illustrate how taxonomy views, activity diagrams, and supporting notes work together to refine the system capabilities, system interactions, and provide a structured path from high-level capabilities down to detailed operational activities.

System Specification Using Level 1 Activities

Building upon the TRD and previous documents, as shown in Figure 3-21, we can produce the system specification. Details of what is required for the system specification are outlined in several documents available on the internet. The key guides for government contracts currently are data item description DI-IPSC-81431A [3] and MIL-STD-961E (available from the Defense Logistics Agency ASSIST website) and the outline provided in the data item description. Initially, the focus should be on the level 2 Activities of the OV-5a taxonomy. It is important to keep the identification of activities and requirements in alignment with the test planning. As previously mentioned,

---

[20] Author-created image

test planning should be started early in the program and move in lock step with the development of models and requirements documents. This will reduce future rework and work sequencing issues later in the program.

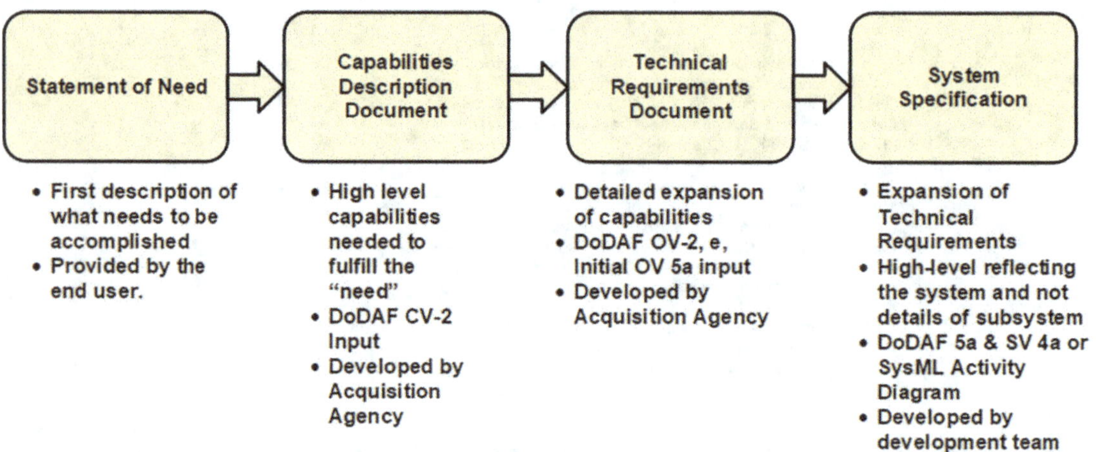

Figure 3-21. *Requirements flow to the system specification*[21]

Continuing the "development thought process," we will use the Perform Cmd & Tlm OV-5a breakout, Figure 3-19, with the supporting activities in this example because our initial concept was to have Perform Cmd & Tlm combined with Perform Communications. Consider how the system requirements would look if all these activities were combined with the Perform Communications activities in the same specification section. It might suffice for just a collection of requirements; however, later during the preparation of test plans and procedures, some test organization and sequencing difficulties may arise.

---

[21] Author-created image

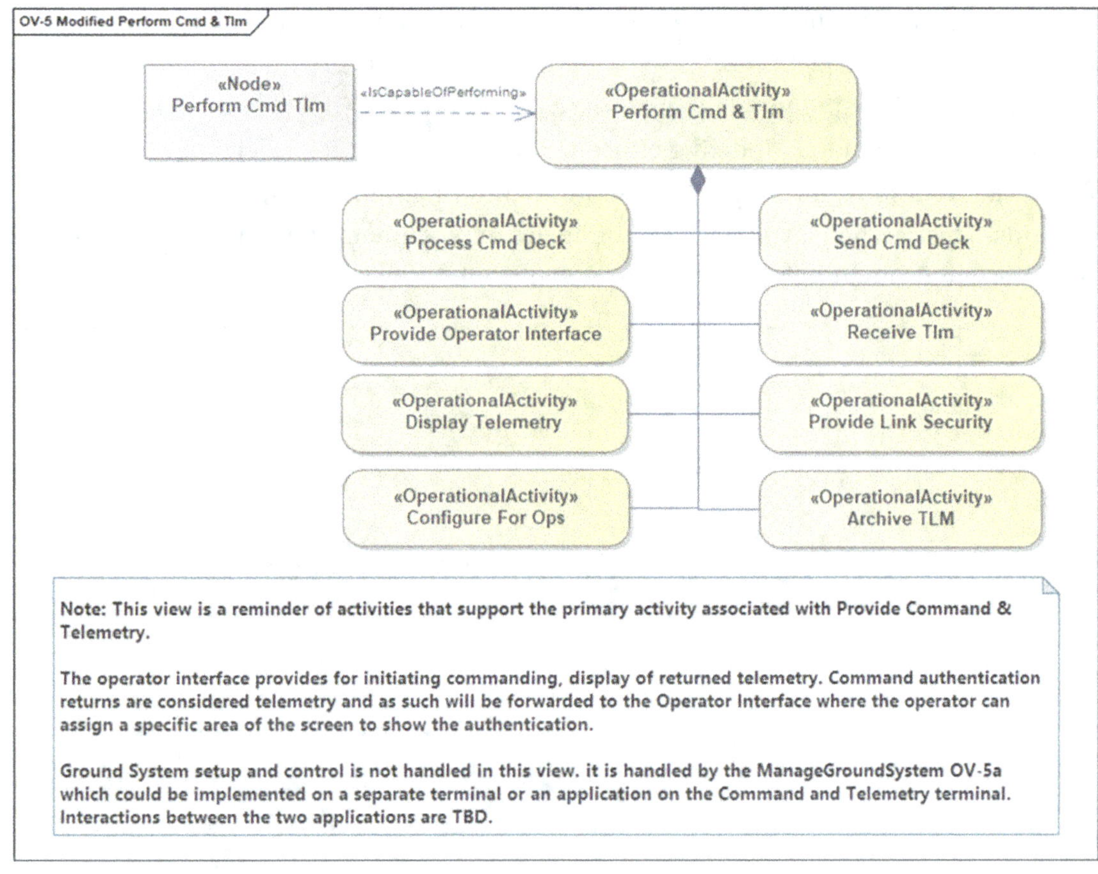

Figure 3-22. *Updated perform command and telemetry activity OV-5a[22]*

The concept thus far has been concentrated upon real-time operations to command the satellite and display the returned telemetry. Now consider that due to satellite anomalies, satellite complexity, and mission complexity, further telemetry analysis may be required. It could be argued that the same software and display terminal could be used for the analysis. On the other hand, consider that this approach could create operational conflicts related to the use of the display terminal. Particularly if the analysis takes a significant amount of time. To avoid this possibility of conflict, telemetry analysis has been separated into a separate subsystem. The operational view of this subsystem is shown in Figure 3-23. The separation of telemetry analysis and Perform Cmd & Tlm also provides some operational resilience since the functions are very different. Perform Cmd & Tlm is tailored to meet the real-time demands of satellite operation, while telemetry

---

[22] Author-created image

analysis is performed after the satellite contact has been completed. The tools employed are tailored for each type of operation. Keeping them separate reduces the complexity of both systems and the potential for errors and conflicts during operation.

A key point is that the Modeling effort provides a basis for the selection distribution of hardware and software within the system. It forms a basis for making/buying decisions. This can help avoid development and deployment problems and operational problems/inefficiencies after the system is deployed.

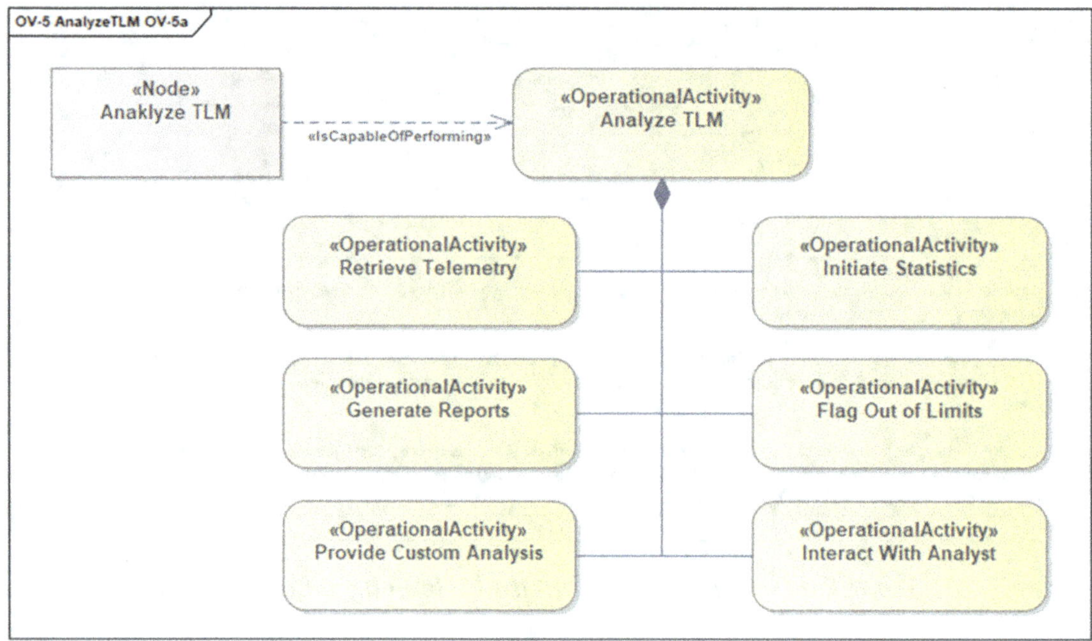

Figure 3-23. *Analyze telemetry activity OV-5a*[23]

When using the model to define operational activities needed, consider the assignment of activities to the components used in the physical implementation. Factors to be considered include items such as

- Use of commercially available software and the selection of which product meets the system operations and analysis needs.

---

[23] Author-created image

- Does the software package include an excess of capability that adds "software bloat" and potential downstream maintenance problems? Remember that problems outside of the primary/desired activity can cause issues with the primary activities.

- Software company stability and potential for going out of business. Remember that you normally are not given the source code needed for maintenance.

- Potential need for custom software to supplement the commercial item.

- Is the activity/function relatively simple to develop, thus eliminating the need for a COTS product? Will the addition of a non-COTS product increase manpower support costs that exceed yearly COTS license costs? It is assumed that the system acquisition provides for the delivery of design data and/or software source code to allow maintenance by the operational organization or any qualified contractor. Note that most often the software vendor will refuse to provide the source code and associated design data. In those cases, the best that can be expected is for the code and design to be placed in escrow in case the company goes out of business.

Process Payload Data

This example shows how to deal with systems/subsystems that are not a direct part of the system being developed. In this case, we have a subsystem that receives data from the system performing interface with and control of the satellite. From a mission standpoint, the Satellite Ground System extracts the payload data from the CCSDS frames and sends it to the end user facility. The processing of payload data is defined as at the end user facility with dedicated computers, as in Figure 3-24.

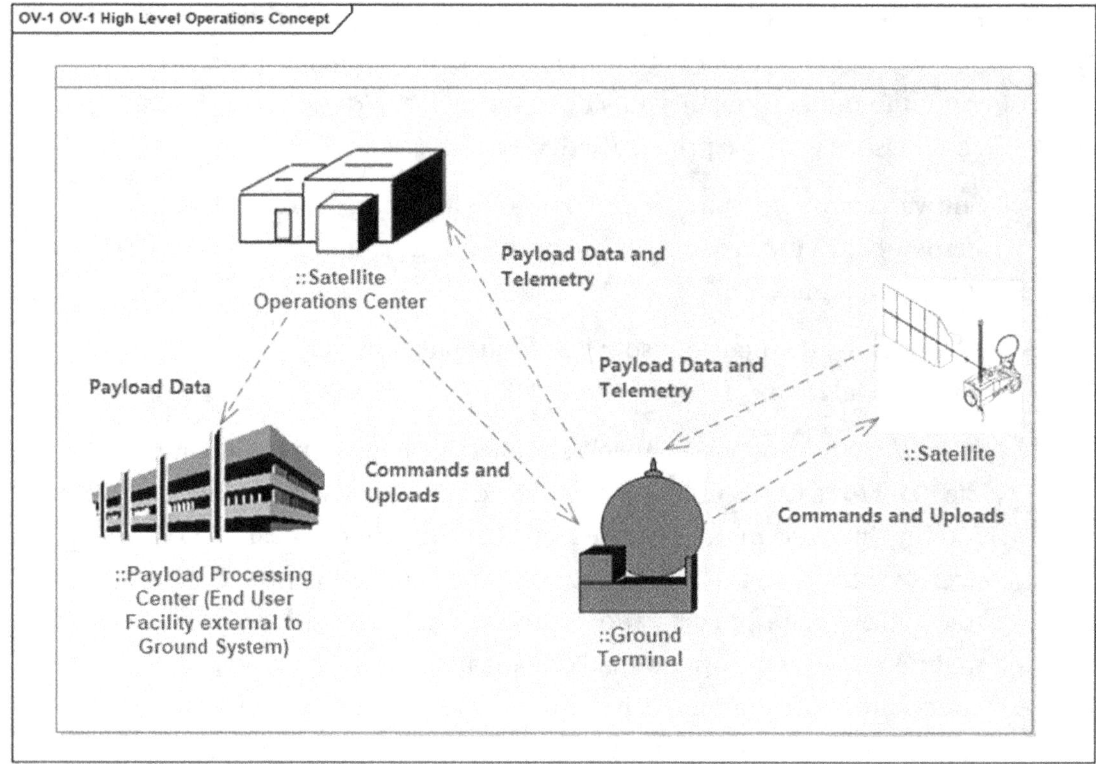

Figure 3-24. *Mission OV-1*[24]

Note that the process payload data in the Use Case view has an <<include>> linkage from Perform Cmd & Tlm (where it receives the raw data) and an <<include>> linkage to Send Pld Data—that is, sent to the end user. This is because payload processing is a part of the overall mission and is performed by the end user; however, processing to extract and preliminarily format the data for transmission to the end user is provided by the satellite ground system within Process Payload Data. For this example, the payload processing system to produce the final products usable by the operational organizations is assumed to be in a different location and developed on another contract Figure 3-26.

---

[24] Author-created image

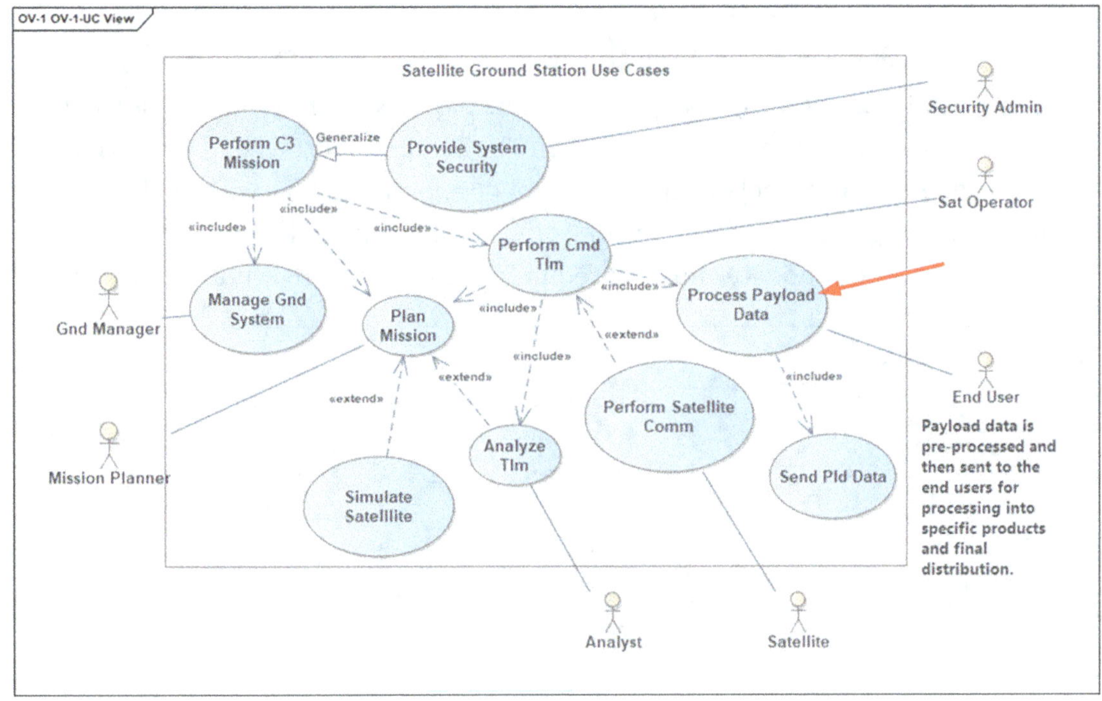

Figure 3-25. *OV-1 use case view*

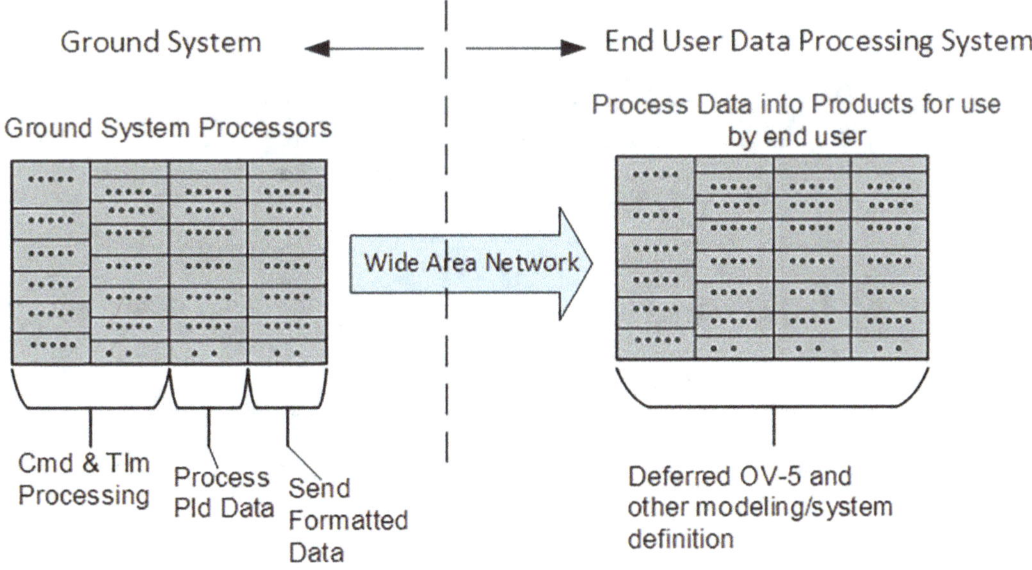

Figure 3-26. *Process payload data showing deferral*

For cases such as this, it is a good idea to generate a placeholder activity view, complete with documentation for reference purposes (Figure 3-27). An explanation covering why this view is being deferred should be provided in the Notes section of the artifact within the Modeling tool (Figure 3-28). The details of the payload processing should be added to the model during the system development. This will provide documentation that may be needed to adjust the ground station design in case changes are necessary to accommodate end-user requirements for data ingestion in their system.

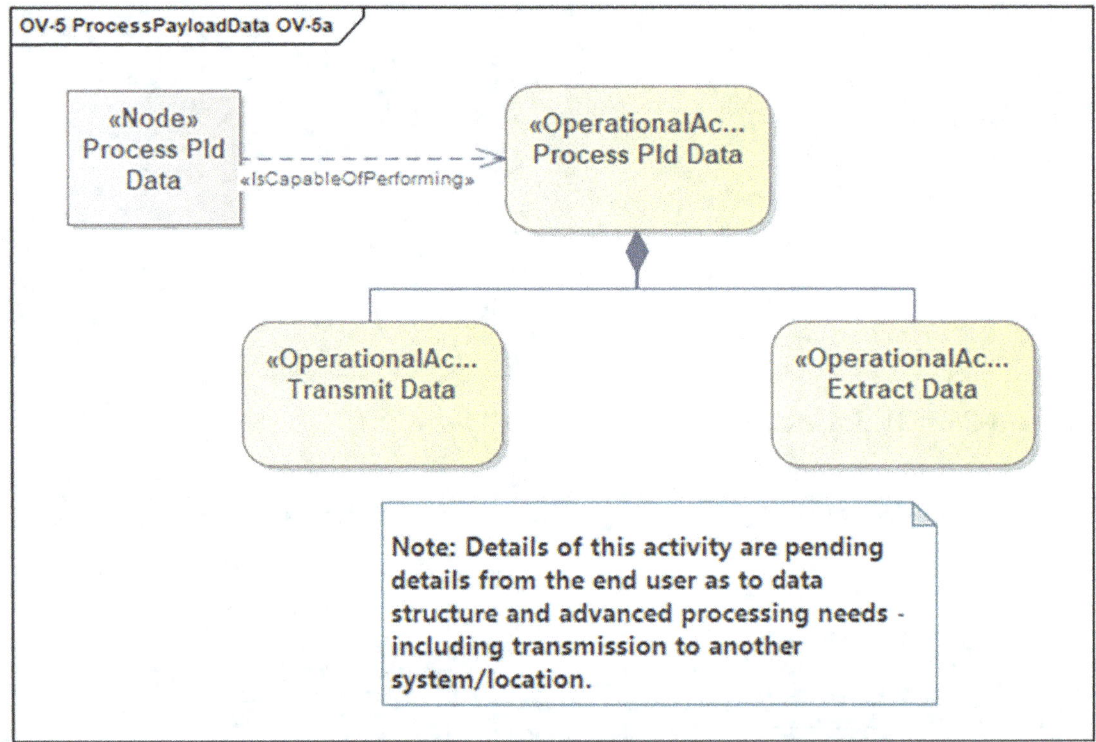

Figure 3-27. Deferral of process payload data design[25]

---

[25] Author-created image

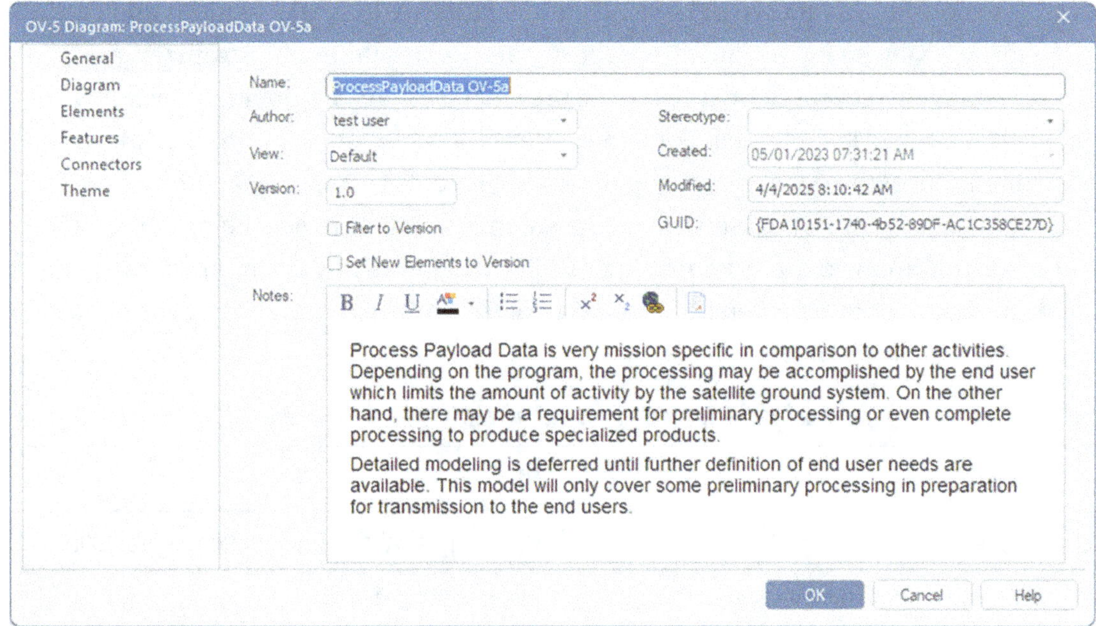

Figure 3-28. *Deferral of process payload data OV-5a*[26]

The complete payload processing model should be developed by the payload processing developer as a part of the payload processing contract. As the processing system model is developed, the two development groups should collaborate on areas of interface and interpretation of required data structures. This will avoid issues late in the development. When both models are completed, consider importing the payload processing model into the Satellite Ground System model to maintain an overall system model.

By deferring the payload processing modeling and development in this model and requirements set and having the acquisition agency and/or end user develop the model additions and requirements, we will avoid scope creep in the current TRD.

System Security

System security has become one of the most expensive items to provide in recent years. Many security issues are not discovered until system testing and accreditation, which is the most costly point in the schedule to address problems. Incorporating security measures from the beginning will help reduce these costs. There are 20 families of

---

[26] Author-created image

controls to consider, as shown in NIST SP 800-53 (Table 3-1). These families and controls are typically reviewed by the end-user security officer, development organization, and, for larger development organizations, the Chief Systems Engineer, Chief Software Engineer, and Security Engineer. For large systems, it is also advisable to consult with select members of the development team and payload data end-user at the start of the program to ensure no critical security items are missing. This review helps to select which controls apply to the system being developed. Identifying the required controls and documenting the accepted interpretation of the control requirements will aid in controlling development costs.

Table 3-1. *Security and privacy control families*[27]

Id	Family	Id	Family
AC	Access Control	PE	Physical and Environmental Protection
AI	Awareness and Training	PL	Planning
AU	Audit and Accountability	PM	Program Management
CA	Assessment, Authorization, and Monitoring	PS	Personnel Security
CM	Configuration Management	PI	PII Processing and Transparency
CP	Contingency Planning	RA	Risk Assessment
IA	Identification and Authentication	SA	System and Services Acquisition
IR	Incident Response	SC	System and Communications Protection
MA	Maintenance	SI	System and Information Integrity
MP	Media Protection	SR	Supply Chain Risk Management

At this point, the applicable control families should be evaluated relative to the OV-5a views. The NIST SP 800-53 controls are worded in a manner that describes the operational and administrative operations. After evaluating each control, consider what the system must do to implement/support the control and formulate a requirement. Evaluate each of these against each of the OV-5a activities. Linking the controls to OV-5a activities has the advantage of starting the evaluation process for the use of custom or COTS software. The OV-5a provides a first indication of what the complexity may entail.

---

[27] NIST SP 800-53 Revision 5, page 8 Table 1, available at `https://doi.org/10.6028/NIST.SP.800-53r5`

Remember that the modelling provides a basis for a checklist to evaluate COTS products and also assess the complexity and cost/schedule of developing the software for the controls in-house.

A good way to perform and document the assignment of requirements to activities is to develop an OV-5a view of the security controls in terms of categories. This helps to account for the fact that the implementation of a control may span more than one operational activity. An example of this categorization is shown in Figure 3-29a and Figure 3-29b. Note that in each case, the security family and control are shown in the diagram element. This will make it easier to assign the controls to one or more activities, as shown in the assignment matrix in Figure 3-30. This process should be conducted by the engineer assembling the model and the program's security engineer to ensure accurate and complete assignment of controls to activities. This will come in handy when developing requirements for lower-level activities, at which time the security engineer should be a part of the requirements development activity. Note that in this case these requirements are for the Technical Requirements Document level of documentation.

The security requirements may be expanded in the SV-4a and/or SysML Activity views, as well as the System and Subsystem Specifications. Rewording of the security control statements may be required to better describe the control in terms of the function/activity being described. Note that additional matrices can be developed, and it is acceptable to go back and update the previous requirements and relationships as the lower-level design progresses—that is, some controls may not be needed for one activity but should be assigned to another.

As the model and system definition progress, it is recommended that the modeling engineer and security engineer go back to NIST SP 800-53 and further evaluate the controls to see if any additions to the model functions/activities are required. Remember, modeling should aid in the thinking process for developing the system. Do not treat modeling as a product. It is the development and documentation of the design definition, including security controls, used to build the system.

Development Checkpoint

Upon completing the operational views, a cross-check should be accomplished to ensure that the capabilities identified in the CV-2 are accounted for in the OV-5a activity views. A handy way to accomplish this task is a matrix approach. Note that this capability is provided in tools such as SPARX EA and other modeling tools. For this example, we have discovered that the Manage Ground System and satellite simulation have not been covered. The model was updated by adding the applicable OV-5a view (Figure 3-31). Note that since modeling tools are built upon a database and the matrix is populated by the database, the addition of the new model activity is automatically added to the matrix (Figure 3-32). The intersection between the new activity and the corresponding capability will be empty. This is the default for adding a new column or row. The model developer is required to assign a linkage at the intersection of the empty row and column.

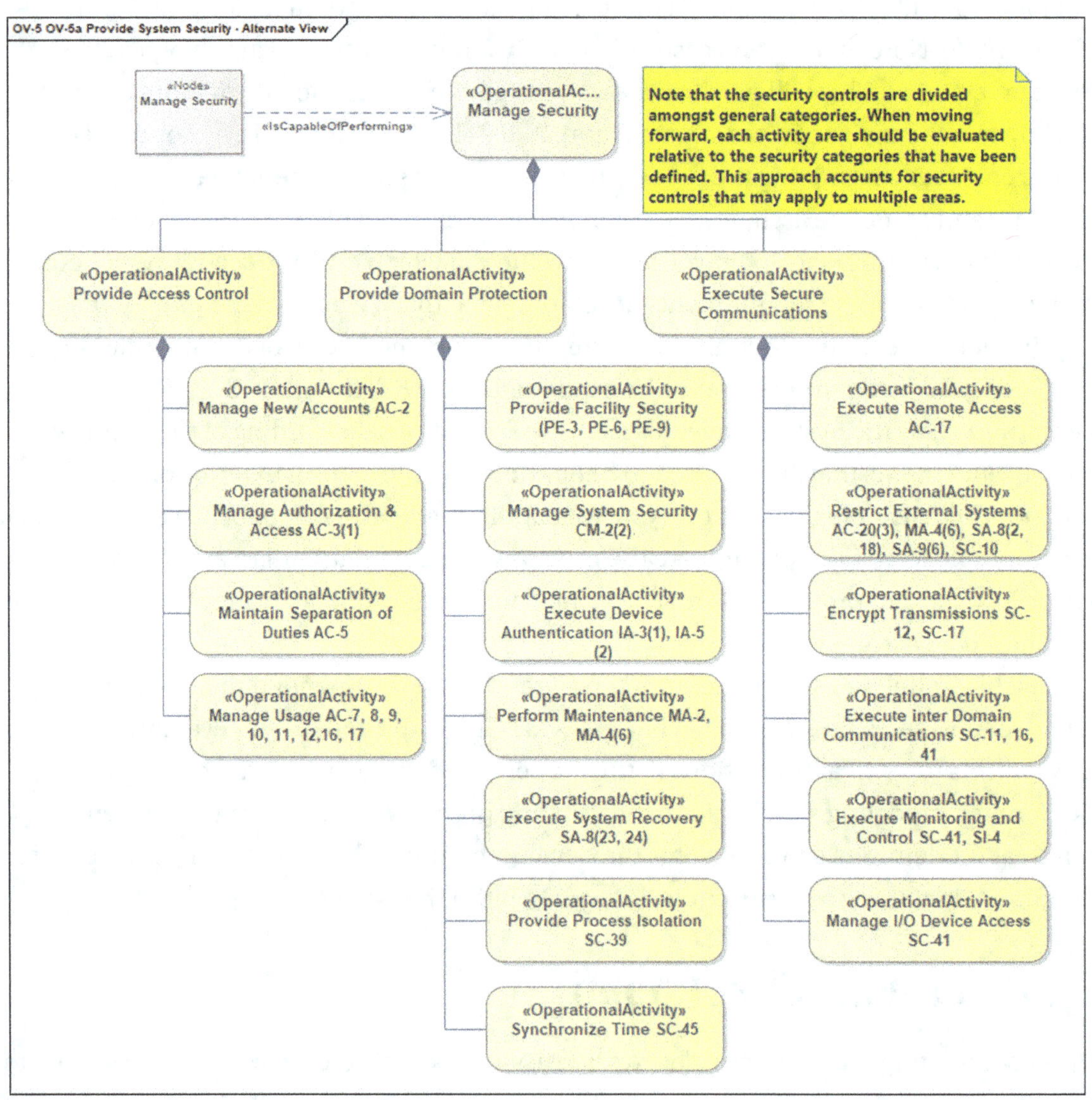

Figure 3-29a. *Security OV-5a example*[28]

---

[28] Author-created image

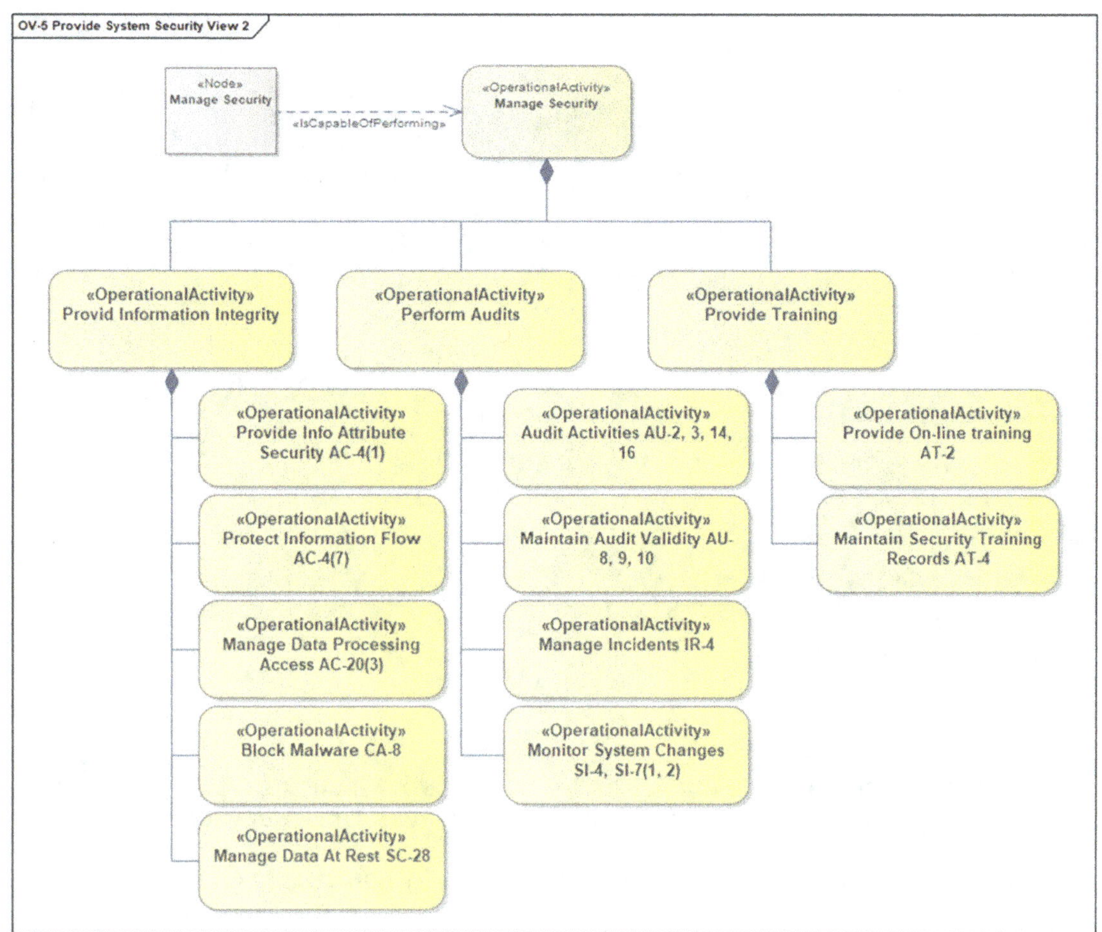

Figure 3-29b. (*continued*)

Source	OV-5a PerformMission::Analyze Telemetry	OV-5a PerformMission::Manage Gnd System	OV-5a PerformMission::Manage Security	OV-5a PerformMission::Plan Mission	OV-5a PerformMission::Process Payload Data	OV-5a PerformMission::Simulate Satellite
800-53-Controls::SEC-001 New Accounts Management [AC-2(1)]			✓			
800-53-Controls::SEC-002 Automatically Manage Temporary Accounts. [AC-2(2)]			✓			
800-53-Controls::SEC-003 Automatically Disable Accounts. [AC-2(3)]			✓			
800-53-Controls::SEC-004 Automatic Audit Account Creation or Modification. [AC-2(4)]			✓			
800-53-Controls::SEC-005 Automatic Logout [AC-2(5)]	✓	✓	✓	✓		✓
800-53-Controls::SEC-006 Privilege Management [AC-2(6)]	✓		✓			
800-53-Controls::SEC-007 Priveleged Accounts [AC-2(7)]	✓		✓	✓		
800-53-Controls::SEC-008 Dynamic Account Management [AC-2(8)]			✓			
800-53-Controls::SEC-009 Shared Account Restrictions [AC-2(9)]			✓			

Note: this is only an example portion of the total matrix which has a total of 88 rows. The first intersection for the column that shows empty is further down the list.

Figure 3-30. *Partial matrix view example of security controls to OV-5*[29]

---

[29] Author-created image

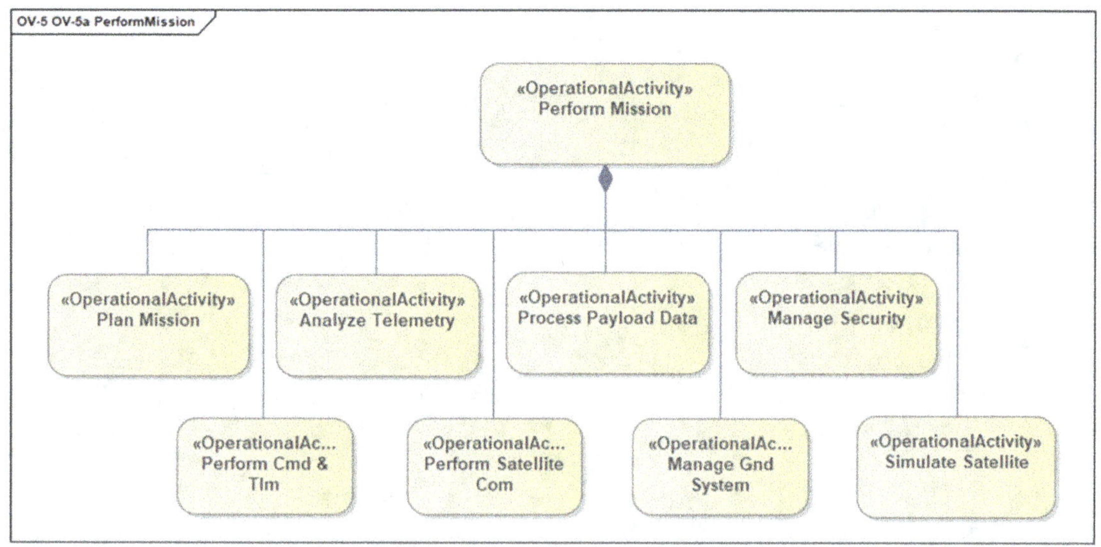

Figure 3-31. *Revised OV-5a for status matrix comparison*[30]

---

[30] Author-created image

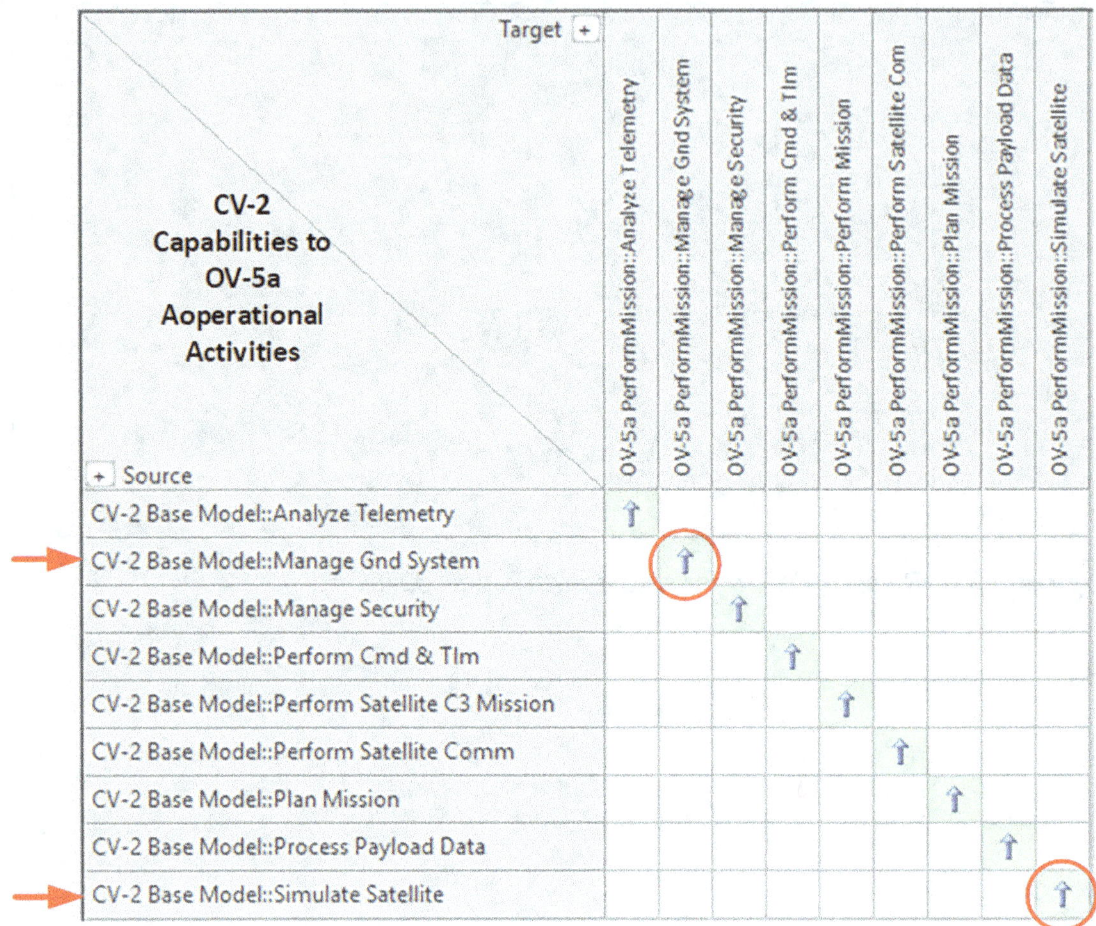

Figure 3-32. *Capability to OV-5a matrix comparison*

Considering Off-the-Shelf Products

Section Guidance for Managers and Engineers:

This section illustrates how Modeling can help to evolve the system and in this case, the ground system management subsystem. It shows that the initial view can be modified because of reviews after the initial model is completed. A functional view is used in addition to the activity view to highlight the changes due to the security review.

System Management Example

Ground system management is an item that is often overlooked or given limited attention. In past years, the view was to just select a network management product. This would be a grave mistake. Modern systems have greatly increased functionality and are not properly controlled via manual interaction with each component. Figure 3-33 shows Manage Gnd System with the supporting activities. The Manage Gnd System operational activity model element contains the high-level requirements. Key among the requirements is the requirement to use the Simple Network Management Protocol (SNMP) for managing the system. This is important for the selection of an off-the-shelf product or creating custom software since alternative protocols such as Network Configuration Protocol (NETCONF) exist.

Trading products and standards against each other requires that the developer consider what features are most important. For example, for our network management, consider that SNMP V3 emphasizes protocol-level security while NETCONF relies upon the transport layer for security. This may seem like a minor point; however, consider that it will drive the entire system's security approach. Also consider that SNMP V3 is primarily designed to monitor and configure network devices. NETCONF provides full configuration and state management of network devices. An independent model of the two approaches can be used for the team to consider the advantages and disadvantages. You need not add this model to the complete ground system mode. Just use it as an aid to discuss the approach and document the rationale for selection. Keep in mind that the selection of standards and products affects the entire system.

Note that from a ground system management perspective, the details are contained in an SV-4 taxonomy as shown in Figures 3-34a and 3-34b. The number of supporting functions that need to be addressed by ground system management greatly expands the management process. Consider the impact of spreading these functions among the operations team. Then consider how operations can be improved if the ground system is managed as one large enterprise from a single point. Note that once the system design matures, the number of functions may increase.

Once the operations view and supporting functional views are developed, review the security controls previously developed and documented in the model. Update the SV-4a functional taxonomy view to add security where required, as shown in Figures 3-35a and 3-35b. Note how the blocks are shaded. Within the Support Secure Operation column, the top grey block indicates that the requirements have been modified. The bottom three blocks are new.

Note that Figures 3-35a and 3-35b are fashioned as called for by DoDAF 2.02 with functions taking the place of the operational activities as was the case in Figures 3-34a and 3-34b. This DoDAF 2.02 representation was chosen to illustrate how the SV-5 is used to show the relationship between operational views.

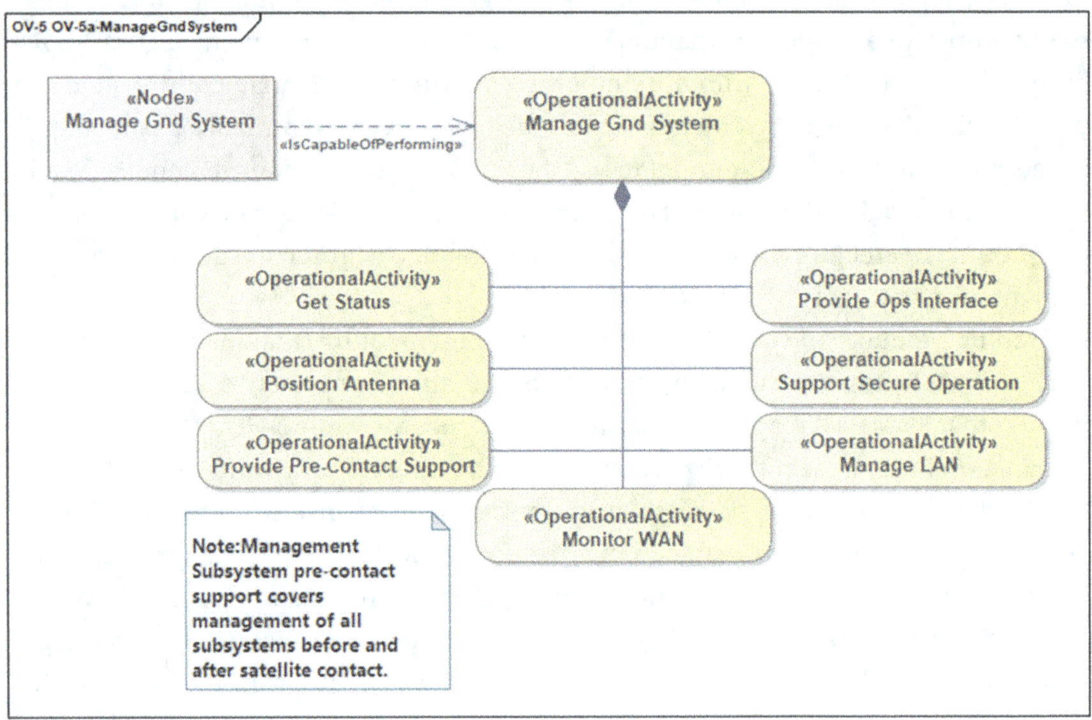

Figure 3-33. *Manage ground system OV-5a[31]*

---

[31] Author-created image

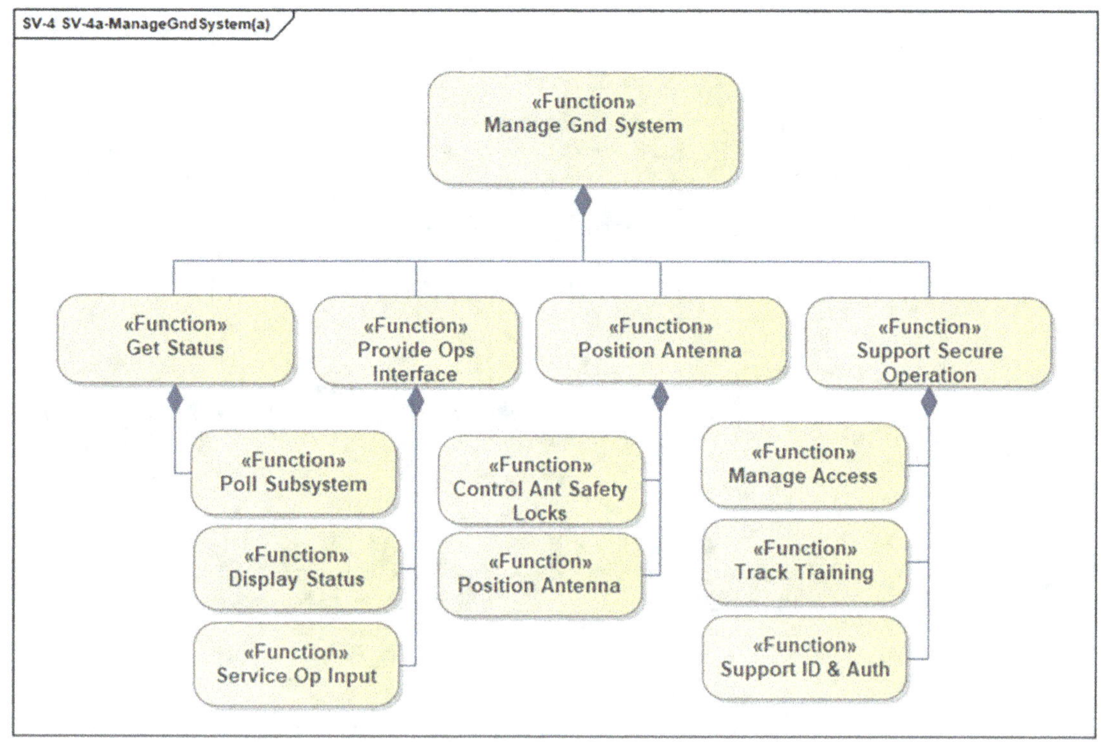

Figure 3-34a. *Manage ground system SV-4a*[32]

---

[32] Author-created image

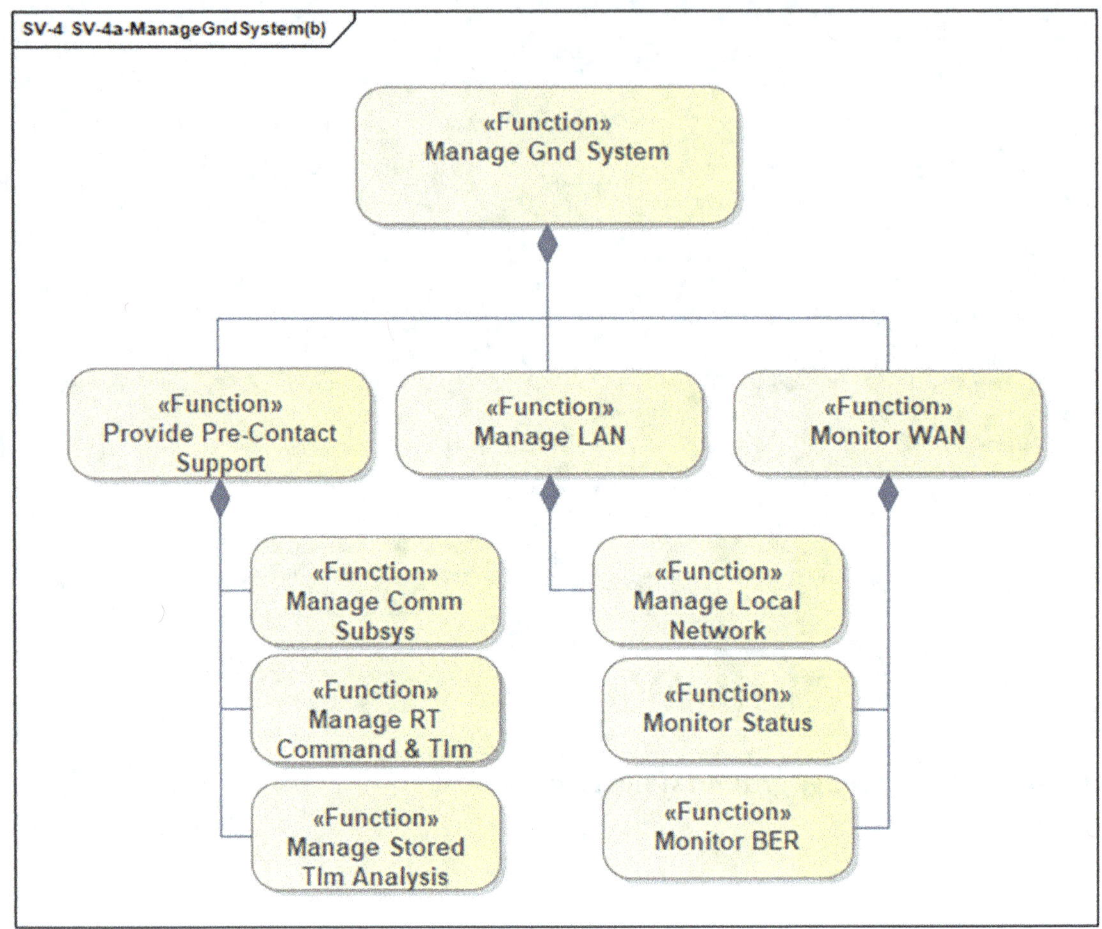

Figure 3-34b. *(continued)*

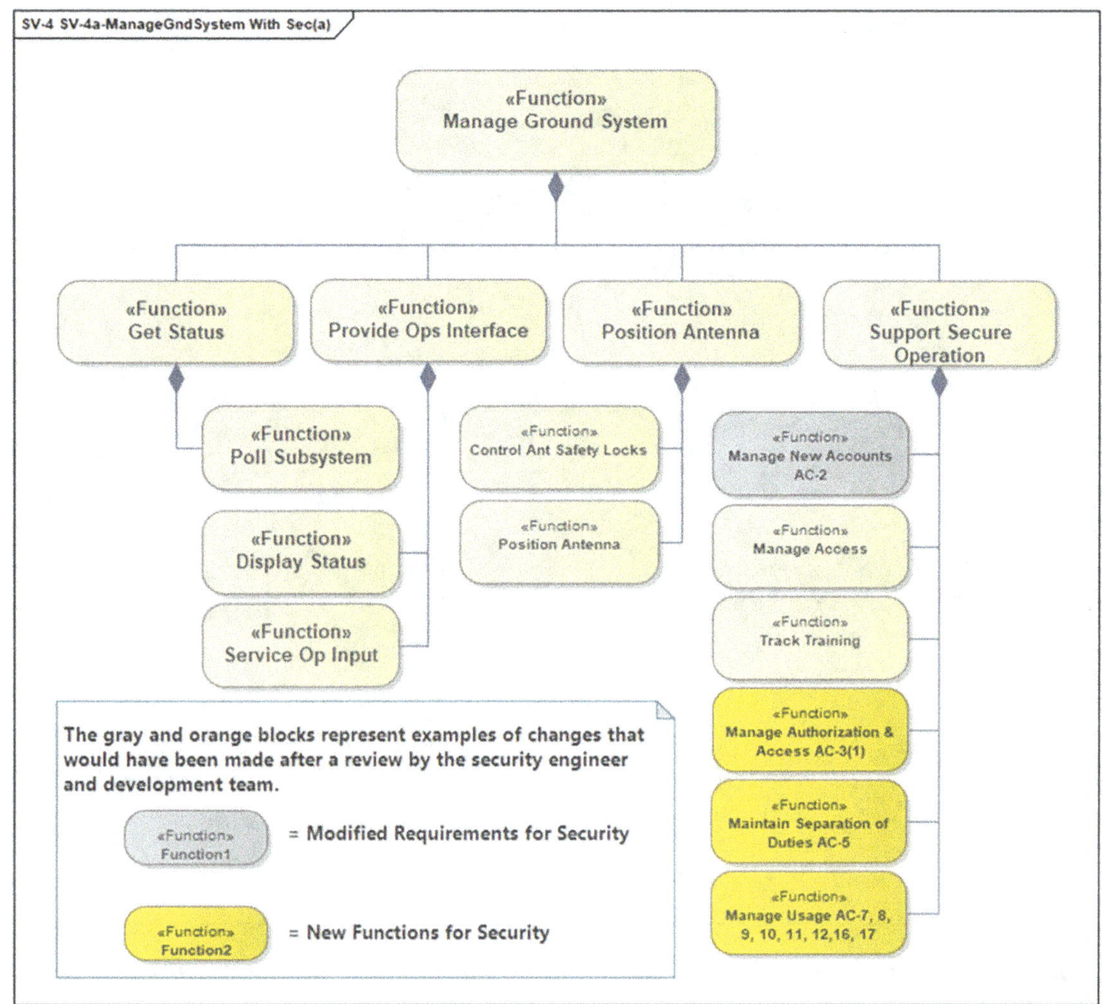

Figure 3-35a. *SV-4a manage ground system DoDAF 2.02 style[33]*

---

[33] Author-created image

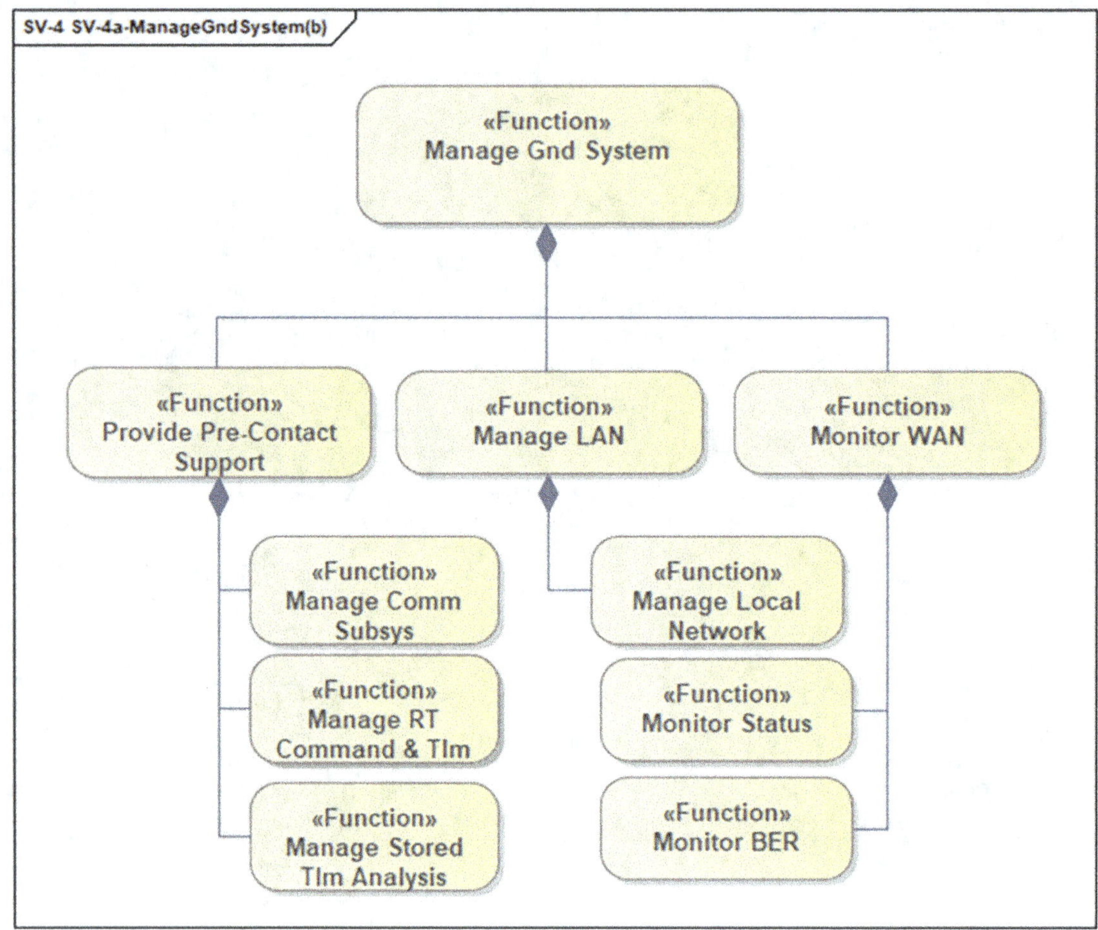

Figure 3-35b. *(continued)*

CV-2 Capabilities to OV-5a Aoperational Activities (Target / Source)

Source	OV-5a PerformMission::Analyze Telemetry	OV-5a PerformMission::Manage Gnd System	OV-5a PerformMission::Manage Security	OV-5a PerformMission::Perform Cmd & Tlm	OV-5a PerformMission::Perform Mission	OV-5a PerformMission::Perform Satellite Com	OV-5a PerformMission::Plan Mission	OV-5a PerformMission::Process Payload Data	OV-5a PerformMission::Simulate Satellite
CV-2 Base Model::Analyze Telemetry	↑								
CV-2 Base Model::Manage Gnd System		↑							
CV-2 Base Model::Manage Security			↑						
CV-2 Base Model::Perform Cmd & Tlm				↑					
CV-2 Base Model::Perform Satellite C3 Mission					↑				
CV-2 Base Model::Perform Satellite Comm						↑			
CV-2 Base Model::Plan Mission							↑		
CV-2 Base Model::Process Payload Data								↑	
CV-2 Base Model::Simulate Satellite									↑

Figure 3-36. *Manage ground system SV-5 matrix view*[34]

A graphical version of the matrix view is shown in Figure 3-37. For large systems, this view can become cumbersome to manage and difficult to read. For those cases, the matrix view is recommended. To show a complete view for our example, separate SV-5 diagrams should be used to break down functions supporting operational activities. It is recommended that for large systems, the matrix view be used. Early use of the matrix view will help to catch missing features and functionality and avoid locking in a product that may be deficient.

---

[34] Author-created image

At this point in system definition, the team can start considering, but not committing to, the potential use of off-the-shelf components. Consideration of off-the-shelf components before development of the operational views, and the later functional views, can lead to significant modifications to the system later in the design or even after the system is activated. This is because focusing on the off-the-shelf components at the start of the development may result in missing essential requirements. It can also result in the selection of components with added features which could be the source of problems downstream. Focus on the OV-5 views and requirements will provide a basis for initial off-the-shelf consideration and potentially provide for selection of several competing products or off-the-shelf items. Later, the lower-level requirements developed in the SV-4a (or SysML activity) views will identify the functionality required to perform each activity. The functions provide the lower-level details that will aid in the selection of the best candidate amongst the originally selected components. This is essential for making final decisions on off-the-shelf usage.

Ultimately the Modeling allows the use of the model descriptions and requirements to be used as a checklist to evaluate the candidates. A checklist matrix view of requirements against the candidate component should be generated to provide a starting point from the standpoint of the model. Differences between the model and candidate off the shelf component can be evaluated and then used as a basis for rejecting the component or modifying the model and requirements. Evaluating the interfaces described in the model relative to potential inter-product interfaces can help to avoid future costs for implementation and maintenance. The point is that using the model in this way allows the development team to make an informed decision early and avoid costly rework later.

Before transitioning from the OV-5a to DoDAF SV-4a or to SysML, collect the requirements gathered with each activity that make up the TRD. Critically evaluate each requirement against each activity and each activity diagram. Look at the requirements in context with each other and use the activity diagrams to evaluate activity inter-action. Uncovering issues with activity interaction early can avoid selection of off-the-shelf components that may require extensive (and expensive) modification to provide operational needs.

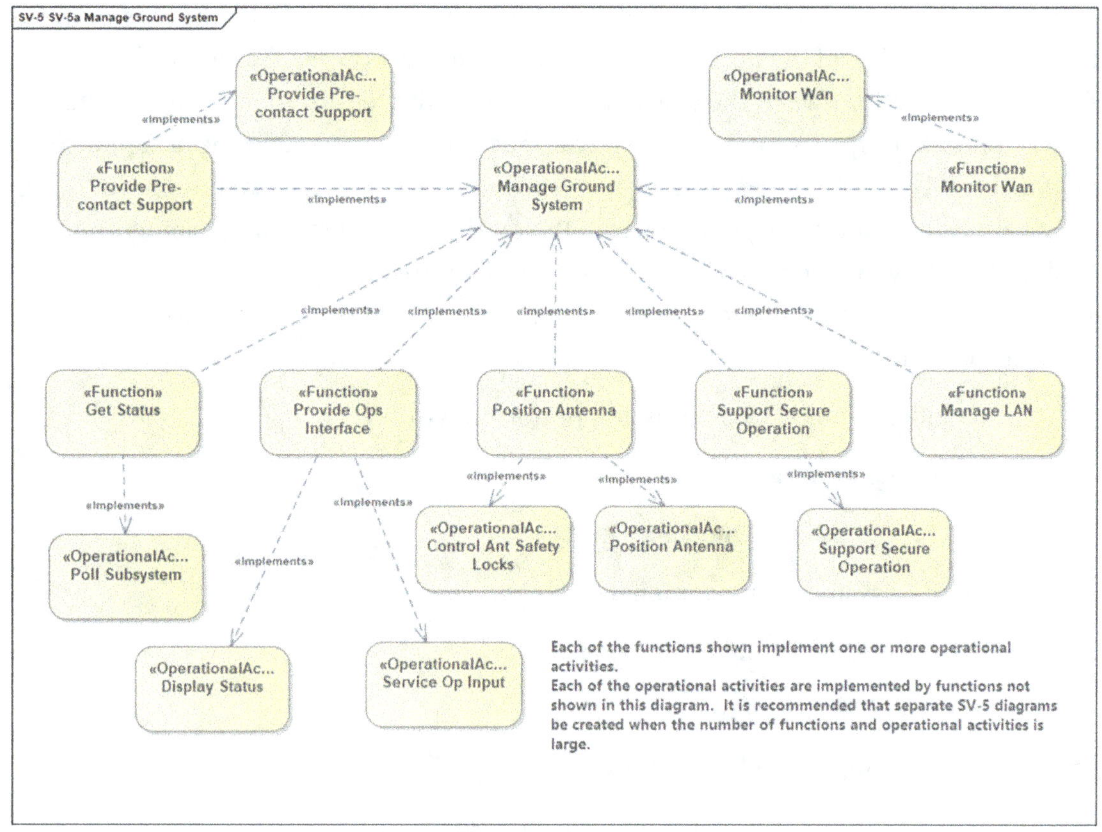

Figure 3-37. *SV-5 Manage ground system diagram view*[35]

Test Planning

The testing procedures that link to the TRD requirements should be collected at this point. The test procedures gathered when defining each of the OV-5a activities should be grouped under the previously defined headings generated from the capability view development. It is expected that these test procedures will be at a high level at this point since the functional design and system specification requirements have not been developed yet. These lower-level requirements and associated test procedures will be developed when the DoDAF system views (SV)/SysML activity views are developed.

---

[35] Author-created image

Developing preliminary test steps early—while the model is still being constructed—supports the creation of the acceptance test plan and procedures. This approach ensures traceability between the tests, the model, and the requirements linked to each model element. It's important to note that although most teams build the acceptance test plan based on system and subsystem specifications, the requirements within those specifications are themselves derived from the model and its associated elements.

Excluding any overhead paragraphs that may be imposed by government data item description or organizational requirements, the start of the test procedures document should look like this:

Satellite ground system mission performance

Mission planning

Test steps for related activities.

Ground system management

Test steps for related activities.

Security Management

Test steps for related activities.

Perform command and telemetry operations

Test steps for related activities.

Satellite communications

Test steps for related activities.

Analyze telemetry

Test steps for related activities.

Simulate satellite

Test steps for related activities.

Process payload data

Test steps for related activities.

The details of the test steps will be expanded as the Modeling proceeds. It is important that the test engineer does the initial conversion of model elements and associated requirements into the test steps. The initial test steps will then be peer reviewed by the program/project systems and software engineers to ensure that the test steps accurately represent the activity operations. Upon completion of these reviews and potential updates resulting from the reviews, the test procedures should be reviewed with the end users/acquisition organization. This will uncover any potential misunderstandings of how the system should operate and how the operation is proven during acceptance testing later in the program/project.

Operational View and Specification Detailed Planning

This chapter expanded upon the activities introduced in Chapter 2, adding details intended to support the development of the System Specification and to serve as a foundation for the Subsystem Specifications, including both hardware and software. As the system definition is refined and detailed allocations are made to individual operational views, agile approaches to planning and scheduling may become viable. The agile approach to scheduling provides a means to adapt the schedule tasking to match the team workflow to how the model is segmented—i.e., areas of the mission view, breakout of mission activities into supporting activities, etc. These smaller work areas become more manageable than one large piece of work and highlight the ability to take portions of the effort and execute in parallel. This phase may also justify expanding the development team, assigning personnel to focus on each major Operational View and the breakdown of supporting activities and their associated requirements. The breakout of activities in the agile schedule and discovery of areas of potential parallelism will help to ensure that the project is not over or understaffed.

The Gantt chart schedule shown in Figure 3-38 is a summary extract that illustrates how specification development can be linked to the system model. Although the example omits organizational tasks such as meetings, peer reviews, and acquisition management activities, the key point is the direct relationship between specification sections and the primary model activities. This includes extracting requirements from the model and, if necessary, refining the grammar of the associated requirements and constraints for inclusion in the specification.

ID	Task Name	Start	Finish	Duration	Dec	Jan	Q1 26 / Mar	Q2 26 / Apr
1	**Create Ground Station OV-1**	**12/26/2025**	**1/2/2026**	**6d**				
2	Create Use Case OV-1	12/26/2025	12/29/2025	2d				
3	Review UC specification (for each UC)	12/30/2025	12/30/2025	1d				
4	Update high level requirements in each specification	12/31/2025	1/2/2026	3d				
5	**Create Ground System bdd**	**1/5/2026**	**1/12/2026**	**6d**				
6	Develop "Subsystem Based bdd" (look at mission nodes in OV-2)	1/5/2026	1/6/2026	2d				
7	For each block document assign site pertinent constraints	1/7/2026	1/12/2026	4d				
8	**System Specification Requirements**	**1/13/2026**	**1/16/2026**	**4d**				
9	Command & Telemetry Section Requirements & Constraints	1/13/2026	1/16/2026	4d				
10	Mission Planning Section Requirements	1/13/2026	1/16/2026	4d				
11	Telemetry Analysis Section Requirements & Constraints	1/13/2026	1/16/2026	4d				
12	Satellite Communications Section Requirements & Constaints	1/13/2026	1/16/2026	4d				
13	Ground System Management Section Requirements & Constraints	1/13/2026	1/16/2026	4d				
14	Security Management Section Requirements & Constraints	1/13/2026	1/16/2026	4d				
15	Satellite Simulator Section Requirements & Constraints	1/13/2026	1/13/2026	1d				
16	Payload Data Section Requirements & Constraints	1/13/2026	1/13/2026	1d				
17	**System Specification Publishing**	**1/15/2026**	**2/2/2026**	**13d**				
18	Incorporate Requirements & Constraints	1/15/2026	1/16/2026	2d				
19	Operational Requirements & Constraints	1/19/2026	1/21/2026	3d				
20	Support Hardware Requirements & Constraints	1/22/2026	1/23/2026	2d				
21	Facility Requirements (to house subsystems) & Constraints	1/26/2026	1/27/2026	2d				
22	Electrical Power & Constraints	1/28/2026	1/29/2026	2d				
23	Temperature and Humidity Requirements & Constraints	1/30/2026	2/2/2026	2d				
24	**Format Contents**	**2/3/2026**	**2/20/2026**	**14d**				
25	Organize Content	2/3/2026	2/5/2026	3d				
26	Stakeholder Review	2/6/2026	2/12/2026	5d				
27	Incorporate comments & Corrections	2/13/2026	2/19/2026	5d				
28	Release Specification	2/20/2026	2/20/2026	1d				

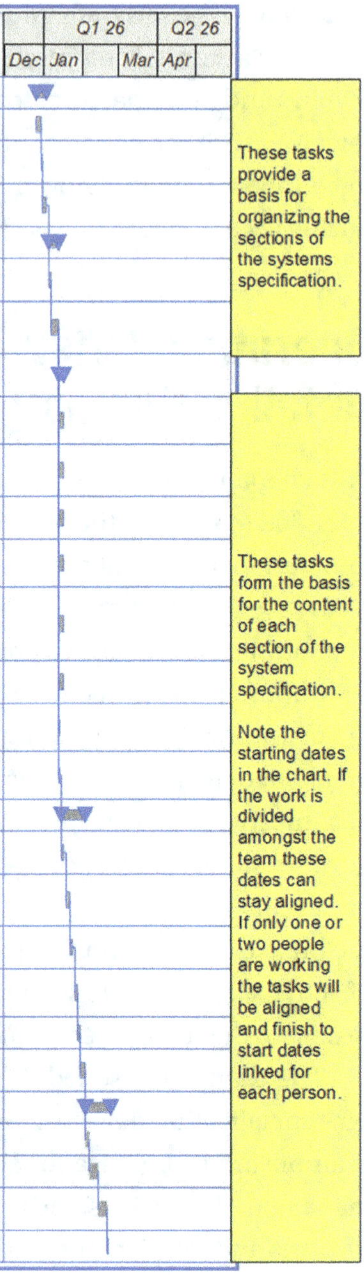

These tasks provide a basis for organizing the sections of the systems specification.

These tasks form the basis for the content of each section of the system specification.

Note the starting dates in the chart. If the work is divided amongst the team these dates can stay aligned. If only one or two people are working the tasks will be aligned and finish to start dates linked for each person.

Figure 3-38. *Example schedule for system specification*[36]

---

[36] Author-created image

Chapter Lessons Learned

- An OV-5a operational taxonomy set of views can be used to expand each capability into one or more operational activities.

- When creating the OV-5a details the process aids the thought process needed to evaluate the capabilities and, if necessary, change a capability to an activity.

- Evaluation of operational activities may determine that one or more of the activities are base capabilities.

- The activity development in the model should be accompanied by the development of requirements for each activity.

- Activity requirements provide a basis for the Technical Requirements Document (TRD) or other form of specification that the organization may use as a basic system specification. Note that the formal system specification should be completed by the development organization.

- The TRD contains primarily Level 1 requirements. These are the highest-level requirements from which lower-level detailed requirements are based.

- The program/project should begin assessing security needs and incorporate into the activity OV-5a views and requirements associated with each operational activity.

- Once the initial activities are documented in an OV-5a, an OV-5b view can be used to show how the activities interact to perform specific operations.

- Update test planning that was started in the previous phase.

- Update Gantt schedules to reflect the effort necessary to develop the operational views and requirements documents. The effort may employ an Agile approach if normally the case within the organization.

- A good practice is to use this point in the schedule as a checkpoint to ensure that capabilities, operational activities, and associated requirements are accurate and appropriate.

- The Preliminary Design Review (PDR) should cover review of the OV-5a activities and their interactions via an OV-5b and sequence diagrams.

- Initial subsystem performance measures should use the OV-5b and sequence diagrams as a basis for calculating performance attributes to ensure that contributors to overall performance are accounted for.

References

[1]   IPSC-81431A Defense Logistics Agency ASSIST web site `https://dla.mil/online/start/index.cfm`. You will need to establish an account if you don't already have one.

[2]   NIST SP 800-53 Revision 5, page 8 Table 1, available at `https://doi.org/10.6028/NIST.SP.800-53r5`

[3]   MIL-STD-961E, Defense and Program-Unique Specifications Format and Content,ASSIST web site `https://dla.mil/online/start/index.cfm`

Acronym List

Acronyms	Definition
Ant	Antenna
Auth	Authorization
bdd	Block Definition Diagram
BER	Bit Error Rate
CCSDS	Consultative Committee for Space Data Systems
CDD	Capability Development Document
Cmd	Command
Comm	Communications

(continued)

Acronyms	Definition
COTS	Commercial off the Shelf
CV	Capability View
DoDAF	Department of Defense Architecture Framework
FFRDC	Federally Funded Research and Development
Gnd	Ground
Info	Information
KPP	Key Performance Parameters
KSA	Key System Attributes
LAN	Local Area Network
MODAF	British Ministry of Defence Architecture Framework
NETCONF	Network Configuration Protocol
NIST	National Institute of Standards and Technology
Op	Operator
Ops	Operations
OV	Operations View
Pld	Payload
RFP	Request for Proposal
RT	Real Time
SNMP	Simple Network Management Protocol
SON	Statement of Need
SP	Special Publication
Subsys	Subsystem
SV	System View
Tlm	Telemetry
TRD	Technical Requirements Document
UPDM	Unified Profile for DoDAF/MODAF
WAN	Wide Area Network

CHAPTER 4

DoDAF Functionality View SV-4a

This chapter focuses on developing system functions from previously defined system capabilities and activities, and how these functions lead to requirements for the system specification. Using the example of a satellite ground system, we demonstrate how the Department of Defense Architecture Framework (DoDAF) system view (SV) aids in defining the requirements necessary for functions such as command and telemetry operations. We also highlight the similarities between the SV and SysML Activity views, showing how these can be useful in transitioning from DoDAF to SysML as part of the overall program/project progression from architecture to system design.

Our goal at this stage of development is to illustrate the flow of activities and functions, along with their associated requirements. Given that programs are typically schedule-driven, we present an approach that allows for the rapid collection of functions and recommend transitioning to SysML activity diagrams. To do this, we use a taxonomy view for the SV-4a rather than a graphic like the OV-5b discussed in Chapter 3.

It is important to note that, in an actual program, transitioning to SysML may not be allowed by the contract. The engineering team may need to follow formal DoDAF 2.02 conventions and maintain separate SV-4a and SV-5a views, based on contract requirements.

Guide for Managers and Engineers

This section is intended for both managers and engineers and focuses on the use of a functionality view to develop requirements for the system specification. Activity, function/action, and sequence diagrams generated during this phase of the program also serve as a foundation for the technical content of the Critical Design Review (CDR).

93

© Dennis Hansen 2025
D. Hansen, *Model-Based Systems Engineering and Requirements Definition*,
https://doi.org/10.1007/979-8-8688-2043-4_4

The requirements developed through Model-Based Systems Engineering (MBSE) views will form the basis of the System Specification prepared by the development organization.

Managers are not expected to delve into the modeling details beyond understanding how the model is used to capture and organize system functions. However, they should recognize the scope of effort involved in generating the views, defining requirements, and supporting test planning—critical considerations when estimating costs and developing schedules.

Engineers should note that SV-4a functions correlate with SysML Activities and can serve as a useful starting point for transitioning to SysML or UML representations.

SV-4a Function Identification

Transition to development of the system specification involves identifying the functions or actions necessary to perform the operational activities. At this point, the engineer can consider changing to SysML. If the contract requires an SV-4 view, consider using the SV-4a taxonomy view that provides a means of rapidly collecting functions. On the positive side, this SV-4a can be used as an initial guide to develop SysML activity views. If there is a decision to move directly to SysML, remember that the activities relate to the TRD, and the actions necessary to perform the activities relate to the system specification. An example of the process is shown below. In this case, let's look at a view of the OV-5a activities for Perform Command and Telemetry (Figure 4-1).

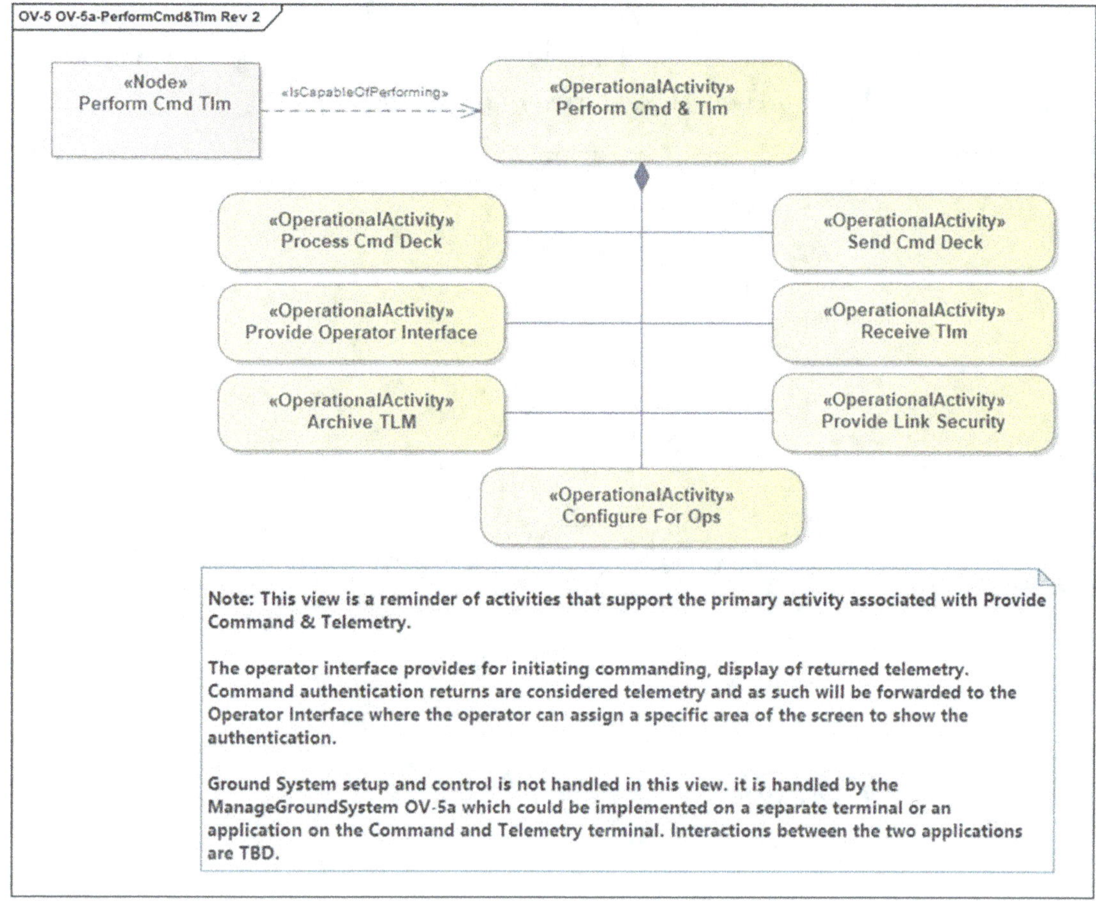

Figure 4-1. *OV-5a perform command and telemetry*[1]

In developing the SV-4a Figures 4-2a, b, c, views consider that the DoDAF Standard only contains the functions. It is convenient to name the SV-4a with the name of the primary activity being performed. In this case, perform Cmd & Tlm. The connectors do not show flow and are shown as an aggregation of functions that are a part of the

---

[1] Author-created image

primary function. An SV-5 matrix view, as shown in Figure 4-2d, is used to show the relationship between the functions and the OV-5a activities. In this way, the matrix view complements the SV-4a and helps to avoid overlooked functions.

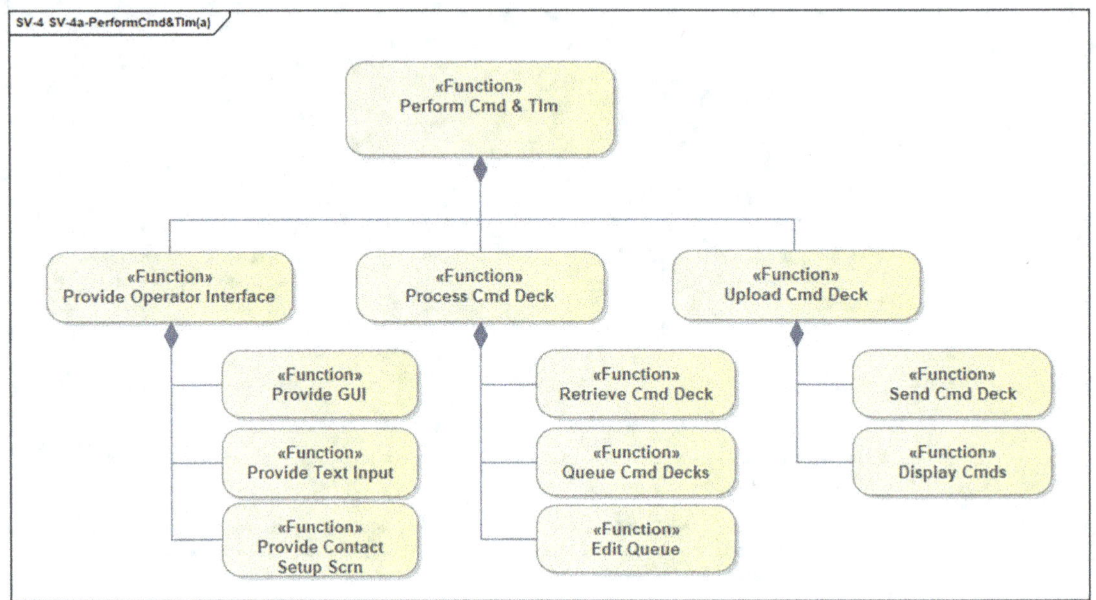

Figure 4-2a. *SV-4a perform command and telemetry*[2]

---

[2] Author-created image

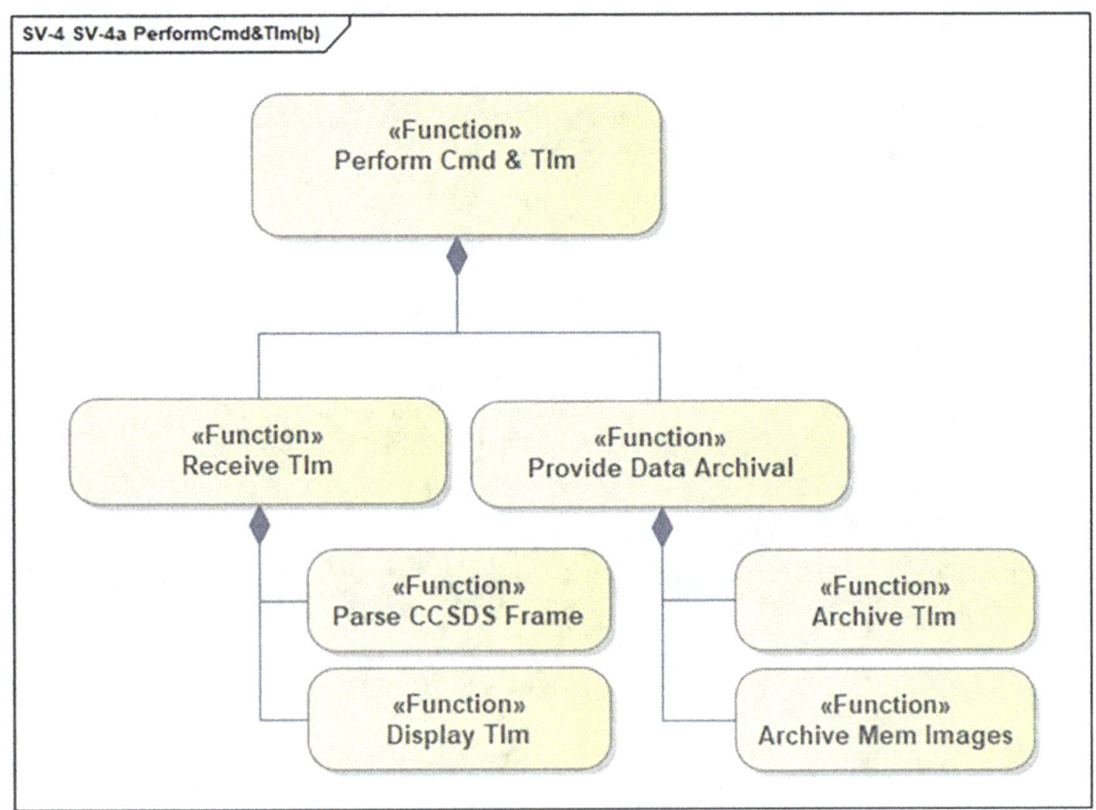

Figure 4-2b. *(continued)*

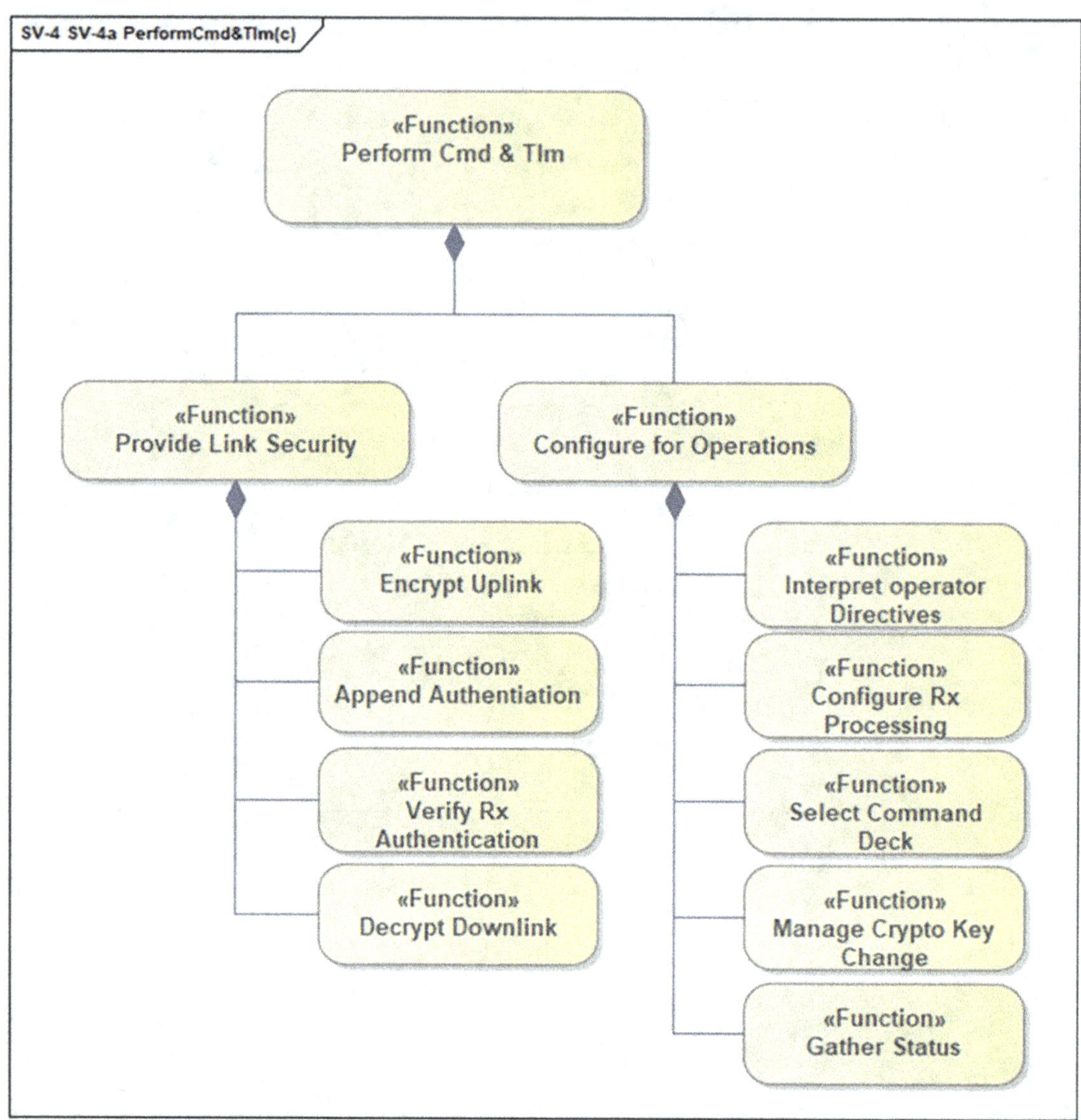

Figure 4-2c. *(continued)*

Source \ Target	OV-5a-PerformCmd&Tlm::Configure For Ops	OV-5a-PerformCmd&Tlm::Perform Cmd & Tlm	OV-5a-PerformCmd&Tlm::Perform Cmd Tlm	OV-5a-PerformCmd&Tlm::Process Cmd Deck	OV-5a-PerformCmd&Tlm::Provide Data Archival	OV-5a-PerformCmd&Tlm::Provide Link Security	OV-5a-PerformCmd&Tlm::Provide Operator Interface	OV-5a-PerformCmd&Tlm::Receive Tlm	OV-5a-PerformCmd&Tlm::System Specification	OV-5a-PerformCmd&Tlm::test	OV-5a-PerformCmd&Tlm::Upload Cmd Deck
PerformCmd&Tlm::Append Authentiation						↑					
PerformCmd&Tlm::Archive Mem Images					↑						
PerformCmd&Tlm::Archive Tlm					↑						
PerformCmd&Tlm::Configure for Operations	↑										
PerformCmd&Tlm::Configure Rx Processing	↑										
PerformCmd&Tlm::Decrypt Downlink						↑					
PerformCmd&Tlm::Display Cmds											↑
PerformCmd&Tlm::Display Tlm								↑			
PerformCmd&Tlm::Edit Queue				↑							
PerformCmd&Tlm::Encrypt Uplink						↑					
PerformCmd&Tlm::Gather Status	↑										
PerformCmd&Tlm::Interpret operator Directives	↑										
PerformCmd&Tlm::Manage Crypto Key Change	↑										
PerformCmd&Tlm::Parse CCSDS Frame								↑			
PerformCmd&Tlm::Perform Cmd & Tlm			↑								
PerformCmd&Tlm::Process Cmd Deck				↑							

Example of accounting for test document attached to model,

Figure 4-2d. *(continued)*

As before, collect the notes, requirement statements, and constraints during the development of the SV-4a in the modeling tool, as shown in Figures 4-3 and 4-4 for the Provide Graphical User Interface (GUI) function.

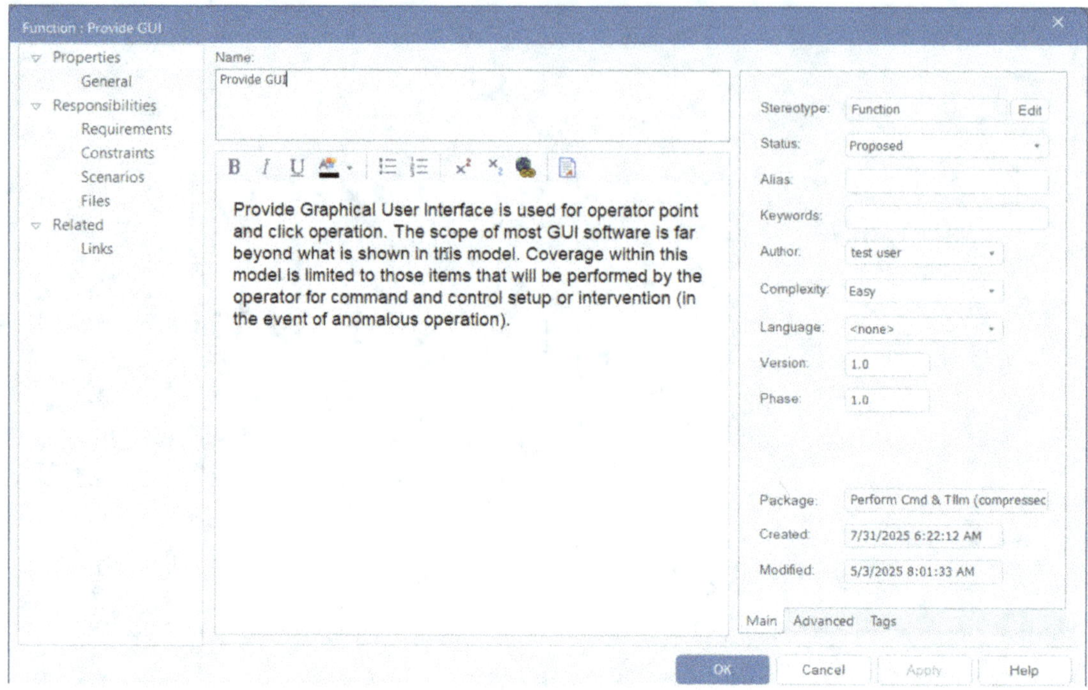

Figure 4-3. *Notes for provide GUI functionality*[3]

---

[3] Author-created image

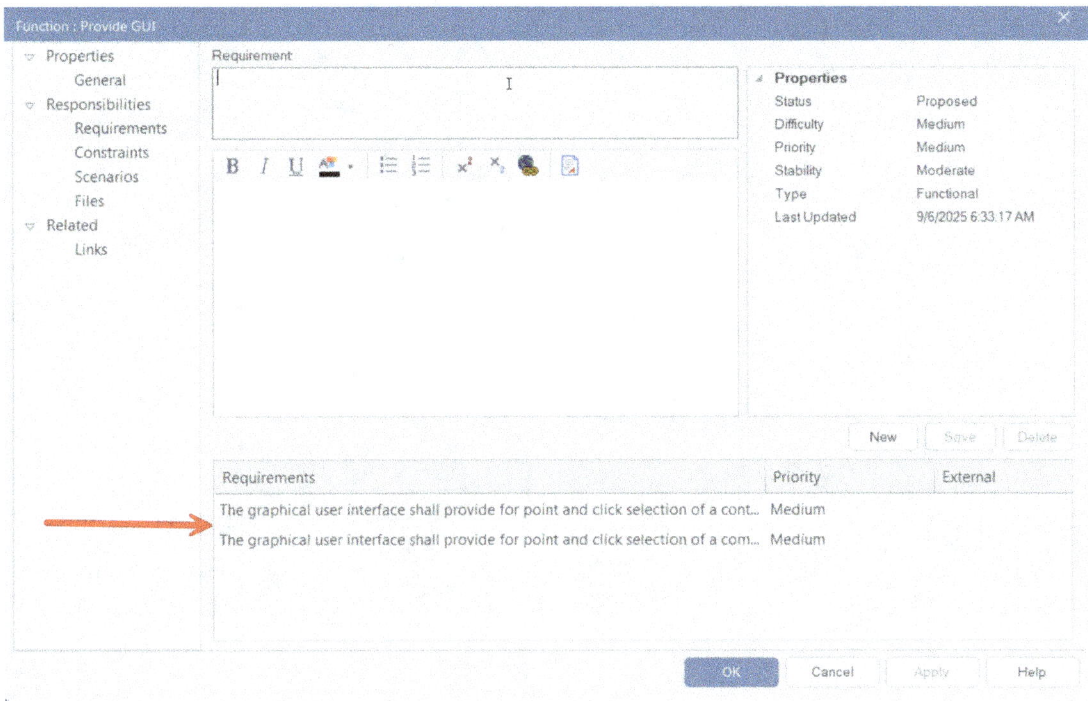

Figure 4-4. *Provide GUI function requirements example[4]*

As previously stated, the SysML activity view can be used in place of the SV-4. This is especially the case if you are considering a Swimlane version of the SV-4, like that shown for the OV-5b (Figure 3-14). Notice how at the Perform Mission level activity diagram (Figures 4-5a and 4-5b), we have all the primary activities shown. In this case, we have circled the Perform Cmd & Tlm structured activity for the reader's convenience. Within the Modeling tool, if we click on the structured activity for Perform Cmd & Tlm it opens into the more detailed view shown in Figure 4-6. These lower-level activities show the lower-level system view details of Perform Cmd & Tlm. Each of the items with the pitchfork in the lower right corner is an action call behavior and when clicked in the Modeling tool will open to further detail for each of the action calls.

---

[4] Author-created image

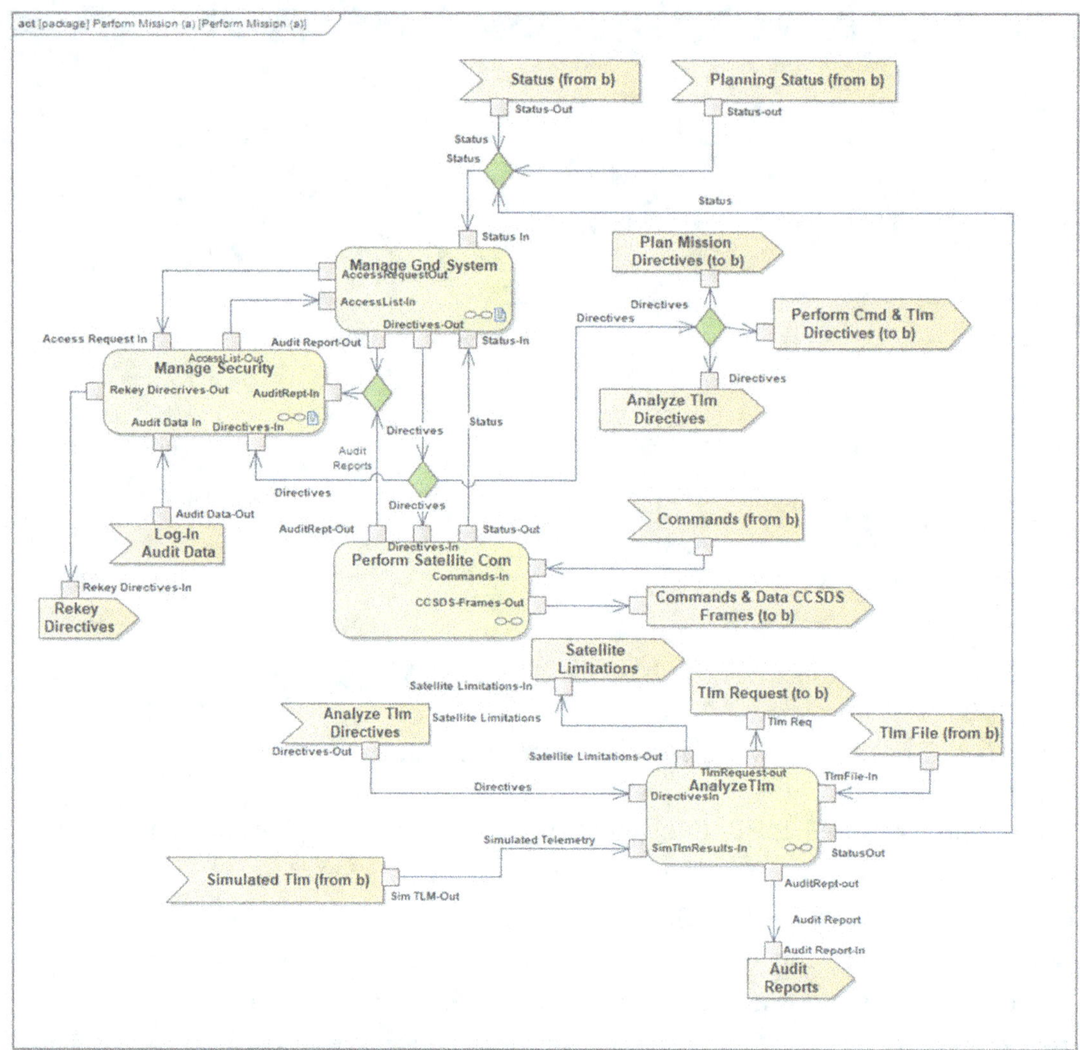

Figure 4-5a. *Annotated perform mission activity view*

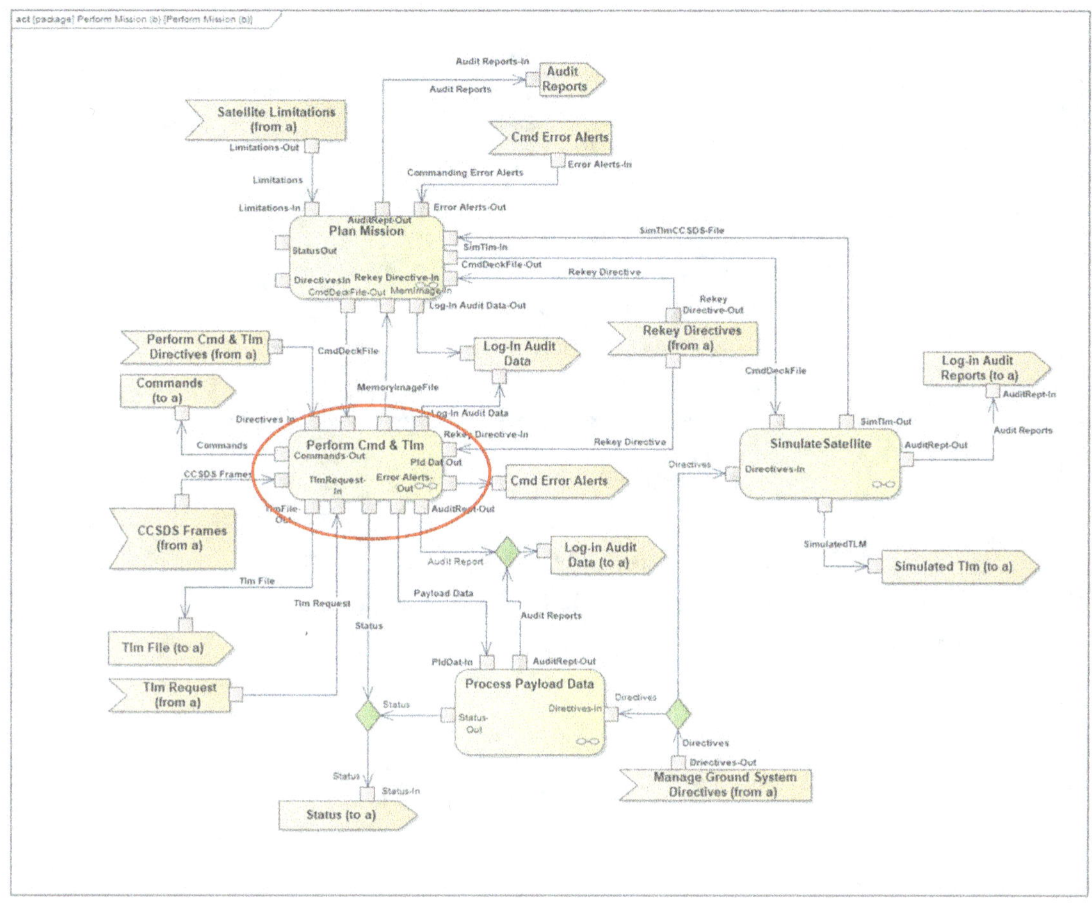

Figure 4-5b. *(continued)*

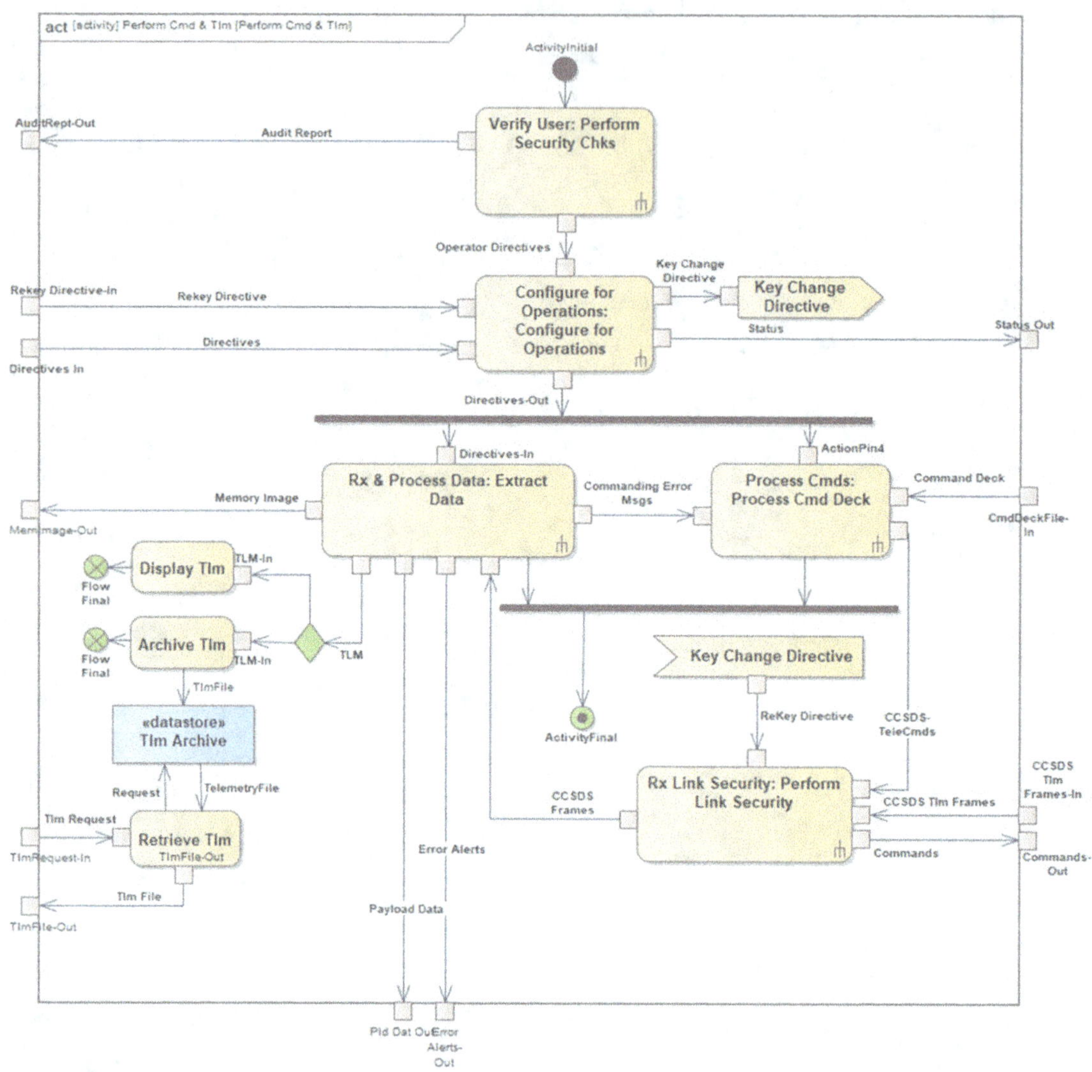

Figure 4-6. *Perform command and telemetry SysML activity[5]*

This view is technically equivalent to an SV-4b. The primary difference is that the actions are not assigned to swim lanes. Thus, the decision to move from DoDAF to SysML can be made when considering the development of the SV-4 views. As stated before, development of the SV-4a can be of use to help think through the required DoDAF Functions which relate to SysML Activities.

---

[5] Author-created image

The perform command and telemetry activity provides digital processing for the Perform Cmd Tlm activity for commanding and telemetry processing, as shown in the OV-1 in Use Case Form (Figure 4-7). It is also shown as a node with the same name in Figure 4-8 node view. The Perform Satellite Comm use case shown at the bottom, just above the *satellite actor*, Figure 4-7, provides for all the RF (analog) functionality. Note that a *<extend>* connection is used between the Perform Cmd Tlm and Perform Satellite Comm. An extend connector type was used because the Perform Satellite Comm is a fragment of the overall command and telemetry activity. The RF handling of commands and telemetry directly supports the input and output of the Perform Cmd Tlm use case.

The Perform Satellite Communications OV-5, Figure 4-9 shows the four supporting operational activities. Note that they are associated with RF and RF-to-digital conversion. Their separation from Perform Command and Telemetry serves to isolate the RF functions from the data processing and display functions. Functions implementing the Perform Satellite Communications operational activity are shown in Figures 4-10a and 4-10b. Considering that the elements shown in these views are, as covered in previous chapters, constructed with supporting data such as requirements, constraints, and notes, it is possible to generate a highly traceable architecture. Access to all the information for each element within the modeling tool provides for ease of evaluation of constraints. For example, the linkage between the Perform Cmd Tlm and Perform Satellite Comm would be a point for trades. For example, should the linkage between subsystems be digital or RF? In this case, the constraint could be "Uplink/downlink systems shall be separated from the command-and-control center by XXX feet." Short distances would favor an RF or intermediate frequency connection. Longer distances would favor a digital interface.

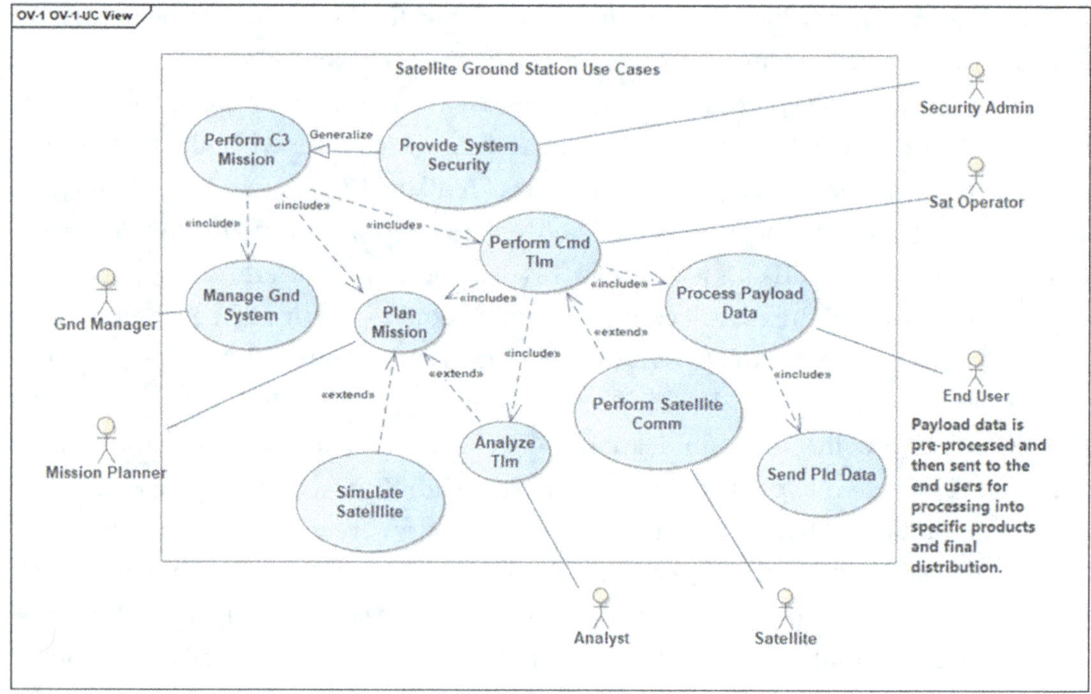

Figure 4-7. *OV-1 use case view*[6]

---

[6]Author-created image

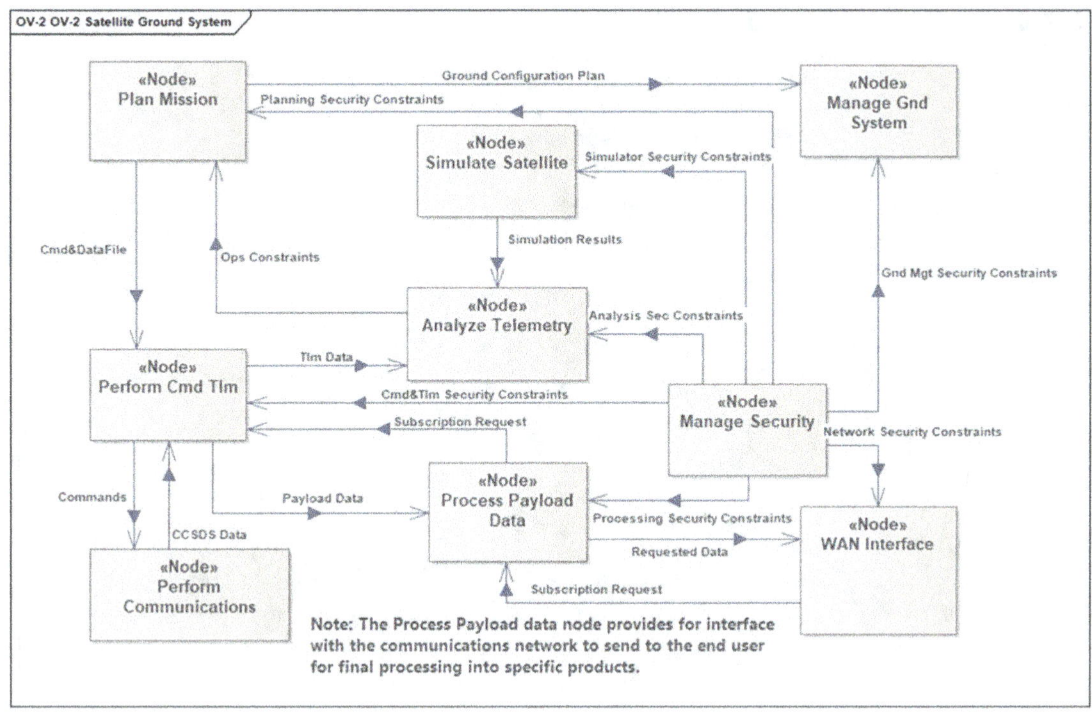

Figure 4-8. *Ov-2 node view*

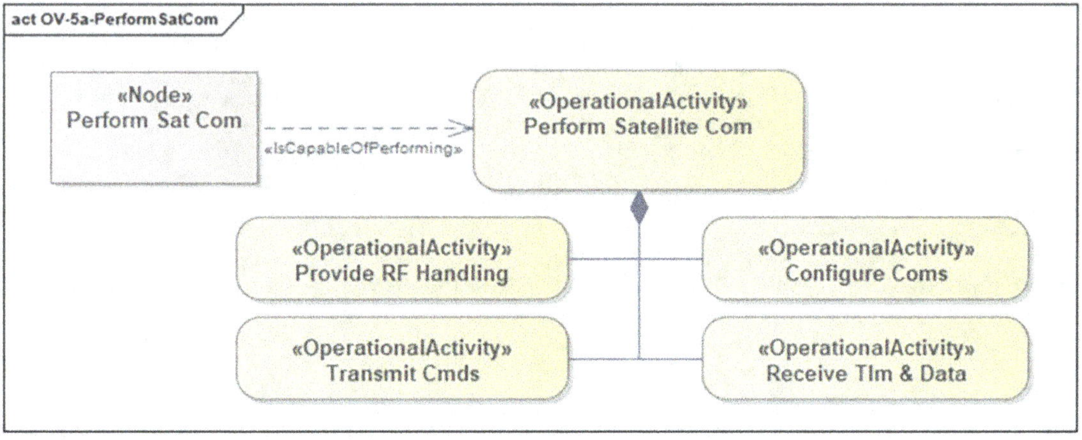

Figure 4-9. *OV-5a perform satellite communications[7]*

---

[7] Author-created image

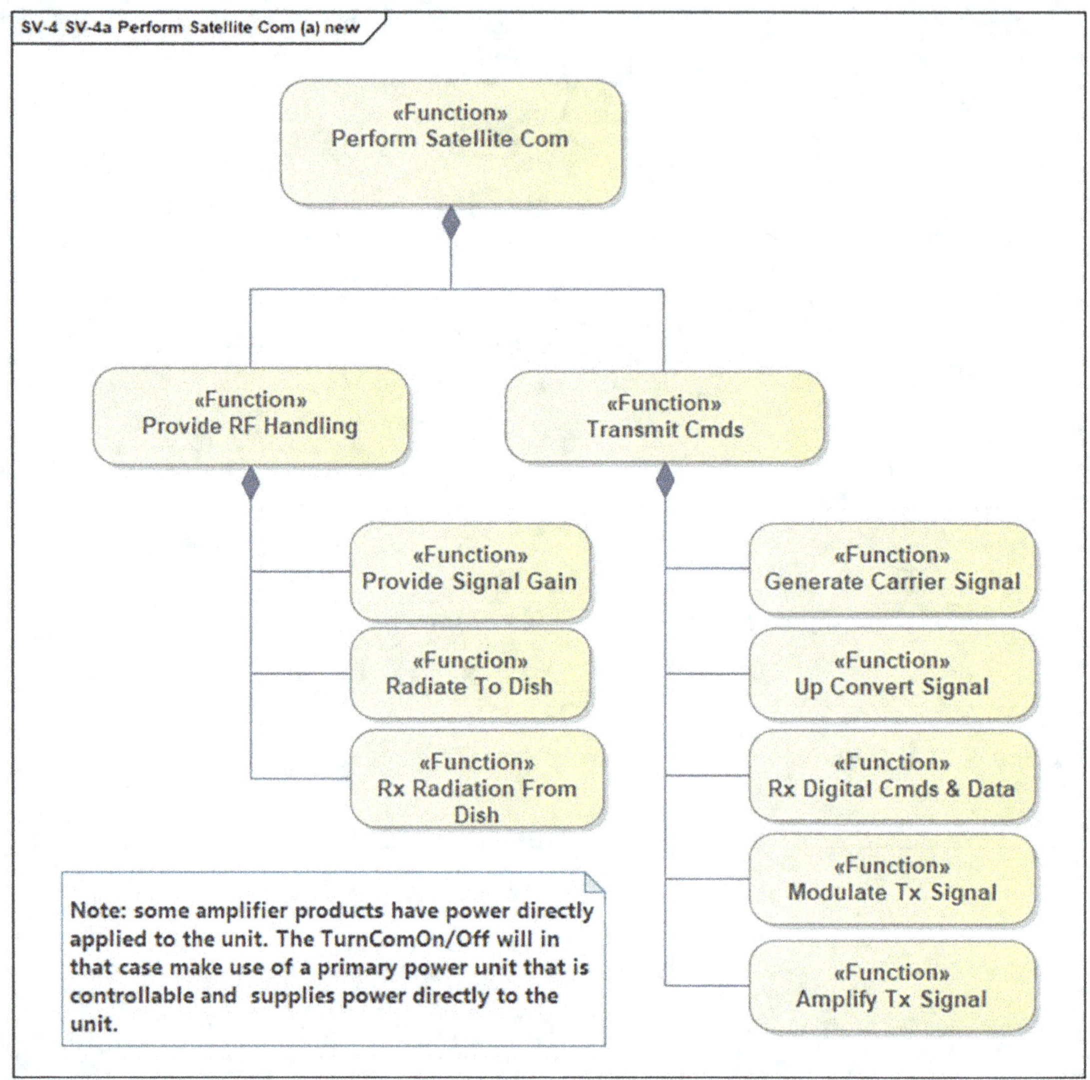

Figure 4-10a. *OV-5a perform satellite communications*[8]

---

[8] Author-created image

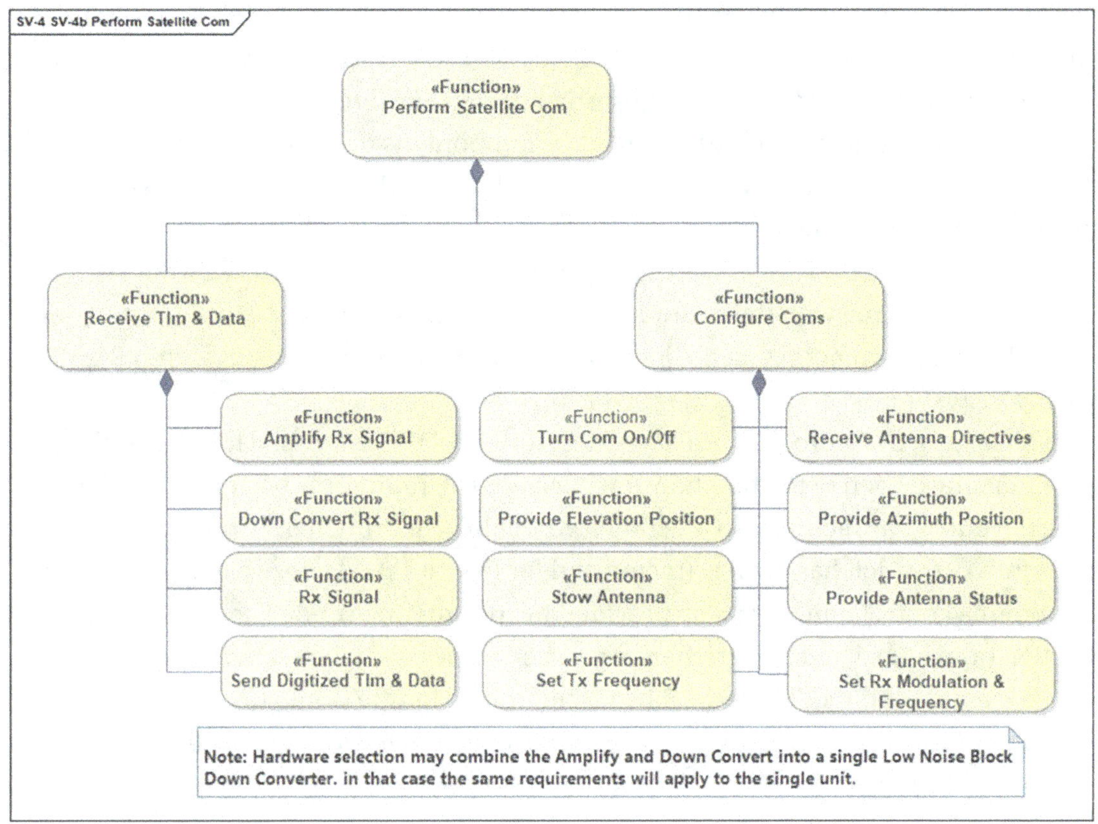

Figure 4-10b. *(continued)*

The Configure Coms operational activity in the OV-5a does not, on the surface, appear to be related to RF. Development of the SV-4a (or an equivalent SysML activity view) reveals that the RF components require some form of control. It is not the model that reveals this requirement. It is the thought process involved with developing the model view that should reveal this need. Within the SV-4a or SysML activity view, the need for control is expressed as Configure Coms. Within the focused Configure Coms functional view, Figure 4-11, we have added three notes.

The top note is a reminder that there is a need for external support for amplifier power turn-on. The reminder highlights that the components may have network-managed capabilities; however, detailed examination of specific components reveals that the on-off function is controlled by the application of electrical power. The note on the right is an example of considerations for off-the-shelf components and the effect of their selection on the model. Note that for the case of the activity Receive Tlm Data, the decision to use COTS may affect the component functions and associated requirements. Requirements gathered for two functions might be combined relative to the component specification; however, from a modeling point of view *the functions* are still separate. The functions may be performed by separate components or combined into a low-noise block downconverter. Conversion of the received RF to a digital form for transmission to processing elements downstream.

For each function in the SV-4a Perform Satellite Communications view in Figure 4-10, continue with the definition of requirements and constraints as discussed earlier. It is recommended that the logic of each function be carried out within SysML Activity Views.

Notice how, in Figure 4-10, the activities from the OV-5a are used to head each set of functions. Each of the functions for each activity represents what needs to be done to perform the activity. To illustrate, we will look at the activity Configure Coms in Figure 4-10, which has been extracted and for Figure 4-11. Here, we recognize that the antenna control unit, normally provided by the antenna vendor, should have a function (and associated requirements) to receive operational directives, each of which will have associated requirements. The requirements for the Configure Coms activity supporting function Receive Antenna Directives are shown as an extract from the model in Figure 4-12.

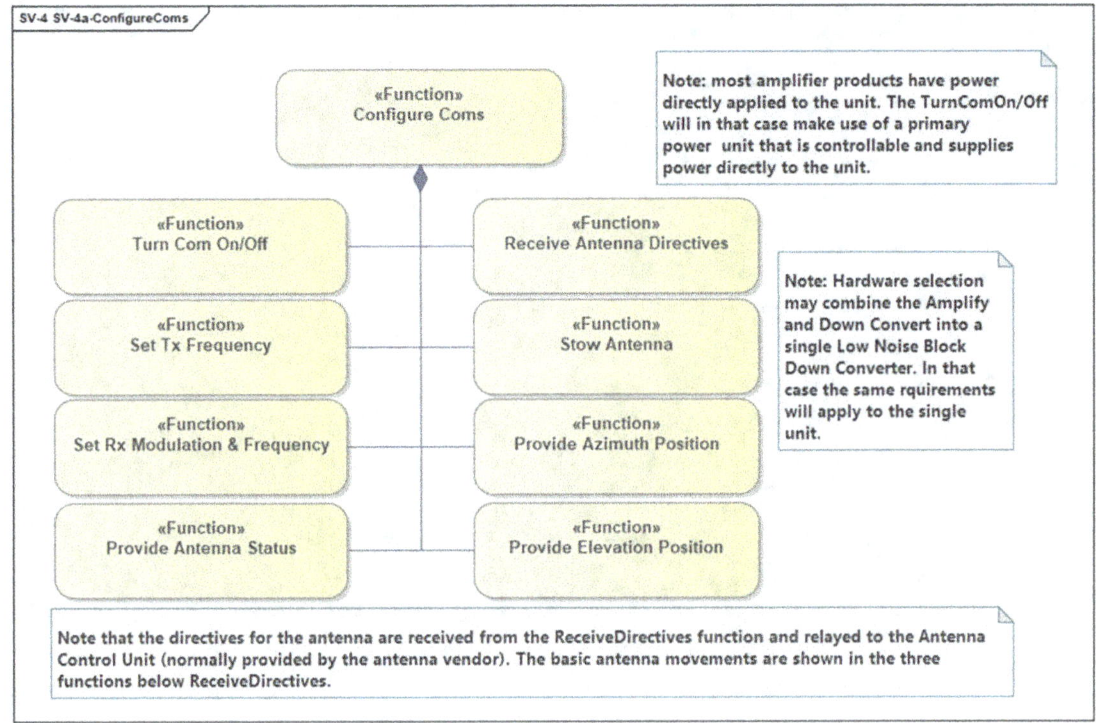

Figure 4-11. *Configure communications SV-4a*[9]

---

[9] Author-created image

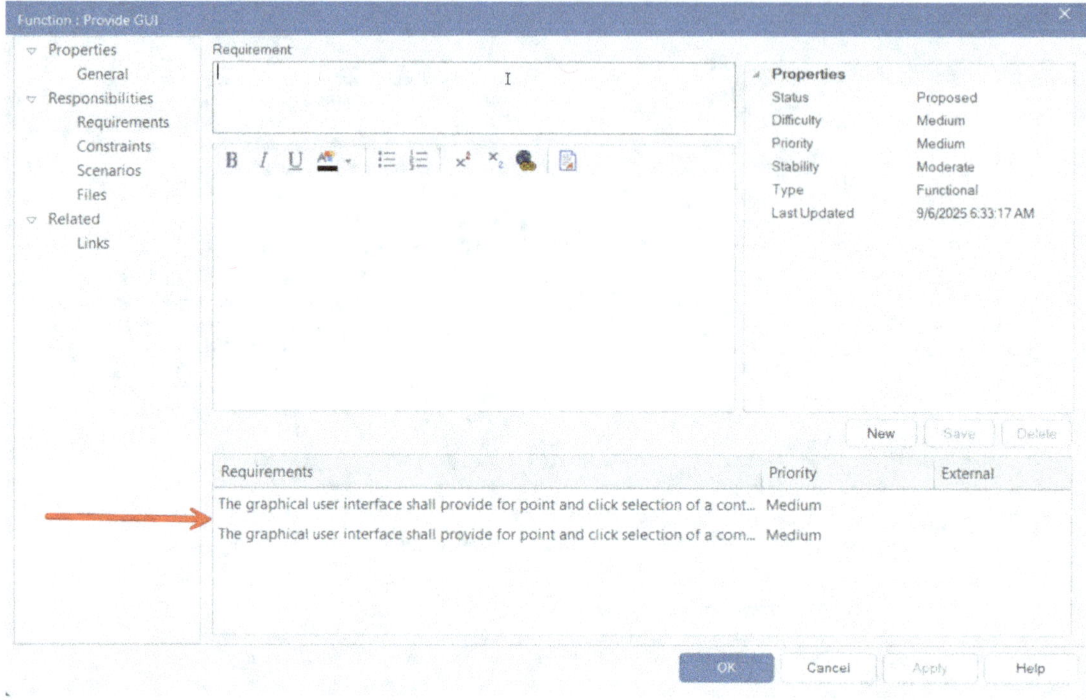

Figure 4-12. *Receive directives requirements example[10]*

Command and telemetry operations naturally span from the operator console to signal transmission and reception at the antenna dish. Breaking down this functionality reveals that, from a modeling perspective, the associated activities and functions can be separated without disrupting the overall system logic. This separation allows a single system specification to define overarching requirements, while detailed requirements for each functional area can be delegated to individual subsystem specifications.

It's important to note that these requirements were initially developed during the creation of modeling views, such as Figure 4-11. As previously discussed, they are linked from the model to the requirements management tool. In most cases, subsystem specifications are generated directly from this tool. When executed properly, the flow—from element definition in the modeling tool to the requirements tool and ultimately to the specifications—ensures consistency throughout the development process and into the final system implementation.

---

[10] Author-created image

Subsystem Planning and Scheduling

In this chapter, we have been developing the elements that lead to a complete subsystem specification. Figure 4-13 presents a schedule extract that supports this effort. The structure of the schedule is designed to support an agile approach to specification development. This approach allows the work to be distributed among different members of the development team and enables iterative progress. Initially, the schedule can be built by repeating a core sequence of tasks for each subsystem. Once all subsystems are accounted for, more detailed, subsystem-specific tasks can be incorporated.

A key component in this process is the use of SysML activity diagrams, which are linked to their corresponding requirements. These views are essential for ensuring that each subsystem specification is complete. Additionally, tasks can be scheduled to initiate test planning and procedure development for each subsystem early in the process.

By combining agile scheduling with model-based development, teams can significantly reduce the risk of omitted requirements and incorrect or unnecessary requirements, both of which can cause serious issues during system and subsystem testing.

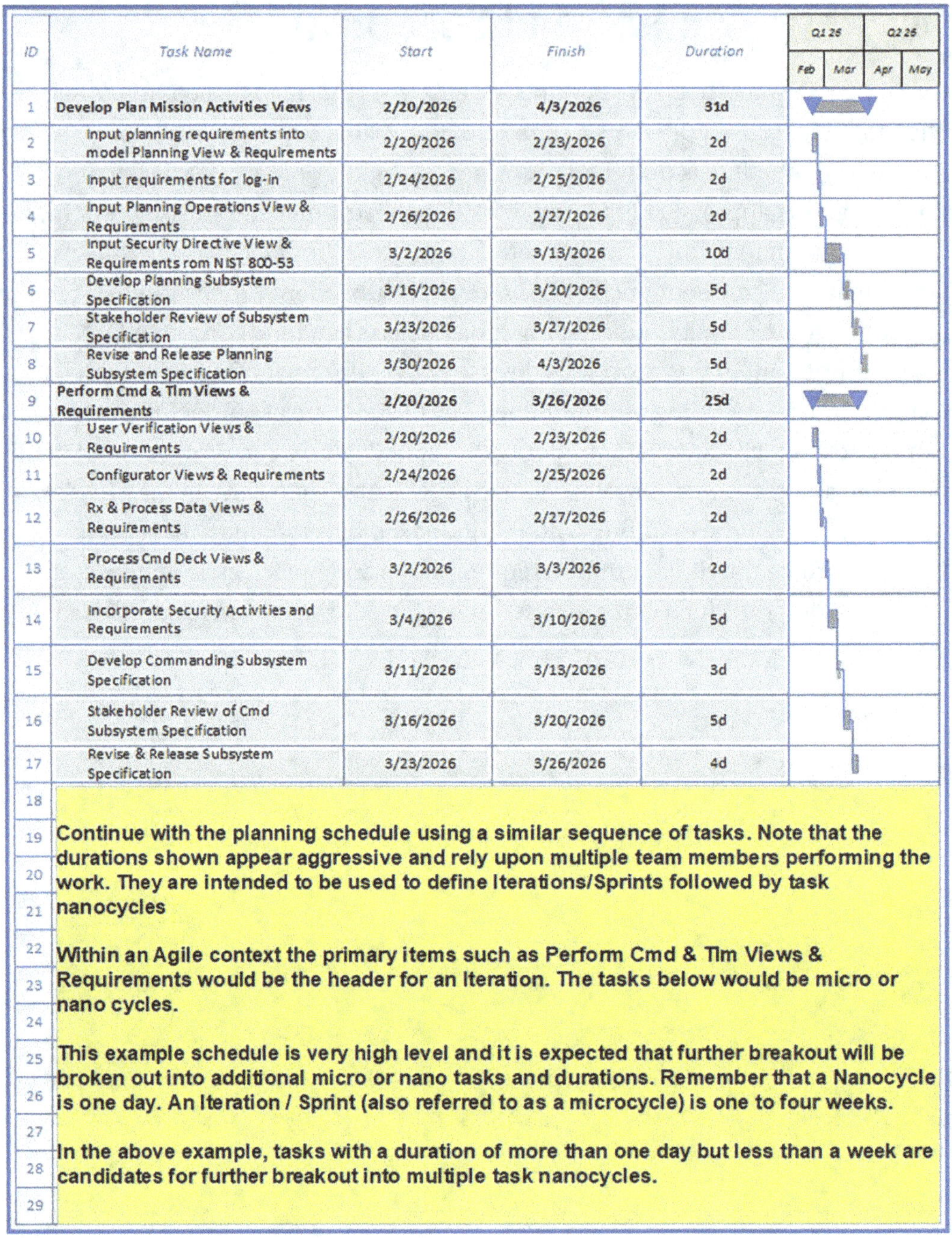

ID	Task Name	Start	Finish	Duration	Q1 26		Q2 26	
					Feb	Mar	Apr	May
1	**Develop Plan Mission Activities Views**	2/20/2026	4/3/2026	31d				
2	Input planning requirements into model Planning View & Requirements	2/20/2026	2/23/2026	2d				
3	Input requirements for log-in	2/24/2026	2/25/2026	2d				
4	Input Planning Operations View & Requirements	2/26/2026	2/27/2026	2d				
5	Input Security Directive View & Requirements rom NIST 800-53	3/2/2026	3/13/2026	10d				
6	Develop Planning Subsystem Specification	3/16/2026	3/20/2026	5d				
7	Stakeholder Review of Subsystem Specification	3/23/2026	3/27/2026	5d				
8	Revise and Release Planning Subsystem Specification	3/30/2026	4/3/2026	5d				
9	Perform Cmd & Tlm Views & Requirements	2/20/2026	3/26/2026	25d				
10	User Verification Views & Requirements	2/20/2026	2/23/2026	2d				
11	Configurator Views & Requirements	2/24/2026	2/25/2026	2d				
12	Rx & Process Data Views & Requirements	2/26/2026	2/27/2026	2d				
13	Process Cmd Deck Views & Requirements	3/2/2026	3/3/2026	2d				
14	Incorporate Security Activities and Requirements	3/4/2026	3/10/2026	5d				
15	Develop Commanding Subsystem Specification	3/11/2026	3/13/2026	3d				
16	Stakeholder Review of Cmd Subsystem Specification	3/16/2026	3/20/2026	5d				
17	Revise & Release Subsystem Specification	3/23/2026	3/26/2026	4d				

Continue with the planning schedule using a similar sequence of tasks. Note that the durations shown appear aggressive and rely upon multiple team members performing the work. They are intended to be used to define Iterations/Sprints followed by task nanocycles

Within an Agile context the primary items such as Perform Cmd & Tlm Views & Requirements would be the header for an Iteration. The tasks below would be micro or nano cycles.

This example schedule is very high level and it is expected that further breakout will be broken out into additional micro or nano tasks and durations. Remember that a Nanocycle is one day. An Iteration / Sprint (also referred to as a microcycle) is one to four weeks.

In the above example, tasks with a duration of more than one day but less than a week are candidates for further breakout into multiple task nanocycles.

Figure 4-13. *Subsystem specification schedule*

When developing the agile schedule and establishing the time duration for individual tasks, it is important to focus on the complexity and scope of the system being developed. Rules of thumb and "similar to" approaches can be used as a cross-check to see if we are missing or not adequately covering an area of design. However, they should not be used as the basis for establishing the schedule durations for the tasks. Consider how much research may be required to model and develop requirements for each area. For example, how many NIST 800-53 controls will apply and how much effort will be required to ensure that the control(s) are supported in the model and requirements. In our satellite ground system example, consider the time required to verify the design necessary to implement CCSDS command and telemetry operations.

For the CDR, do not place an arbitrary limit on the duration of the review. All the model views and their associated requirements and constraints should be covered in the review. This review will verify that we are building the right product—in this example, the satellite ground system. Failure to achieve a mutual understanding of what the system is supposed to accomplish and what technical and security factors apply will result in problems during system testing and certification, as well as issues during system operations.

Chapter Lessons Learned

- The previously developed operational activities need to be broken down into system activities (shown as functions in a DoDAF SV-4a).

- These activities should have associated requirements developed and entered in the Modeling tool as the Modeling progresses.

- A taxonomy SV-4a is a good way to rapidly work through the activities and associated requirements. Leave the details to a set of SysML activity views.

- The SV-4 consists of functions, not activities.

- Activity relation to functions can be shown in an SV-5 matrix.

- The SV-5 is often shown as a graphic using swim lanes for the functions, as shown in Figure 3-14. If contractually allowed, consider migration to SysML instead.

- The requirements collected during the Modeling should be exported to the specification. Don't rewrite the requirements in the specification since errors can occur. Modeling tools often provide publishing capabilities and the ability to export to a requirements tool such as IBM DOORS. The final document is often produced from a word processing program such as Microsoft Word using data that was exported from the requirements tool.

- The materials generated during this phase are the basis for the technical portion of the CDR. The term technical portion is based on the author's previous experience with a heavy focus on program management elements of the program during a review.

Acronym List

Acronym	Definition
Cmd	Commands
DODAF	Department of Defense Architecture Framework
GUI	Graphical User Interface
OV	Operations View
RF	Radio Frequency
SV	System View
SysML	Systems Modeling Language
Tlm	Telemetry
UC	Use Case
UML	Unified Modeling Language

CHAPTER 5

Initial Considerations for Migrating to SysML

Differences in opinion frequently arise concerning the application of DoDAF versus SysML in systems development. This chapter examines the commonalities between the two modeling approaches and outlines key considerations for transitioning from traditional DoDAF views to SysML representations. Programs can effectively leverage both frameworks in a complementary manner. DoDAF is often used by end users and acquisition agencies to define mission objectives, required capabilities, and support operational requirements. Development organizations can then utilize SysML to refine and implement these models within the system design process. Recognizing the appropriate context and timing for migrating between modeling languages is essential for ensuring continuity and traceability throughout the program lifecycle. Overall, acquisition organizations and managers more easily relate to DoDAF and Unified Architecture Framework (UAF) views of the overall architecture while SysML enables detailed design, verification, and traceability at the detail level.

Guide for Managers and Engineers

Differences of opinion often arise between acquisition and development organizations regarding the use of SysML versus DoDAF (or other modeling languages such as UA or MODAF). While DoDAF has evolved to include numerous views intended to fully specify a system, it's important to remember that DoDAF is fundamentally an architectural framework. In contrast, SysML is a system modeling language designed to support system design and can be used to build upon existing DoDAF views.

© Dennis Hansen 2025

D. Hansen, *Model-Based Systems Engineering and Requirements Definition,*
https://doi.org/10.1007/979-8-8688-2043-4_5

DoDAF Comparison to SysML

Crucially, there is a well-established mapping between DoDAF and SysML. This relationship enables the integration of SysML without disrupting the acquisition organization's requirement to produce DoDAF-compliant architectural views. This compatibility is largely due to overlapping language elements, as illustrated in Figure 5-1, and the formal mapping between the two frameworks shown in Figure 5-2 [5]. For example, OV-5a (Operational Activity Model) maps to the SysML Block Definition Diagram (BDD). The BDD can represent behavioral operations using the "operations" compartment within a block. In practice, many find the OV-5a taxonomy more efficient for identifying and organizing system activities, while the BDD is useful for assigning these actions to subsystem-level operations within blocks.

Some methodologies prefer using the BDD over traditional DoDAF operational views, depending on the specific modeling needs and team preferences.

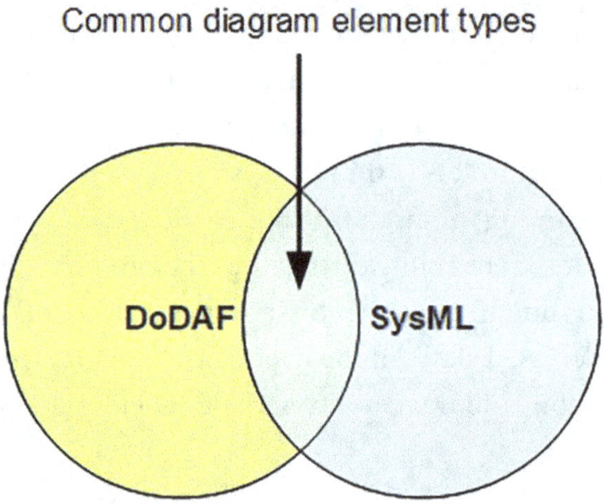

Figure 5-1. *DoDAF and SysML overlap provides a basis for migration between languages*

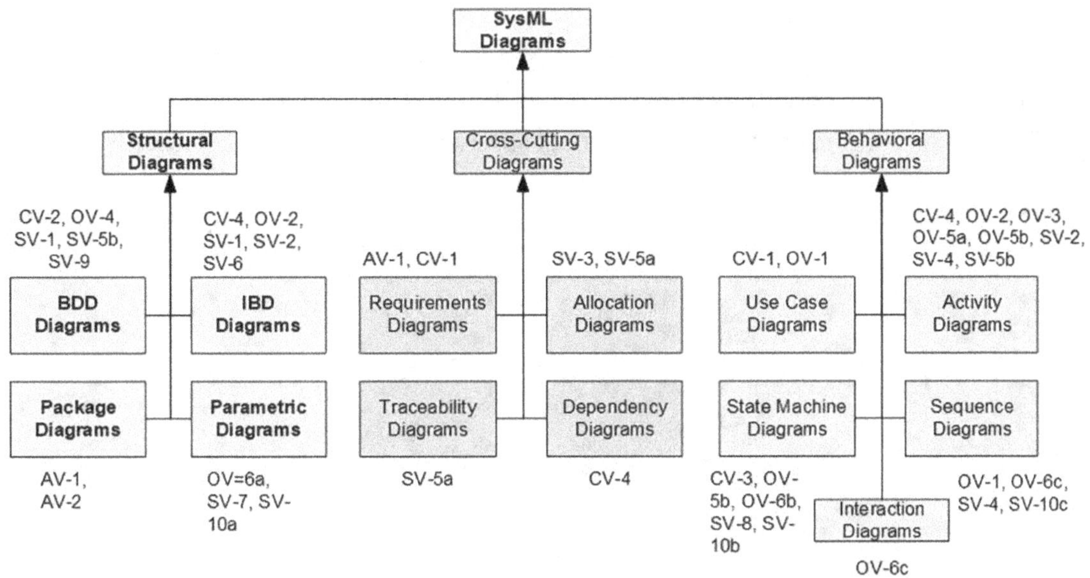

Figure 5-2. *SysML to DoDAF mapping*

Capabilities (CV-2) view to SysML involves converting capabilities to system use cases. As stated in the Introduction, the differences start to be evident in the background system information. For the CV-2, the data emphasis is on capability, i.e., what the capability provides. Consider that the Object Management Group (OMG˙) Unified Profile for DoDAF/MODAF (UPDM) [6] acknowledges that UPDM is built on UML and SysML. Thus, the OV-1 Operational Context is another form (in many cases using better graphics) of SysML Use Cases. Thus, we can present the OV-1 Use Case (Figure 5-3) to SysML Use Cases as shown in Figure 5-4. Note that the only change is the naming of the diagram frame header, shown circled in the figures below.

Note that the capability view (CV-2) does not have a counterpart in SysML. If a decision is made to just develop the SysML approach, then it is still a good idea to generate the CV-2. As discussed earlier, evaluation of the system "needs" can make great use of the CV-2 and provide a linkage to the follow-on SysML views.

Caution must be exercised during the transition from DoDAF to SysML. Some details of the requirements may be missed. The higher-level wording of the DoDAF element will most likely relate to several lower-level requirements in the SysML element. Thus, without diligence, there is a potential to misalign the original high-level requirement and the lower-level supporting requirements in the SysML element. Use of a matrix view similar to that employed earlier in this book can assist in maintaining

119

alignment. Use the architectural requirements along the X axis and the detailed design SysML-derived requirements along the Y axis (there will be many more detailed requirements than architectural requirements. Populating the intersections of the matrix will aid in identifying missing and occasionally misstated requirements.

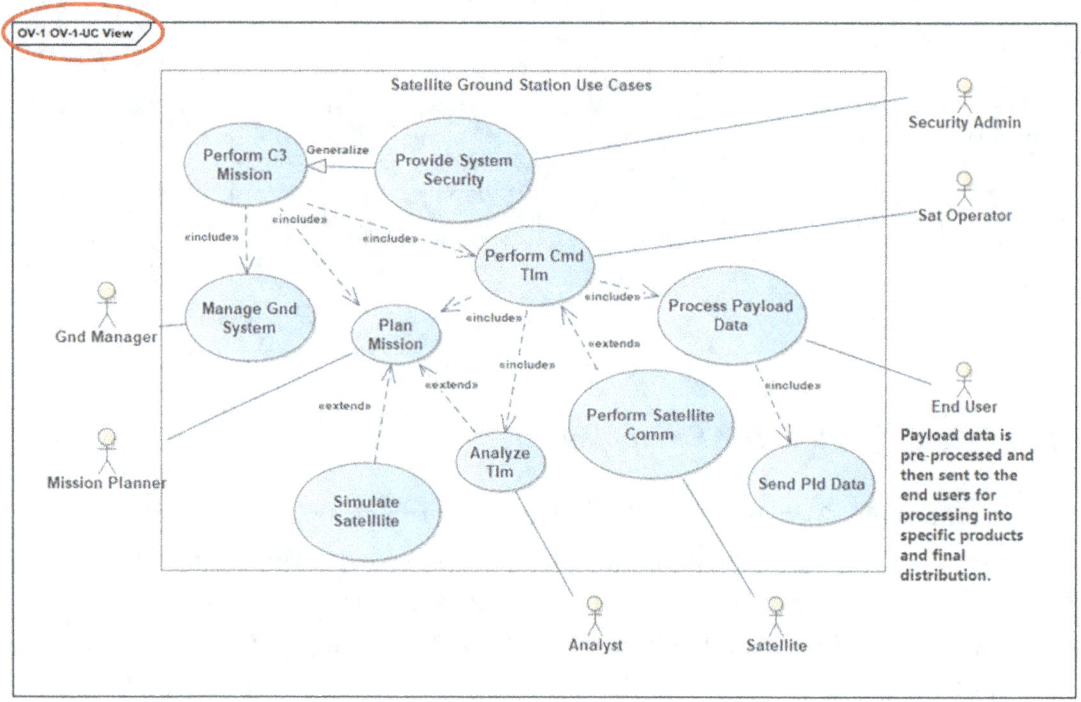

Figure 5-3. *OV-1 operational context use cases differ from SysML use cases in terms of the detail of the data contained in the model element*

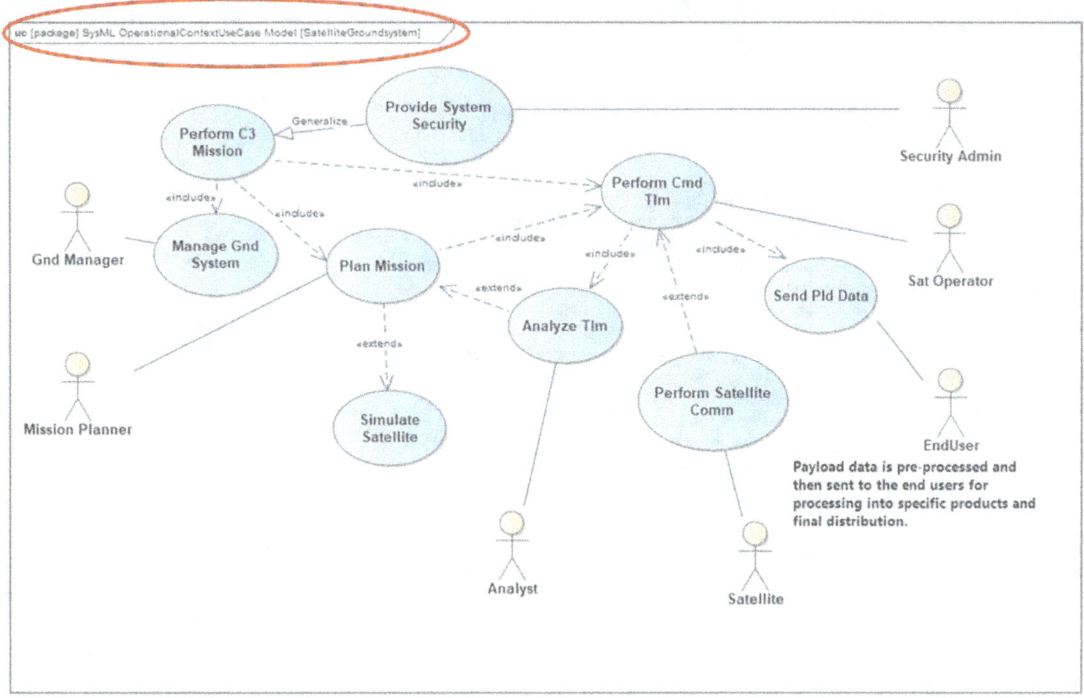

Figure 5-4. *SysML operational context use case provides greater design detail in notes and requirements[1]*

High-level requirements for each use case should be documented in the requirement/constraint area as discussed earlier. During software development, the normal practice is to develop a more detailed software specification. To accomplish this, the detailed specification should be included in the notes section of the use case as shown in Figure 5-5. The listing of requirements shown in the figure is a commonly used framework. The use case specification shown in the figure will provide greater depth in the SysML view than the DoDAF equivalent view.

---

[1] Author-created image

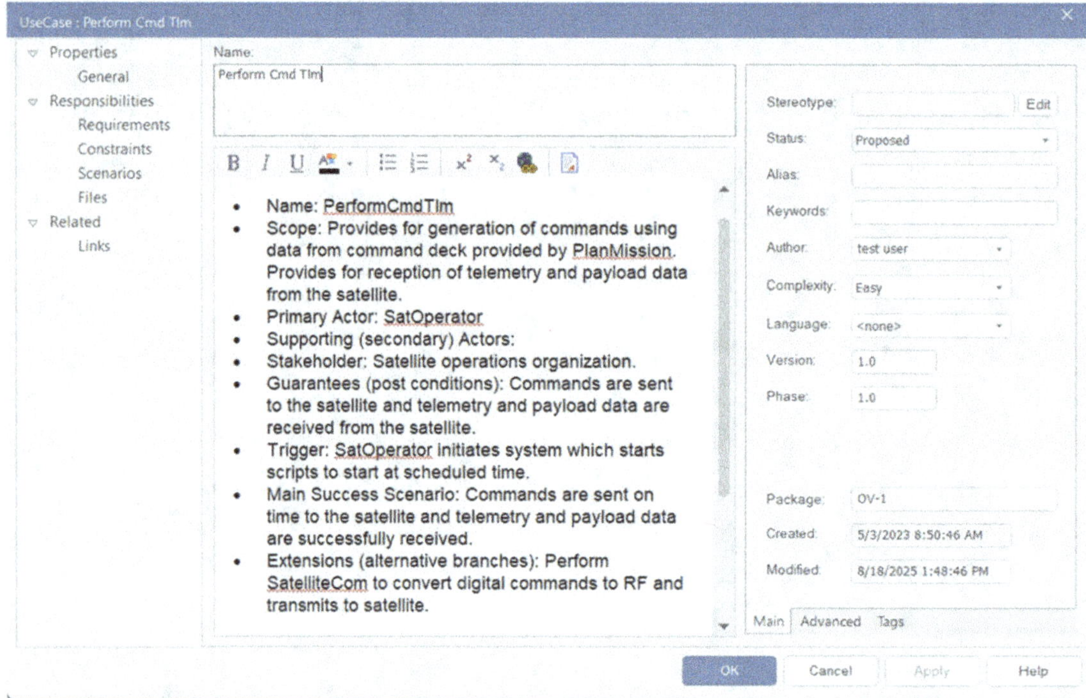

Figure 5-5. *Use case specification[2]*

The structured notes, combined with the use case specifications, provide a starting point for defining the requirements for the activity views. Both DODAF and SysML make use of activity views and use case views. Thus, the development of use case specifications is helpful for the development of both DoDAF and SysML views and aids in eliminating ambiguity as the development team moves to lower levels of design. The important point to remember is that DODAF is primarily an architectural framework. SysML is part of the design documentation where the emphasis shifts from an architectural view, which defines what the system should do, to how the system activities implement actions to provide the capabilities.

As the focus shifts from defining the mission (i.e., what the system should do) to determining how to deliver the required capabilities, it is strongly recommended to complete the CV-2 and immediately develop the use cases and DoDAF OV-5a activity views. The OV-5a views help structure the activity taxonomy and leverage use case specifications to define the topmost layer of the activity hierarchy. Additionally, the

---

[2] Author-created image

OV-5a facilitates the identification and grouping of all supporting activities under this top layer, enabling the construction of a model-based taxonomy that is both logical and easy to assemble. This method allows engineers to clearly map activities to capabilities, strengthening traceability and maintaining architectural coherence throughout the development process.

It provides for organizing the activities and grouping them with their associated capability. This activity could use textual listings of activities; however, the relationship between activities and capabilities is not as obvious and does not provide for retaining additional information about each activity. There is always a danger, especially with a tight schedule and a larger team, that the SysML (system) or UML (software) design will be developed simultaneously with the OV-5a. Ultimately, that approach will result in rework later in the schedule or in the worst-case scenario, there will be design errors not discovered until very late in the schedule. Thus, there will be cost escalation and schedule slip.

The DoDAF methodology normally moves the activity into the development of OV-5b views. This view organizes activities into an activity diagram. The OV-5b activity diagram provides the interaction between architectural elements in the same manner that the SysML Activity diagram does for the system design logic. This is another reason to consider a transition to SysML for the remaining modeling. The initial DoDAF taxonomy views provide the basic information/descriptions necessary to define the program. The transition to SysML allows an easy transition from systems to software development later in the program.

In practice, the development of the SysML activity views can alter the team's view of previously defined capabilities and architectural elements. Occasionally, a capability may be redefined as an activity because it's more of a "how-to" component. In a similar fashion, the team may define an activity in place of a capability. An instance of a CV-2 view that includes an extensive range of capabilities is presented in Figures 5-6a, 5-6b, and 5-6c. The rationale and characteristics of each capability, previously documented in the tool, provide a basis for redefining and moving a capability to an activity view. For example, in Figures 5-6a, 5-6b, and 5-6c, we show a series of capabilities dealing with the Capability "Communicate with Satellite." When working in the development of the OV-5a, OV-5b, and/or SysML activity views, it becomes obvious that the underlying capabilities are "things that need to be accomplished" to communicate with the satellite. They are not capabilities to perform the mission; they support a capability that meets the mission's needs. As a result, the CV-2 was updated as shown in Figure 5-7. The removed capabilities are then added to the applicable OV-5a and SysML activity views.

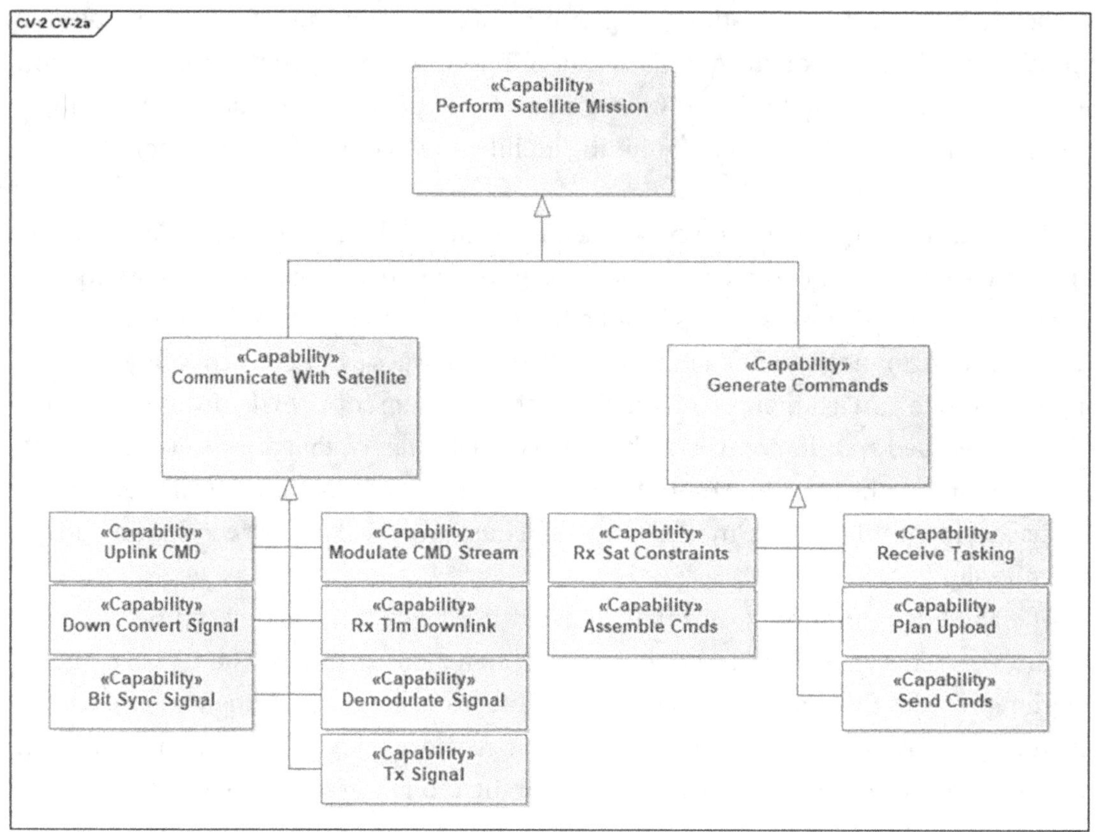

Figure 5-6a. *CV-2 with excess capabilities*[3]

---

[3] Author-created image

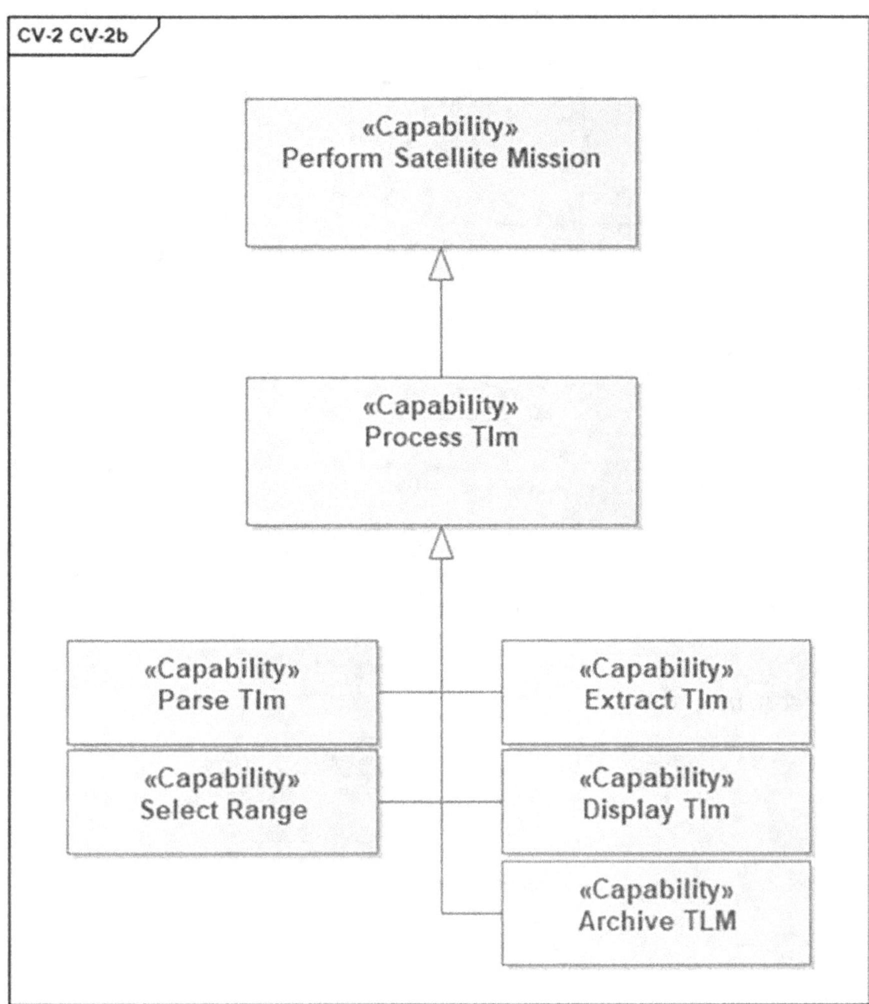

Figure 5-6b. (*continued*)

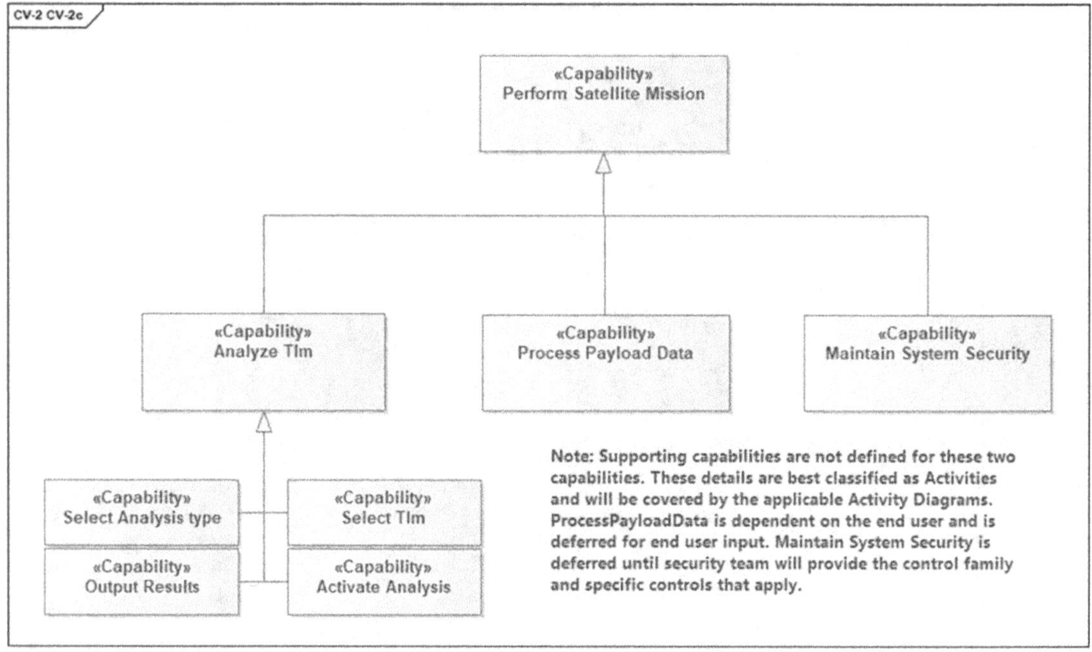

Figure 5-6c. (*continued*)

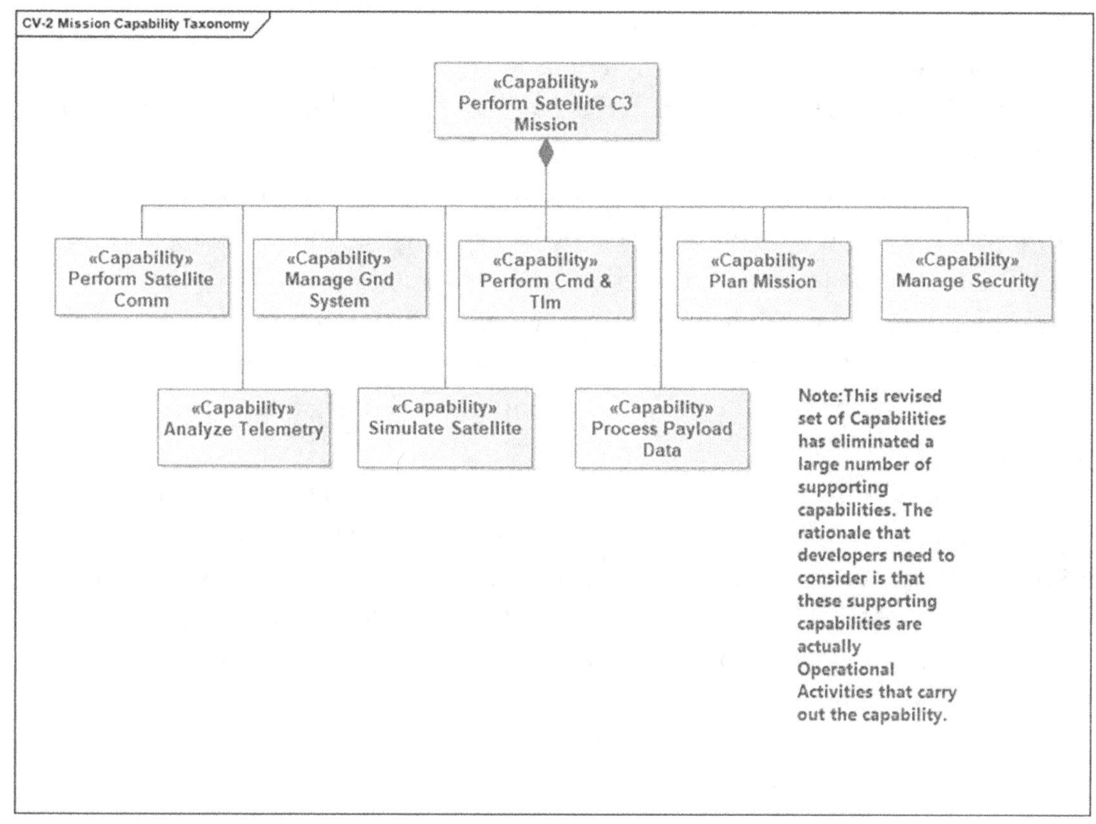

Figure 5-7. CV-2 after movement of capabilities to activity view[4]

Keep in mind, within industry, there is often a view, by managers, that MBSE/ MBSA is just a series of PowerPoint pictures that can be developed in one or two weeks. This is especially the case with managers and executives that only see the roll-up views during a presentation. The evaluation process for capabilities and high-level activities just discussed demonstrates that a few PowerPoint pages developed to meet DoDAF or SysML requirements to meet contractual deliverables is a fallacy.

The approach covered in this book illustrates that the modeling process is one of "organized thought" that moves from high-level capabilities to lower-level descriptions, all of which conform to the onion model shown in Figure 5-8 (the onion model). Each development activity moves from the mission level down to the detailed design and at each layer, corresponding specifications or documentation must be produced to support that level of abstraction.

---

[4] Author-created image

This layered approach applies not only to activities but also to documentation—for example, capability documents, requirements documents, system specifications, and so on. It also highlights the need for interface documents to support integration across specification layers.

When engineers consistently develop notes, requirement statements, and constraints for each model artifact—as previously discussed—the modeling process provides a solid foundation for trade studies and continued system definition. This process extends across multiple phases of development and testing. Issues discovered during testing often stem from insufficient attention to detail during modeling or from introducing new requirements without properly evaluating their impact within the model.

If an OV-5b view is required and there is a plan to transition to SysML, it is advisable to keep the OV-5b at a high level (as shown in Figure 5-9) and reserve detailed modeling for SysML. This is especially important because SysML views can serve as a foundation for subsequent software development using UML (Unified Modeling Language). Keep in mind that there is an area of overlap between DoDAF (or UPDM in British programs) and SysML, as illustrated in Figure 5-9.

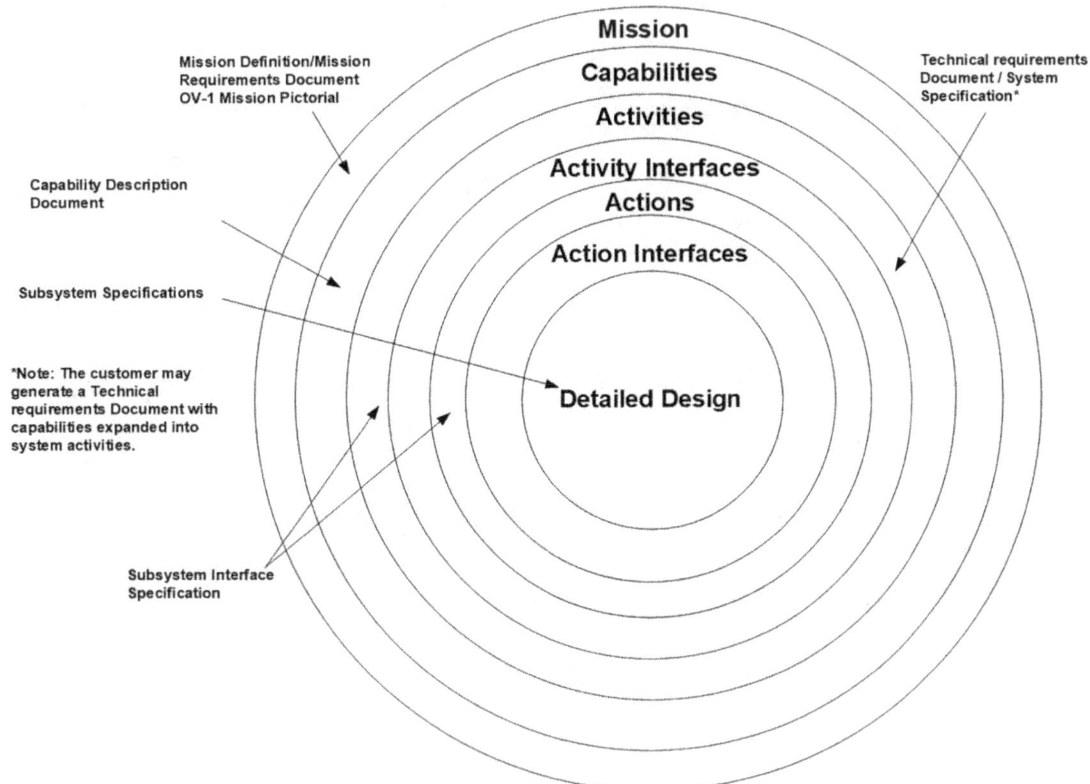

Figure 5-8. *Onion analogy of layered system definition*[5]

____

[5] Author-created image

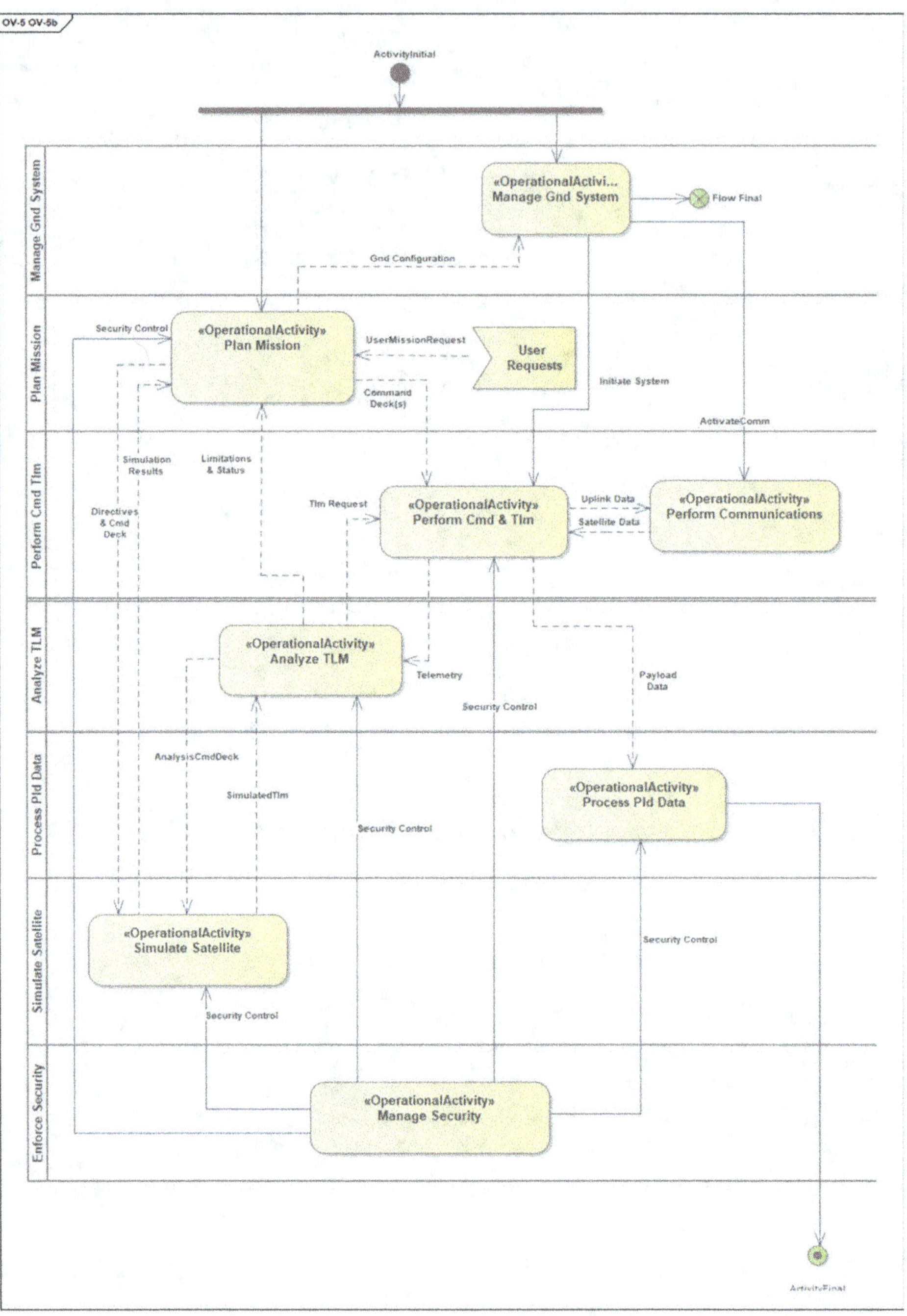

Figure 5-9. *OV-5b example*[6]

---

[6] Author-created image

Chapter Lessons Learned

- If there are plans to shift to SysML for development the best time to make the switch is after creating the SV-4a views.

  - If a transition to SysML is planned, consider omitting the OV-5b view and instead capturing its intended purpose—the relationships between activities—within the SysML activity diagrams. This approach can help avoid the cost and schedule impacts associated with developing the OV-5b. However, this recommendation assumes that the OV-5b is not a contractual deliverable.

- There is an overlap of DoDAF and SysML views that makes it easy to make the switch to SysML at this point in the program/project.

- There is no CV-2 equivalent in SysML; however, it is acceptable to use a DoDAF CV-2 for capability documentation.

- The DoDAF OV-1 can be implemented as a use case diagram, which will aid in conversion to SysML.

- Use cases developed for the program/project should each have an associated specification included as a part of the model element.

- Use case specification material can be used later in defining the activities used to fulfil the use cases.

References

[1]   Model Based Systems Engineering and Systems Modeling Language, Chris Gedo, Defense Information Systems Agency, 2012, page 7

[2]   Object Management Group (OMG) Unified Profile for DoDAF/ MODAF (UPDM)

Acronym List

Acronym	Definition
BDD	Block Definition Diagram
CV	Capability View
DODAF	Department of Defense Architecture Framework
MBSA	Model-Based Systems Architecture
MBSE	Model-Based Systems Engineering
OV	Operations View
SV	System View
SysML	Use Case
UC	Use Case
UML	Unified Modeling Language
UPDM	UML Profile for DoDAF/MODAF

CHAPTER 6

Detailed System Definition

Programs can become inefficient when too many changes are made directly to the top-level system specification. Often, these updates should instead be directed to the relevant subsystem specifications. Transitioning from the Department of Defense Architecture Framework (DoDAF) to the System Modeling Language (SysML) helps prevent overspecification at the system level and encourages more focused development of subsystems. When using a modeling tool, this process can be semi-automated, making use of the SysML element types Structured Activity and Action Calls. By building the model using structured activities and action calls, the supporting activities and actions can be linked. Using this linkage approach, the relationship and layering of activities and their associated requirements will remain connected. This provides a built-in traceability between the highest-level requirements and the detailed requirements, capabilities.

This chapter also explores how system-level activities flow into subsystem development, using the "onion model" to illustrate where key development and documentation efforts occur. It also explains how SysML supports these processes by improving traceability, aligning activities, and enabling a smoother transition to detailed subsystem design.

Guide for Managers and Engineers

Managers should recognize that the details in the system and subsystem are essential to reduce development risk and the risks associated with security certification at the completion of system testing. Taking the time to research the required NIST SP 800-5c controls and communications security and including them in the model will ensure that security requirements are not missed and subsequently discovered during acceptance testing and/or accreditation processing. These late discoveries will significantly affect

© Dennis Hansen 2025
D. Hansen, *Model-Based Systems Engineering and Requirements Definition,*
https://doi.org/10.1007/979-8-8688-2043-4_6

cost and schedule since their resolution will require rework and testing of portions of the system. Engineers will benefit from the model by providing a guide for the lower-level design (software and hardware).

Use of SysML for Definition

From a requirements document standpoint, we are in some cases updating the system specification; however, details of the supporting components/subsystems will normally start at this point. The overall document flow is shown in Figure 6-1.

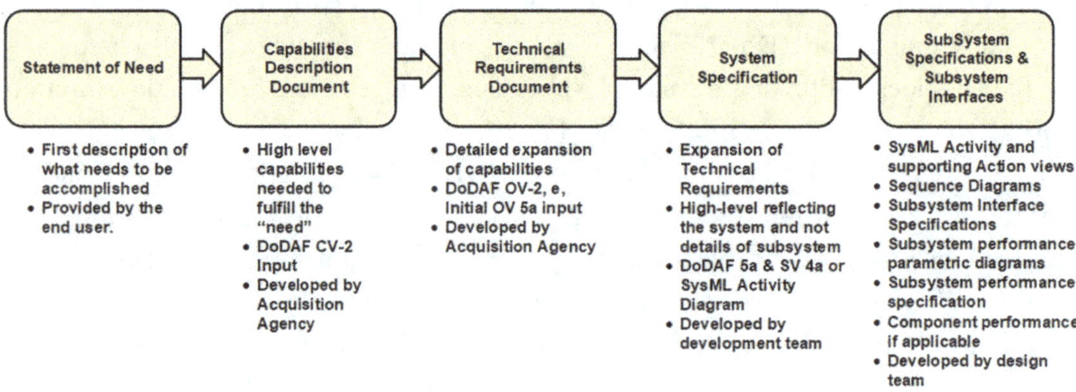

Figure 6-1. *Document development flow*[1]

In keeping with the "onion view" of a system, we are now beginning to define the lower levels of design, including the actions and interfaces within the activities. In Figure 6-2, we see potential points of transition in terms of the activity and functional views. We also see how there are interfaces between activities and actions and between actions and detailed design. Using the modeling tool to develop the SysML views, we note that the connectors between activities and actions represent interfaces at multiple levels of each operational chain of activities in the system. By using the Structured Activities and Action Call features of the language and tool, we see how the linkage is achieved between the layers of the onion. This modelling approach provides early support to subsystem integration and test definition.

In addition, consider that the SV-4a functions can be redefined as SysML actions, admittedly a manual process. Thus, usage of the SV-4a vs. transition to SysML is basically

---

[1] Author-created image

a contractual data requirement or local process. The SysML Activity view representing the transition to a SysML activity diagram view is shown in Figures 6-3a and 6-3b.

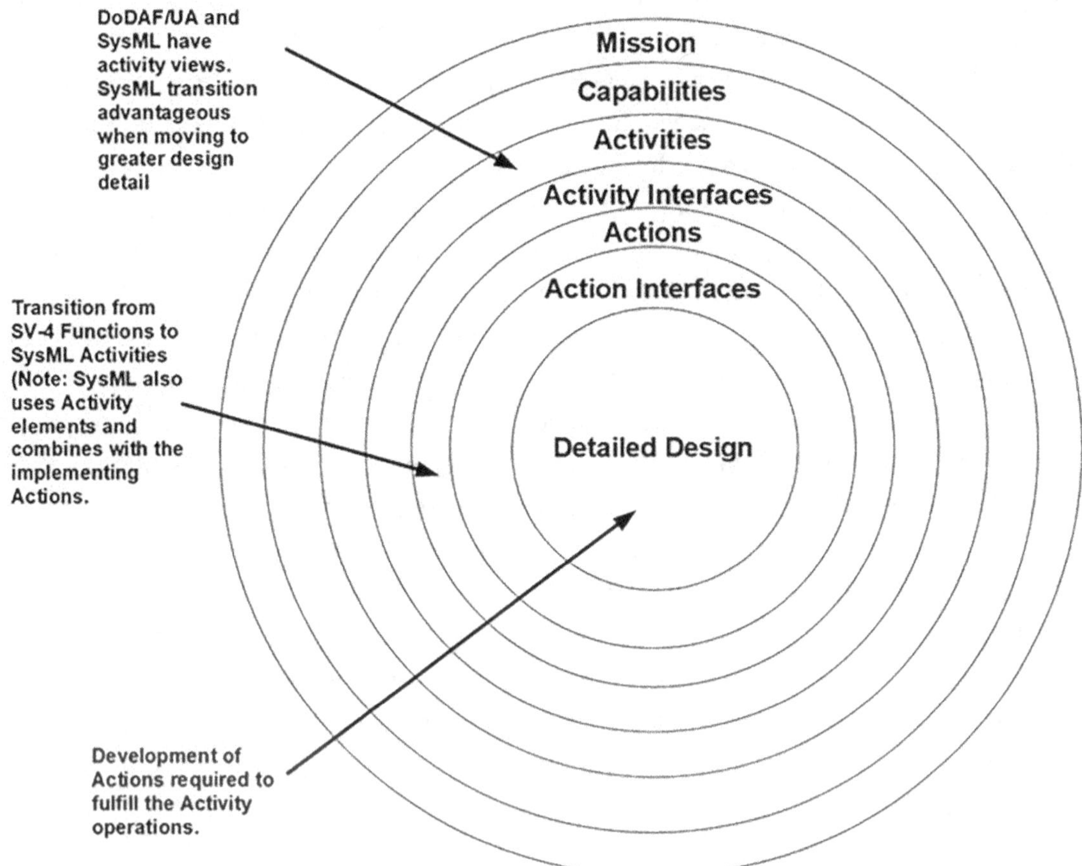

Figure 6-2. *SysML in relation to onion model[2]*

Note the difference between Figures 6-3a, 6-3b, and 6-4. The intent of the OV-5b was to show the operational interaction, including the operational partitions where the activities take place. The SysML diagram shows the activities from a system design perspective. Note the dumbbell symbol in the lower right corner of each activity. The symbol indicates that there is more detail at a lower level. Using a modeling tool normally allows clicking on the activity and automatically jumping to that lower level.

---

[2] Author-created image

If the effort requires the creation of the OV-5b and transition to SysML, caution must be exercised. Depending on the modelling tool capabilities, there may not be a means to link requirements directly between OV-5b activity requirements and the SysML activity view. In this case, the transfer of requirements from the OV-5b (it is assumed that it will be created first) to the SysML activities will be a manual process. A peer review should be conducted upon completion of this manual transfer of requirements to ensure that there is traceability between the two model views.

It is important to keep documenting requirements within the modeling tool when moving forward to SysML detailed modeling. There will be some replication of requirements among the OV-5a, SV-4a, and the SysML activities and actions. This is normal since the operations view requirements may act as a preface to a requirement at the next level. Remember, the OV-5 and associated requirements are the highest-level activity. The SV-4 functions support the higher-level activity. SysML views can start at a level lateral to the OV-5 activities; however, the level of detail begins to escalate as the SysML views mature. The higher-level requirements from the OV-5 still act as the parent for the SysML requirements. The key is to develop requirements at the lower level that support rather than replicate the original higher-level requirement in the OV-5 or System Specification. Previous efforts in years past (before the use of modeling) conducted requirements brainstorming sessions. When the team transitioned to a lower-level specification, invariably, many of the requirements from the higher-level specification were repeated. In some cases, this is acceptable since repetition provides context to the lower-level requirements.

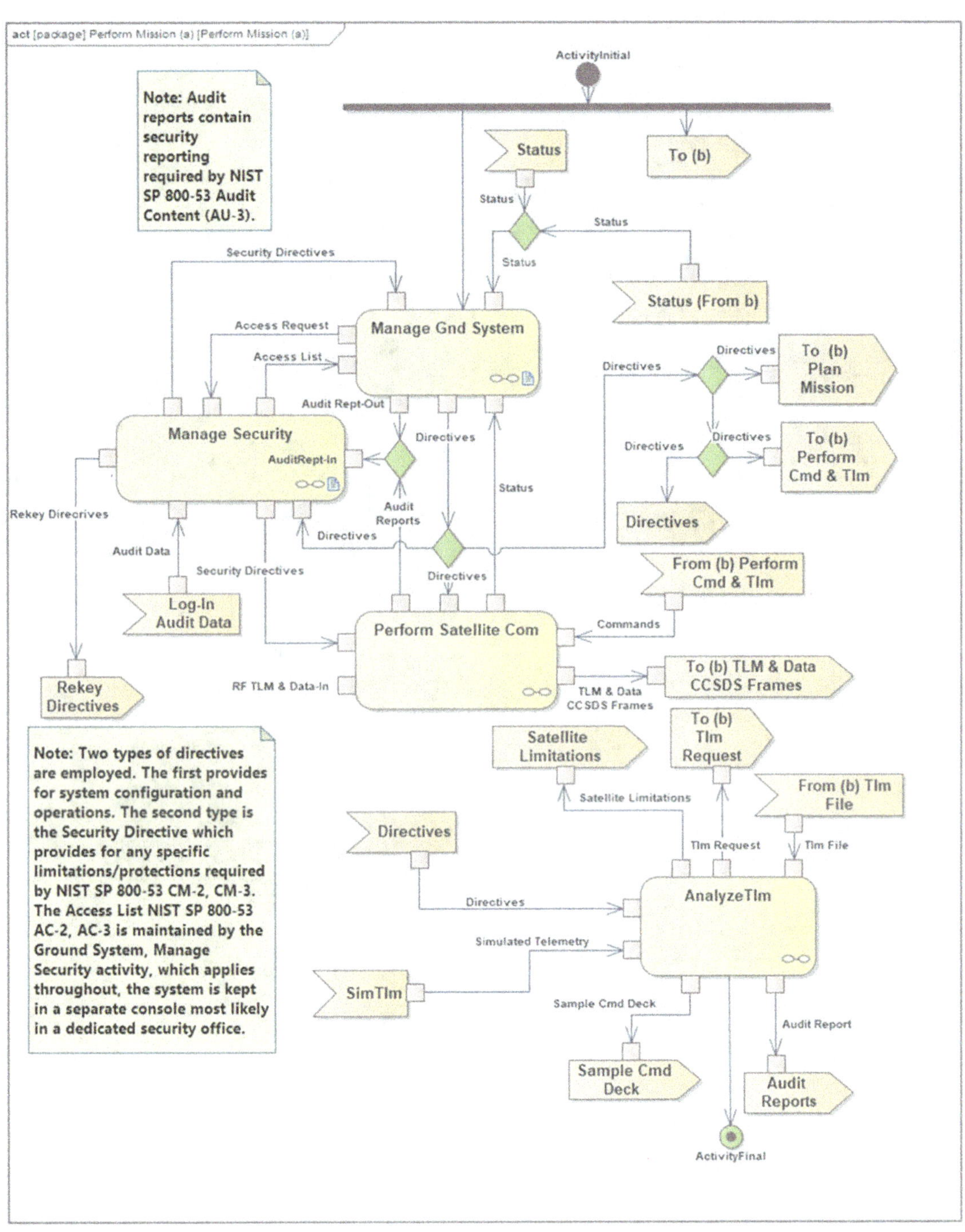

Figure 6-3a. *SysML perform mission activity view*[3]

---

[3] Author-created image

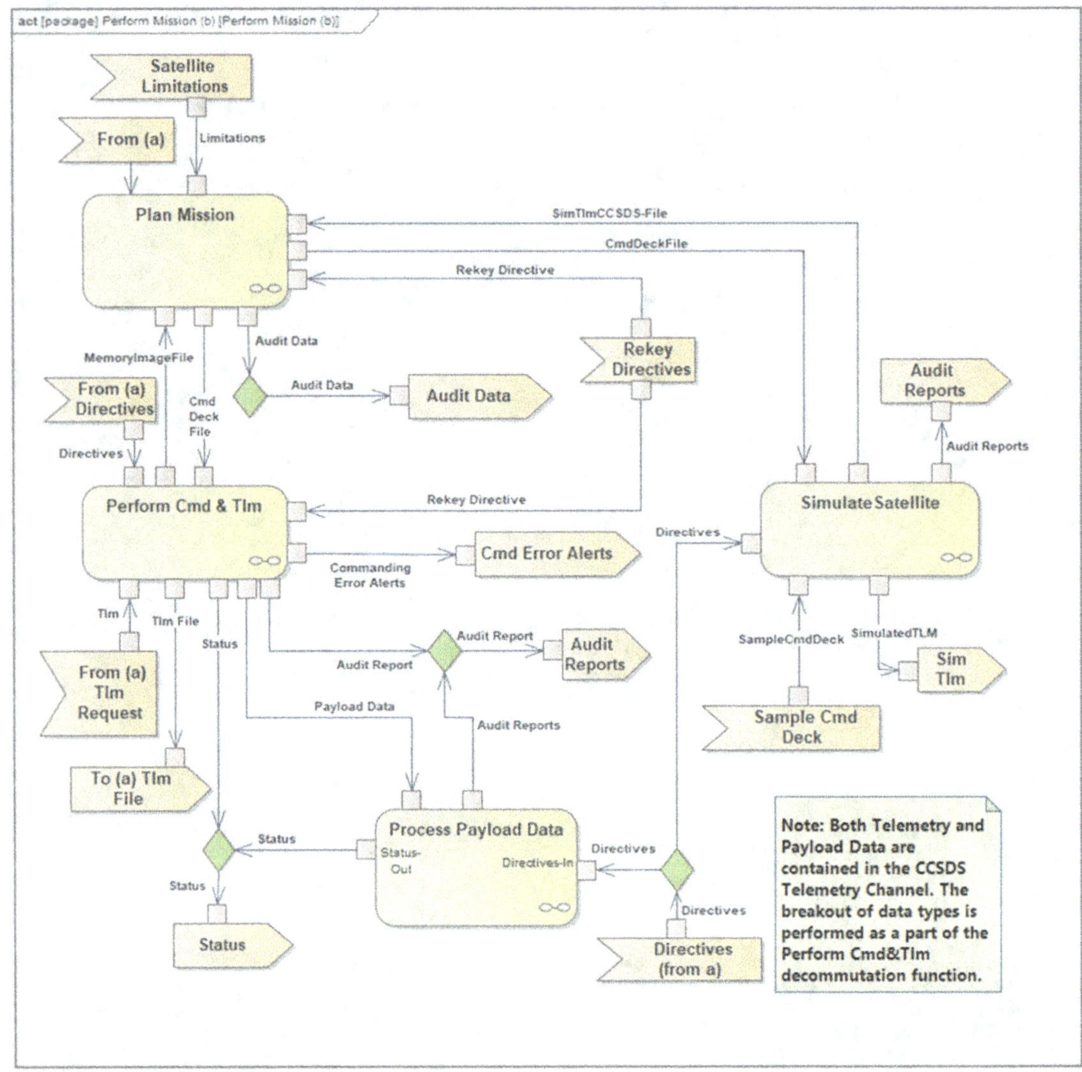

Figure 6-3b. *(continued)*

138

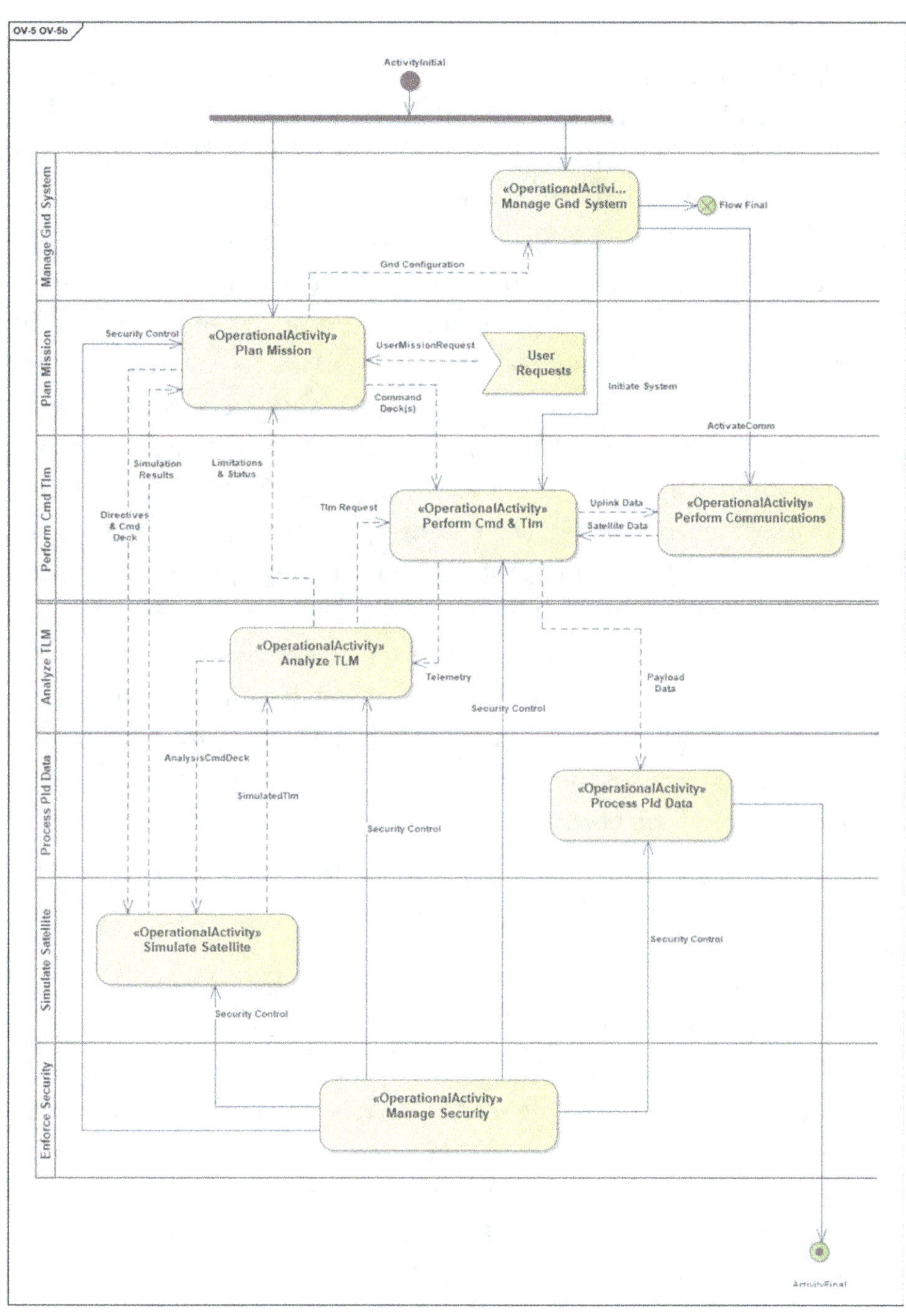

Figure 6-4. *DoDAF OV-5b activity view*[4]

---

[4] Author-created image

Keep in mind that a critical reason for developing requirements in the tool, rather than directly developing the specification, is to provide the basis and background information for each element. When developing any model, especially if you must leave the model for a period, there needs to be a reminder of the model logic. Without the reminders, it is possible for the model to drift from the original intent.

The requirements documented thus far should be downloaded into the initial system specification. The resultant document should be edited to eliminate replication, that is not provided for context and clarify requirement wording. When working through the editing process, consider developing (at a high level) the test methodology to be employed and document it in a separate document. This approach will save time when formal test plans and procedures are developed. If the modeling tool provides a means of storing the test approach for each element, consider adding this information to the tool rather than a separate document. Depending upon the modeling tool being used, there may be an option to document, gather, and export the high-level test procedures/methodology to an editable document.

During the initial stages of ground system design, it is advisable to consider if management should be conducted in physically different locations or from a centralized location. The question of where the function is performed affects the hardware and facility requirements. From a software perspective, the impact is greater. There are COTS software packages available that can perform most of the required functions. The difference between packages may be in the form of functions provided and functions that can be developed (possibly with a scripting language or a feature selection option) to operate within the management structure.

All too often, government and corporate programs/projects decide that "this is a COTS function and does not require time in the schedule, funding, and other resources to implement." This is a big mistake. The use of modeling, in addition to finding missing functionality, can directly support trade studies between custom development and COTS as well as between COTS alternative products.

Development of the SysML activity diagrams and especially the associated data and requirements can mitigate the potential pitfalls such as omission of control links or subsystem activities/actions to carry out a function specified in the system specification. The activity diagrams and requirements/constraints documented can be used to generate an acquisition checklist for the evaluation of potential COTS products. For those functions and features not provided by any of the candidate products, the model data can be used as a basis for developing software to fill in the gaps. If COTS is selected, the model should be updated to show where it fits and how it interfaces with the other activities. The key is that the modeling aids in the detailed examination of what system features are required and how they interact to perform the organization's mission. The scope of ground system management is shown in Figures 6-5a and 6-5b SysML ground system management activity view. Note how the figure shows notes related to the security needs of the management function.

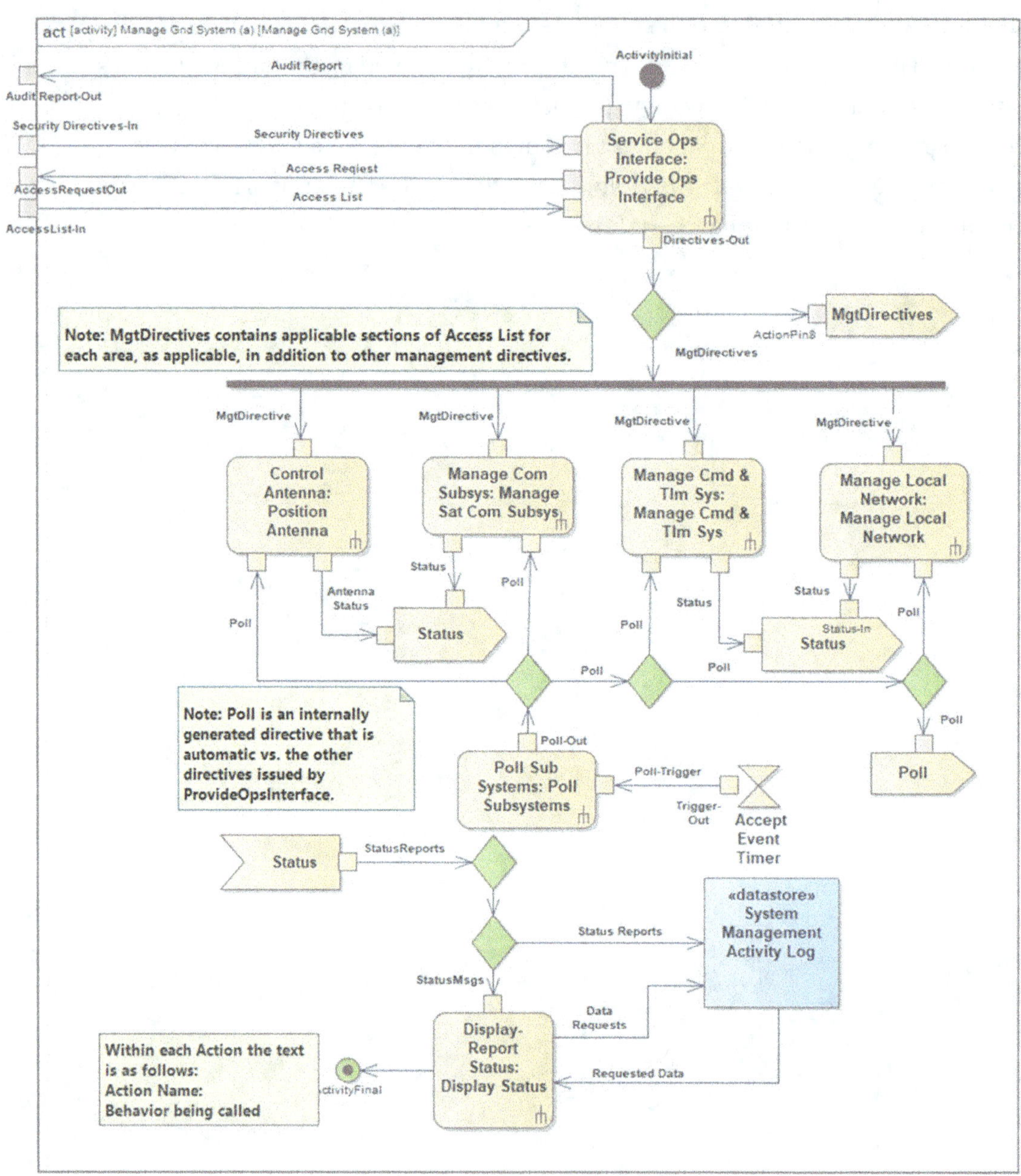

Figure 6-5a. *SysML ground system management activity view[5]*

---

[5] Author-created image

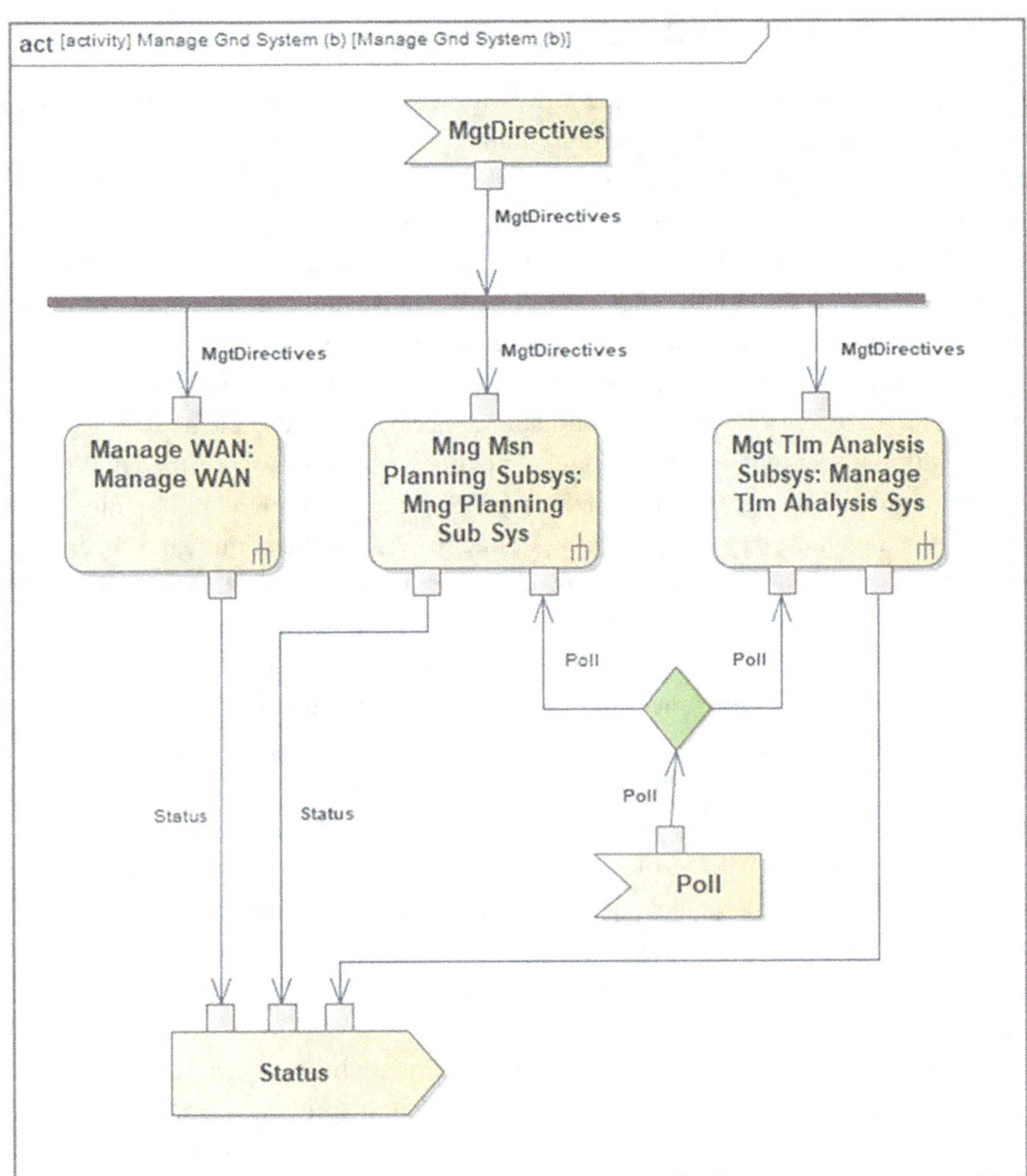

Figure 6-5b. *(continued)*

SysML Manage Security Example

It may seem strange to be addressing security within a system model and design context. Any engineer or program manager that has built a government system in the past has experienced some level of difficulty during final certification for operations. A long list of problems requires a Plan of Action and Milestones (POAM) report. Each POAM requires tracking against a deadline for resolution. It is essential to provide security and the risk management framework as early as possible to avoid downstream costs for rework and, most importantly, potential security breaches during initial operation.

In past years, security was addressed largely as an administrative function. Remember that to perform security administration, provisions must be made for working within the system being developed. Looking at the process described in this book, we addressed security in terms of the capability diagram and the capabilities required. We then moved to the activities required to perform the administration and then the functions required to perform the activities. These DoDAF items are a good way to quickly start evaluating and documenting the physical attributes required.

As mentioned earlier, the engineer and the program need to start looking at the lower levels of detail after the functions have been described and documented in terms of requirements and constraints. A switch to SysML at this stage will aid in considering system security details from beginning to end. Recall that SysML is built upon UML (used by software engineering in particular) and that the SysML model elements can be further developed in UML by software engineering as necessary. For example, note how Manage Security was shown separately from Manage Ground System in the SysML Perform Mission activity diagram (Figures 6-3a and 6-3b). The details of the Manage Ground System activities are linked to the Manage Security activity diagram (Figures 6-6a, 6-6b, 6-6c).

Considerations such as the Manage Security placement become critical when dealing with COTS. All too often, government and corporate programs/projects will have decided that "this is a COTS function and does not require time in the schedule, funding, and other resources to implement." This is a big mistake, especially when looking at functions such as security management. Development of the SysML activity diagrams and especially the associated data and requirements can help to mitigate the potential pitfalls, such as omission of control links or subsystem activities/actions to carry out a function (in this case, security management) specified in the system specification. The activity diagrams and requirements/constraints documented can be used to generate an acquisition checklist for the evaluation of potential COTS products. For those functions and features not provided by any of the candidate products, the model data can be used as a basis for developing software to fill in the gaps. If COTS is selected, the model should be updated to show where it fits and how it interfaces with the other activities. The key is that the modeling aids in a detailed examination of what system features are required and how they interact to perform the organization's mission.

From the standpoint of ground system management, we consider what needs to be accomplished to manage all subsystems and components. We also need to consider that there is a need to manage the security of the system. Now consider if the subsystem management includes security management. In the case presented here, we consider that these are separate activities (refer to Figures 6-6a, 6-6b, 6-6c). The rationale used is that security is required for all activities, including ground system management. Notice how the Manage Gnd System in Figures 6-7a and 6-7b requests and receives the access list from Manage Security. It also receives security directives from Manage Security. These directives will control subsystem security settings, that is, settings that will impact activity performance. A critical security management function involves obtaining/creating cryptographic keys and managing rekey of the systems, as shown circled in Figures 6-6b, 6-7a, and 6-7b.

If desired, a single management console can be used for ground system management and security administration, since, as separate activities, there can be separate software packages. Both packages will require a unique sign-in. Thus, security and ground system management can be performed on a single operator console or on separate consoles that are in the same location or even separate locations. A system trade, using NIST-SP-800-53 SC-32 as a guide, should be conducted before implementing one approach or the other.

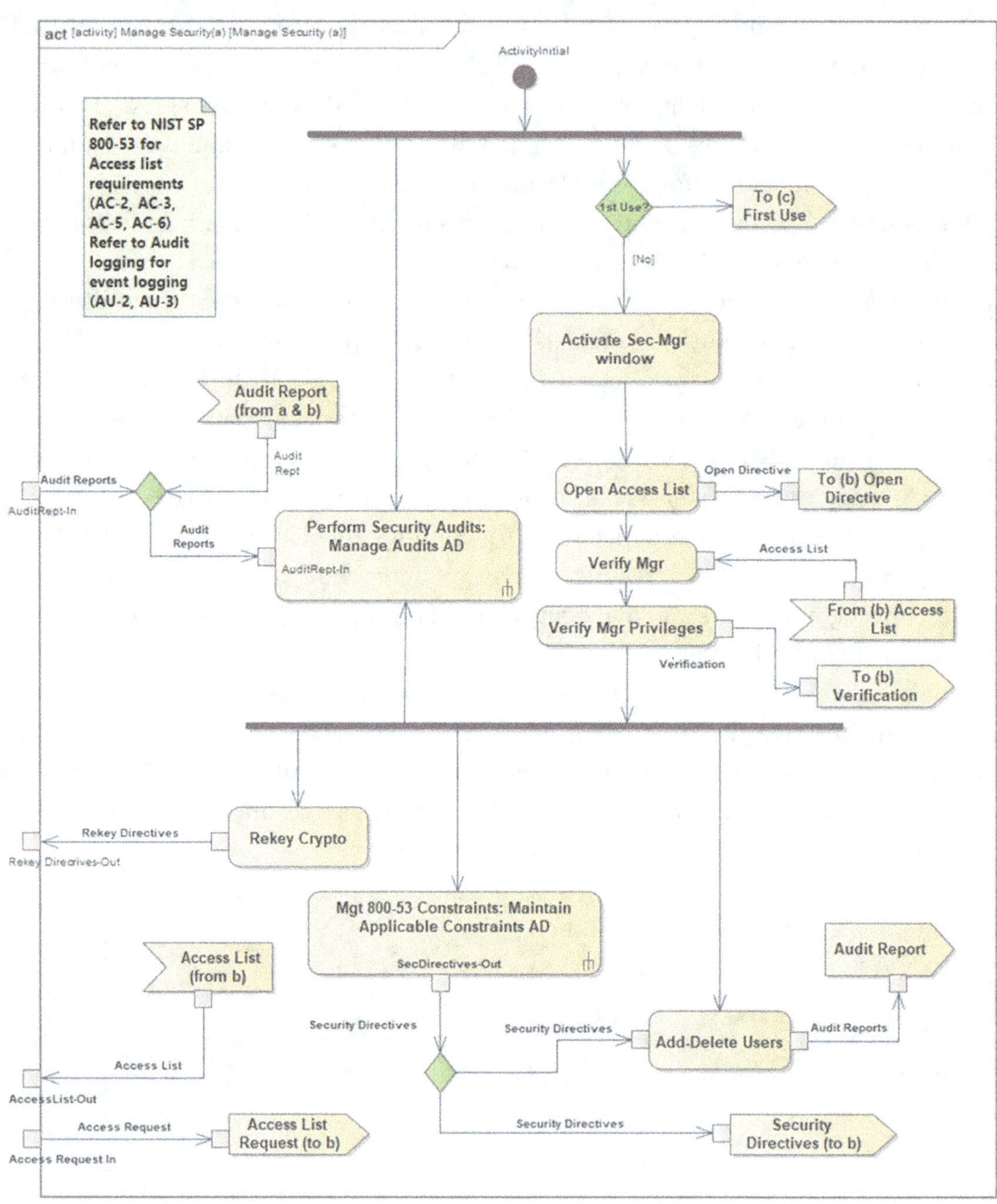

Figure 6-6a. *Manage security activity diagram*[6]

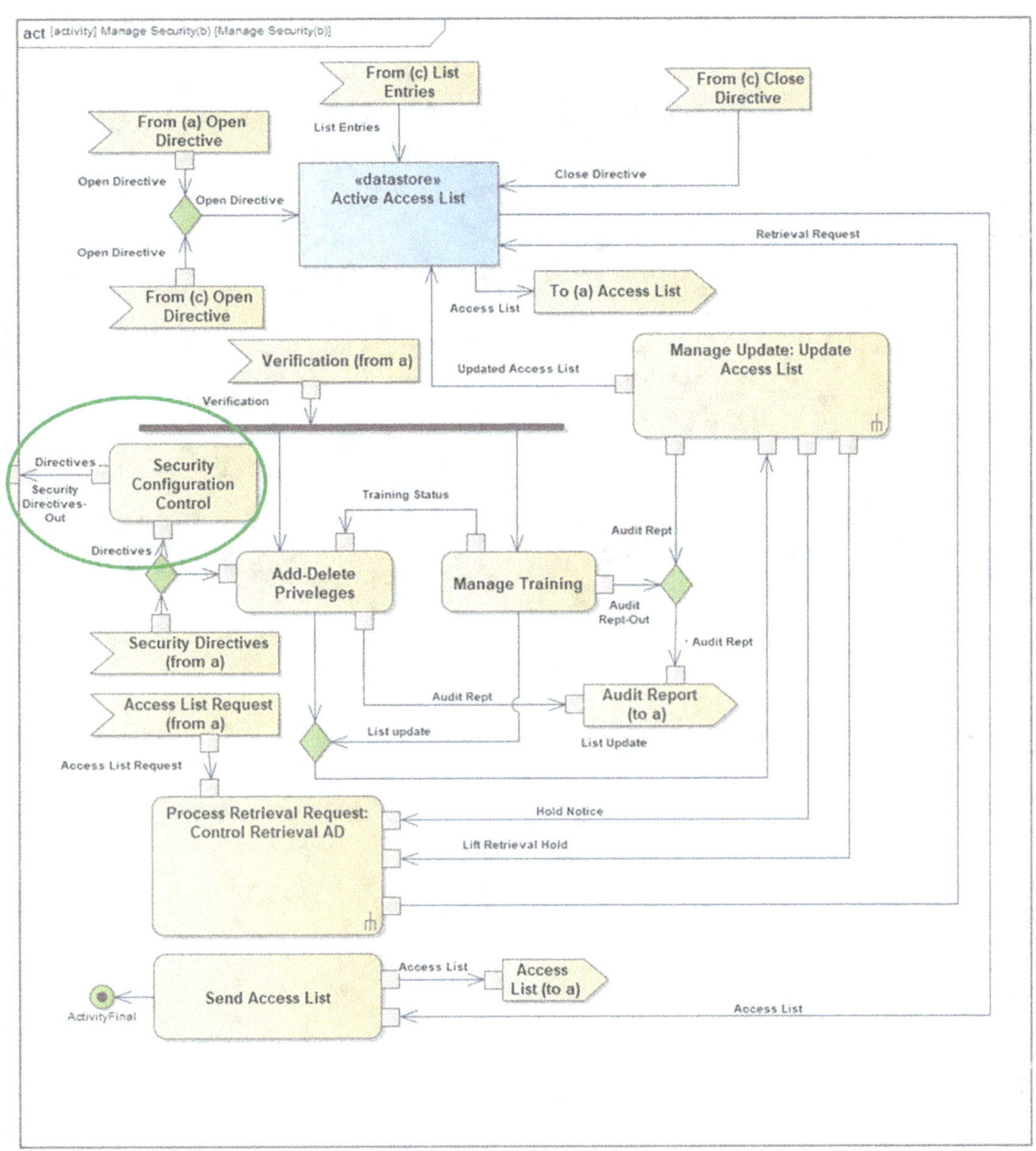

Figure 6-6b. *(continued)*

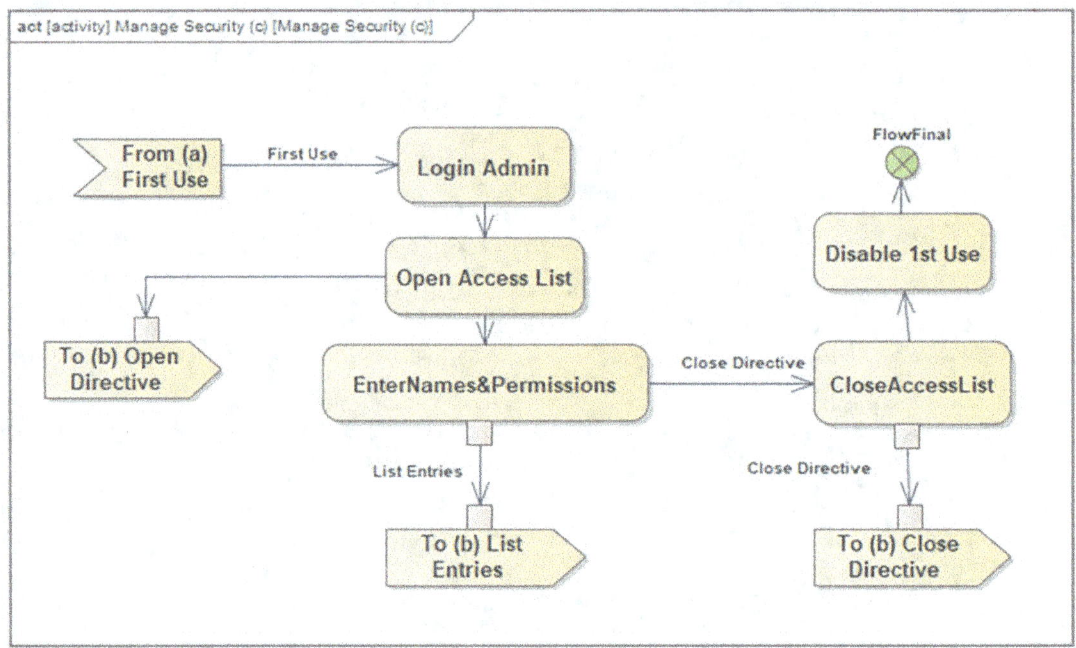

Figure 6-6c. *(continued)*

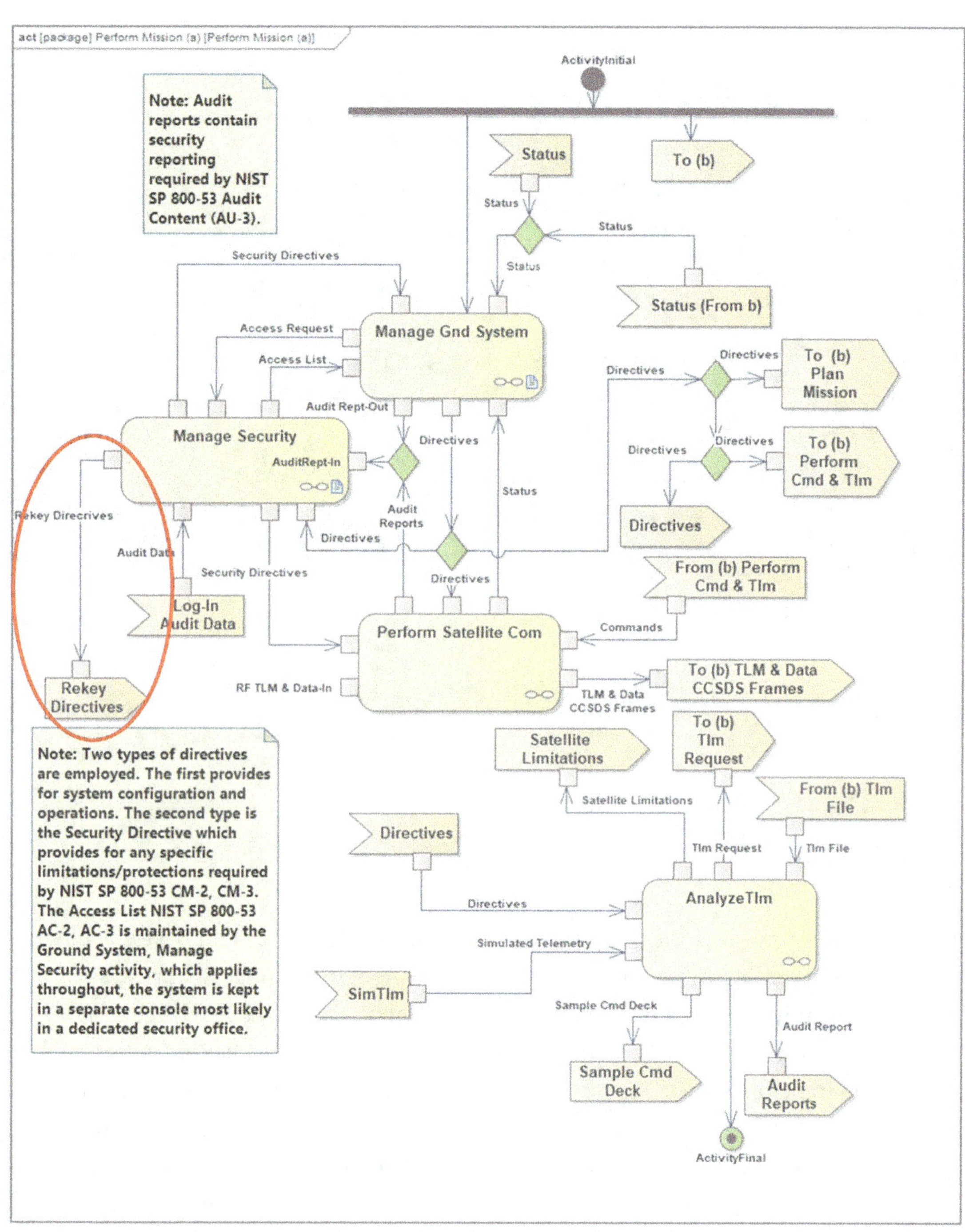

Figure 6-7a. *Perform mission activity diagram*[7]

[7] Author-created image

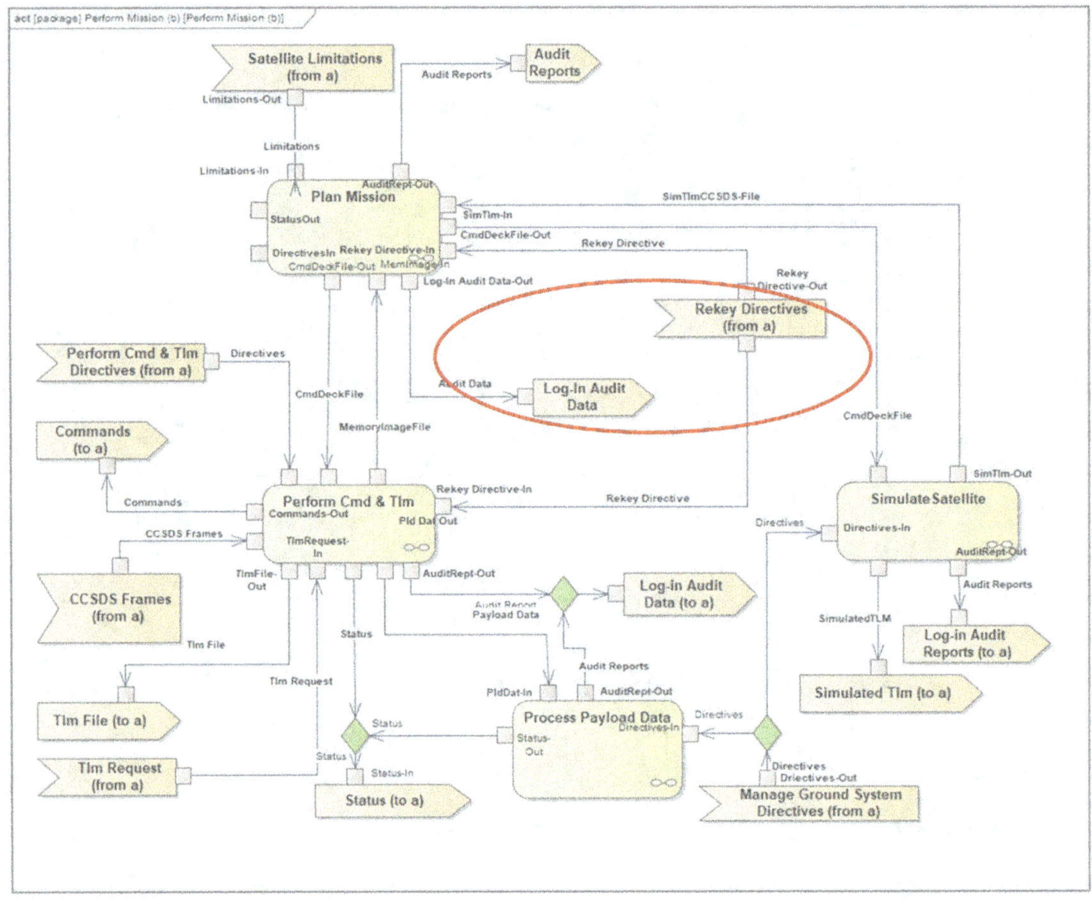

Figure 6-7b. *(contineud)*

Note that there should be security features incorporated within the system activities that implement the security management directives sent by Manage Security. Security directives are shown as the third action pinned down on the left edge of Figure 6-6b. They are shown entering the activity Provide Ops Interface (at the second action pin from the top in Figure 6-5a). The intent is for the ground system manager to have access to all external directives received by the ground system management function. Management directives are relayed to ground system components as necessary.

It may seem strange to be addressing security within a system model and design context. Any engineer, or program manager, that has built a government system in the past has experienced some level of difficulty during final certification for operations. A long list of problems requires a Plan of Action and Milestones (POAM) report. Each

POAM requires tracking against a deadline for resolution. It is essential to provide security and the risk management framework as early as possible to avoid downstream costs for rework and, most importantly, potential security breaches during initial operation.

In past years, security was addressed largely as an administrative function. Remember that to perform security administration, provisions must be made for working within the system being developed. Looking at the process described in this book, we addressed security in terms of the Capability diagram and the capabilities required. We then moved to the activities required to perform the administration and then the functions required to perform the activities. These DoDAF items are a good way to quickly start evaluating and documenting the physical attributes required.

As mentioned earlier, the engineer and the program need to start looking at the lower levels of detail after the functions have been described and documented in terms of requirements and constraints. A switch to SysML at this stage will aid in considering system security details from beginning to end. Recall that SysML is built upon UML (used by software engineering in particular) and that the SysML model elements can be further developed in UML by software engineering as necessary.

Note how Manage Security was shown separately from Manage Ground System in the SysML Perform Mission activity diagram (Figures 6-3a and 6-3b). The details of the Manage Ground System activities are linked to the Manage Security activity diagram (Figures 6-6a, 6-6b, 6-6c).

Security First Use Considerations

First use is often just taken for granted. COTS packages often just use Admin as both the login name and password. Care should be taken for selection of these initial users. To accomplish this, Figure 6-6c provides for Protective First Use Actions. Login Admin provides an initial ability to perform security management. This will most likely be accomplished via simple means such as those already discussed. Administratively, this should be a single, trusted person designated by the Security or Project Manager. After login, the Security Admin can open the access list file in the data store and then enter the initial list of persons and permissions. Upon completion, the data store will be directed to close the access list file.

After the initial list of people and permissions has been completed using NIST SP 800-53 AC-2 as a guide, the system will use the normal login process using the Security Manager Window on the console. All passwords, managers and users, should be changed after the first log-in. Note that the actions shown for normal login are generic and may be altered for callable actions to provide further details for each action. Keep in mind that the process shown is not intended to be directed, and it is only a suggestion of how security administration for the system can be implemented. Using organization directives and design team selection of COTS, software reuse, or new custom software can alter this process. If this is the case and the approach shown in Figures 6-6a, 6-6b, and 6-6c is used as a starting point, the model should be updated.

Access List Routine Update

A preliminary representation of the update process is shown in Figure 6-8. This illustration is not prescriptive; implementation may vary depending on system context. However, all updates must include user information—specifically the authorized password, the date the password was changed, and assigned privileges. Each subsystem relies on this data during its login sequence.

Audit data, including pass/fail authentication results, is forwarded to the Manage Security function. For further guidance, refer to NIST SP 800-53 controls AU-2 and AU-3.

Detailed implementation is intentionally omitted here, as audit handling may differ based on local configurations and the characteristics of commercial off-the-shelf (COTS) equipment. In some cases, COTS products or reused software from legacy systems may already satisfy system requirements. When evaluating COTS solutions, this update approach can serve as a checklist to assess product capabilities.

Ultimately, our objective is to comply with NIST SP 800-53[1] and to fulfill the essential operational requirement: the ability to securely power the system on and off.

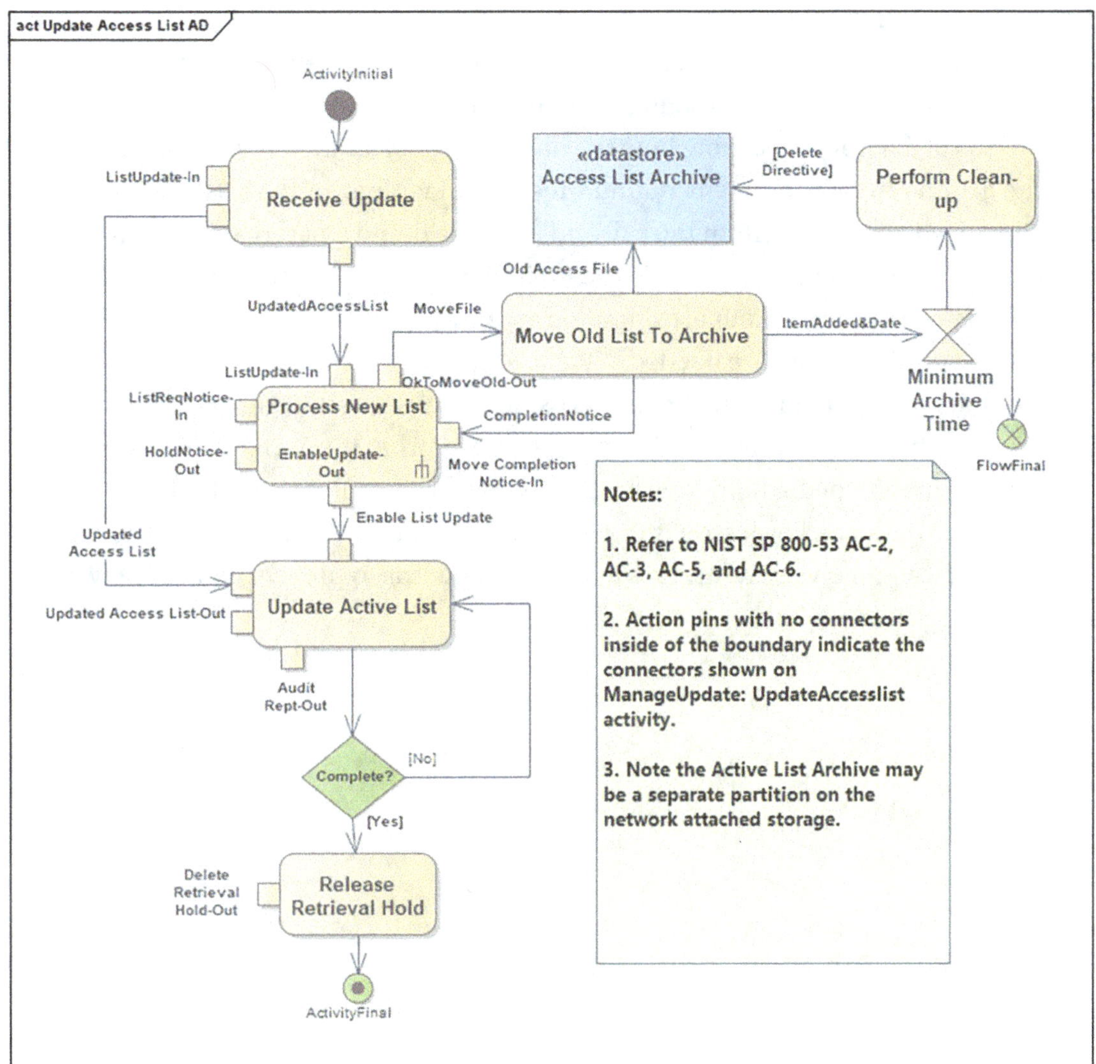

Figure 6-8. *Update access list activity diagram example*[8]

One approach for meeting the needs of routine access list update is shown in Figure 6-8. The sequence of events related to Figure 6-8 are shown in Figures 6-9a and 6-9b. On the surface, this sequence diagram combined with activity diagram may appear rather simple and obvious. Its value is in guiding the thought process of the actions and their relationship. In practice, it is not uncommon to find errors in the interconnect logic

---

[8] Author-created image

and sequence by developing the sequence diagram along with the activity diagram. The development of the operational logic continues with the Process List activity diagram (Figure 6-10) and the associated sequence diagram (Figure 6-11).

In terms of diagram style, note how the higher-level diagrams show connections from the action pins to the activity boundaries. The diagrams for the action calls are a depiction of what goes on within the call and are considered a part of the original activity diagram. An illustration of this point is shown in Figure 6-12. Notice how the Action Pins within the diagram call out are the same as shown on the Action Call. Thus, no connections to a boundary are needed.

The final action is to process the access list retrieval request, Figure 6-13. Note that the retrieval is held based on the Hold Notice received from the Manage Update action call. The elimination of the hold is performed when a Delete Retrieval Hold is received from Manage Update. A key lesson is that a seemingly simple task, such as retrieving an access list, can involve several steps and activity guards to prevent conflict between updates and retrievals.

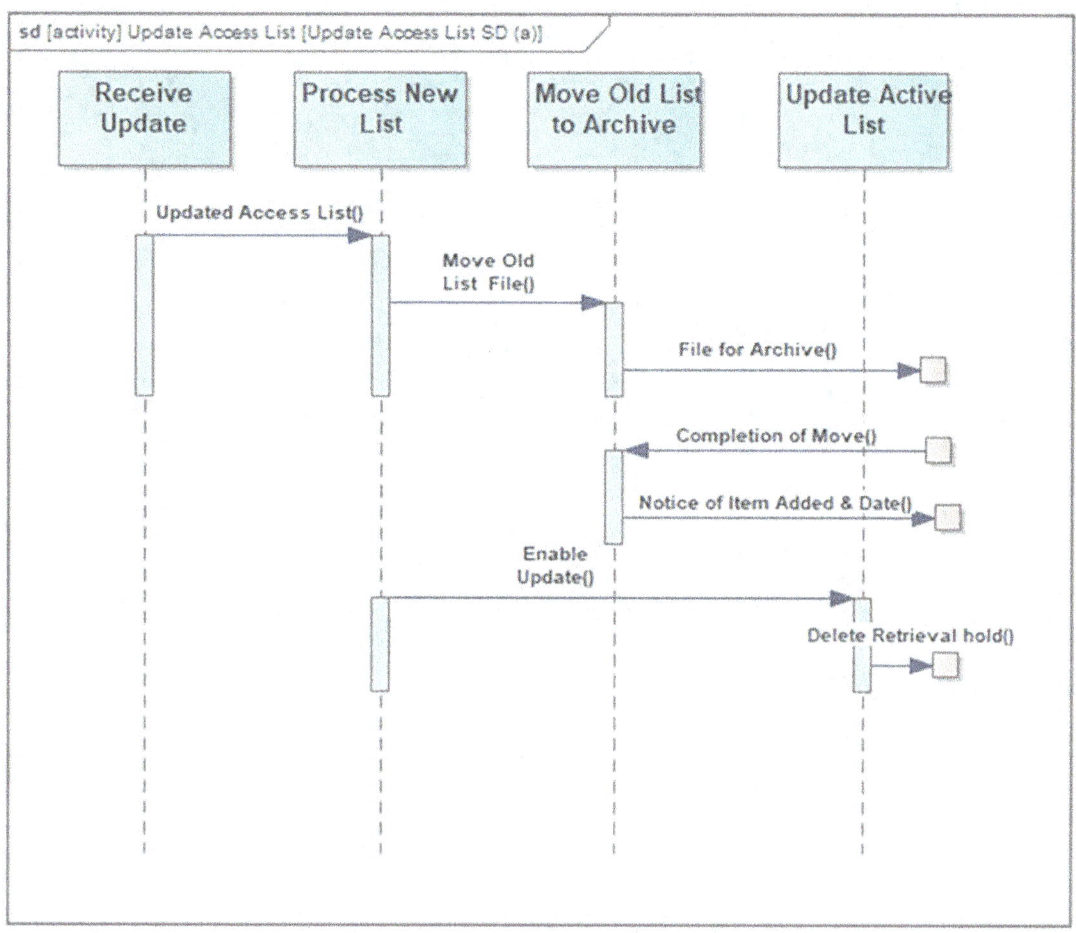

Figure 6-9a. *Update access list sequence diagram*[9]

---

[9] Author-created image

155

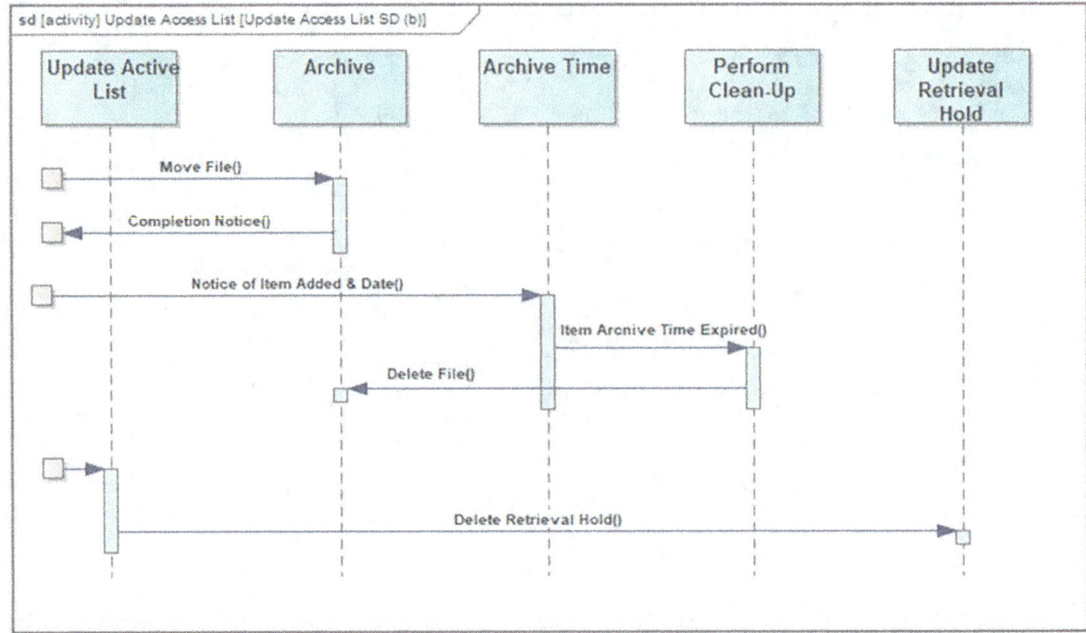

Figure 6-9b. *(continued)*

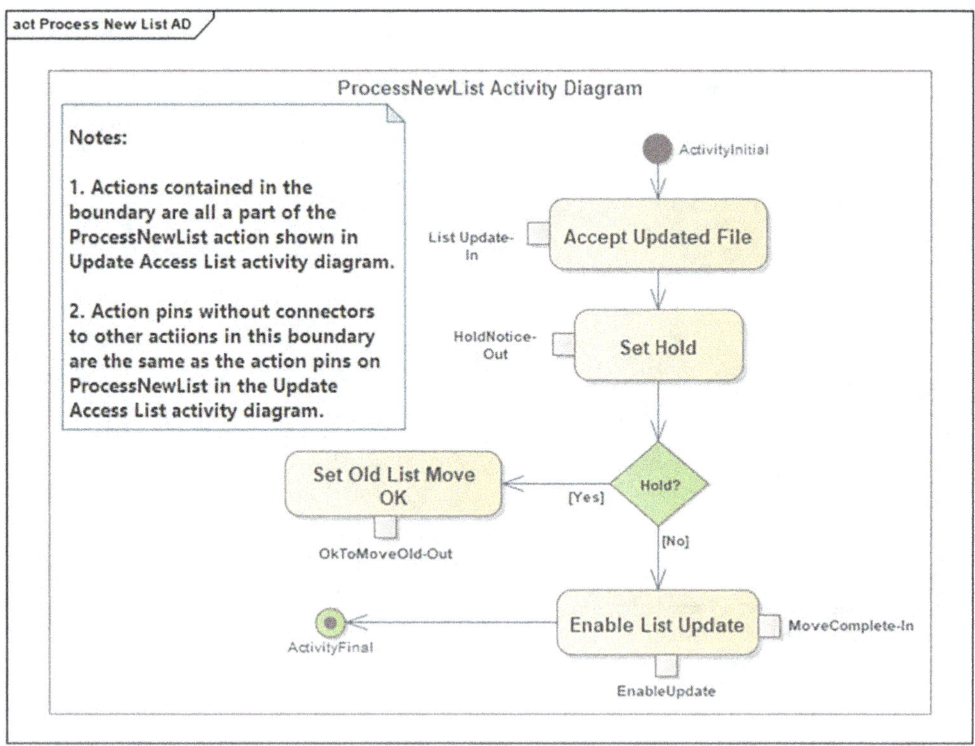

Figure 6-10. *Process new list activity diagram[10]*

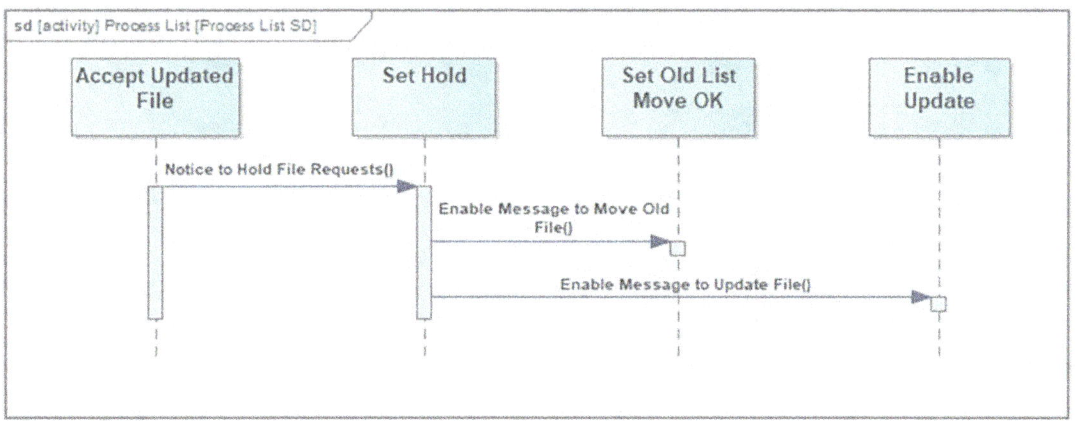

Figure 6-11. *Process list sequence diagram[11]*

---

[10] Author-created image

[11] Author-created image

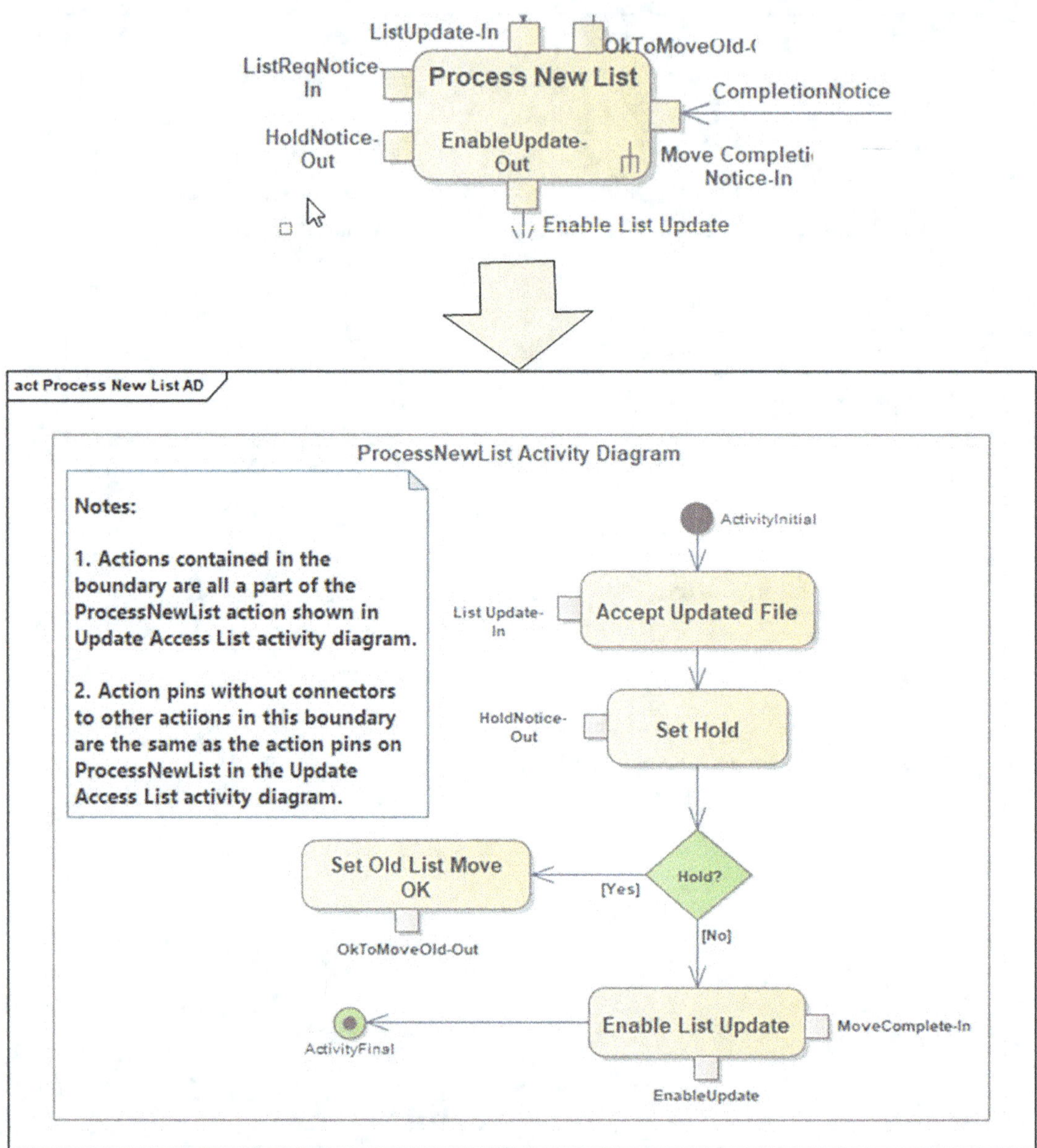

Figure 6-12. *Action call content illustration*[12]

---

[12] Author-created image

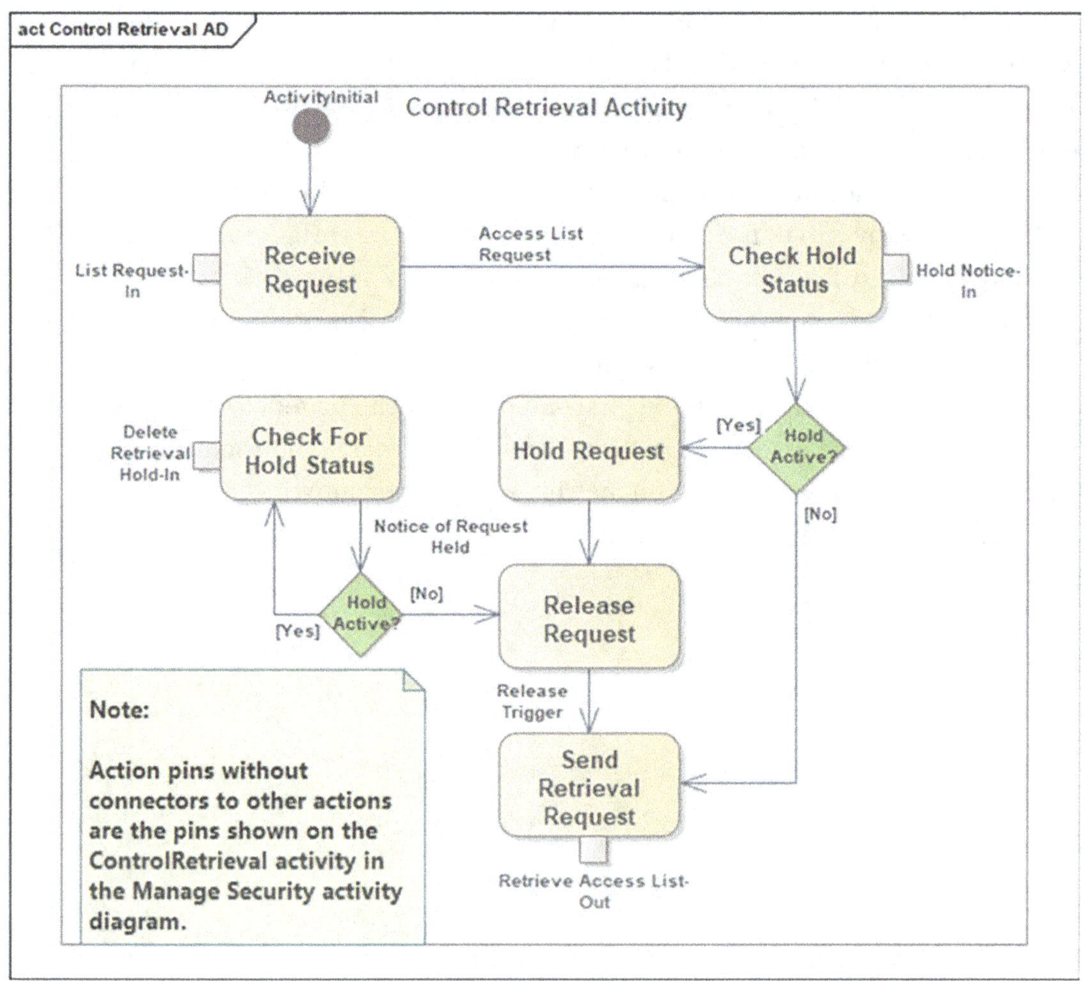

Figure 6-13. *Control retrieval activity diagram*[13]

Security Administration, NIST SP-800-53

This section is particularly useful for managers and engineers working on government programs. It is recommended that all managers and engineers, regardless of their affiliation with the government, follow the guidelines in NIST SP-800-53.

---

[13] Author-created image

Thus far, our example has concentrated on the log-in process. A very important part of security involves system audits (NIST SP 800-53 Au-1) [1]. This section will not cover every possible aspect of system security audits. Obviously, there is a requirement to poll for or otherwise receive audit reports and manage them. Team activities required to gather the information at each subsystem are not included in this section.

During the early part of the system development, it is important to provide an initial definition of security features of the ground system. Figures 6-6a, 6-6b, and 6-6c provided an initial view of security concerns. The ultimate need for security audit was shown as Manage Audits. This action call links to further definition of the action (Figure 6-14). Note that the actions shown are initial placeholders that can be redefined as the system and actions supporting associated security controls evolve. Initial insights into the operational mechanisms of the action may be incorporated into the graphics.

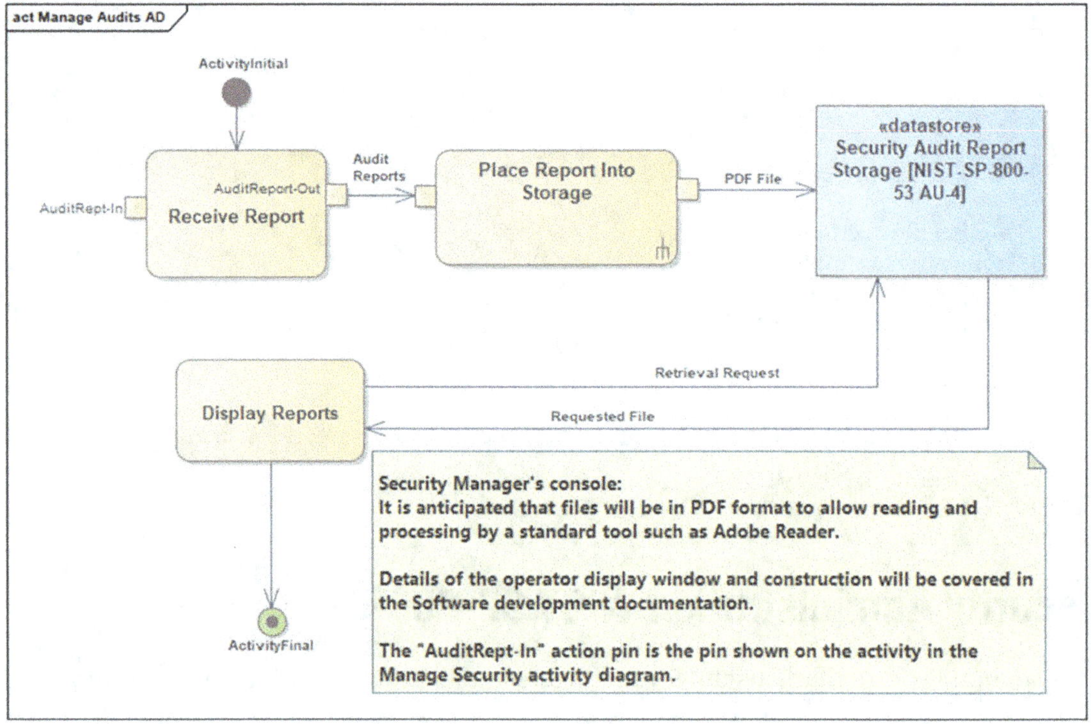

Figure 6-14. *Manage audits[14]*

---

[14] Author-created image

In addition to notes in the graphics, notes should be applied for each of the actions/ activities shown in the graphic, as shown in Figure 6-15. Requirements should be documented as shown in Figure 6-16.

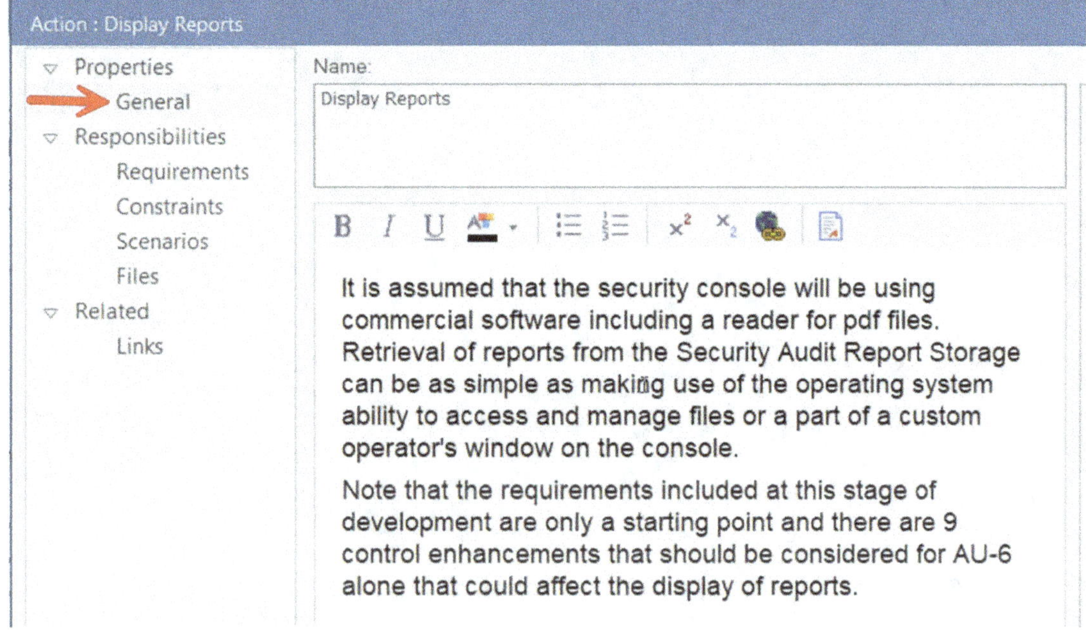

Figure 6-15. *Action notes*[15]

---

[15] Author-created image

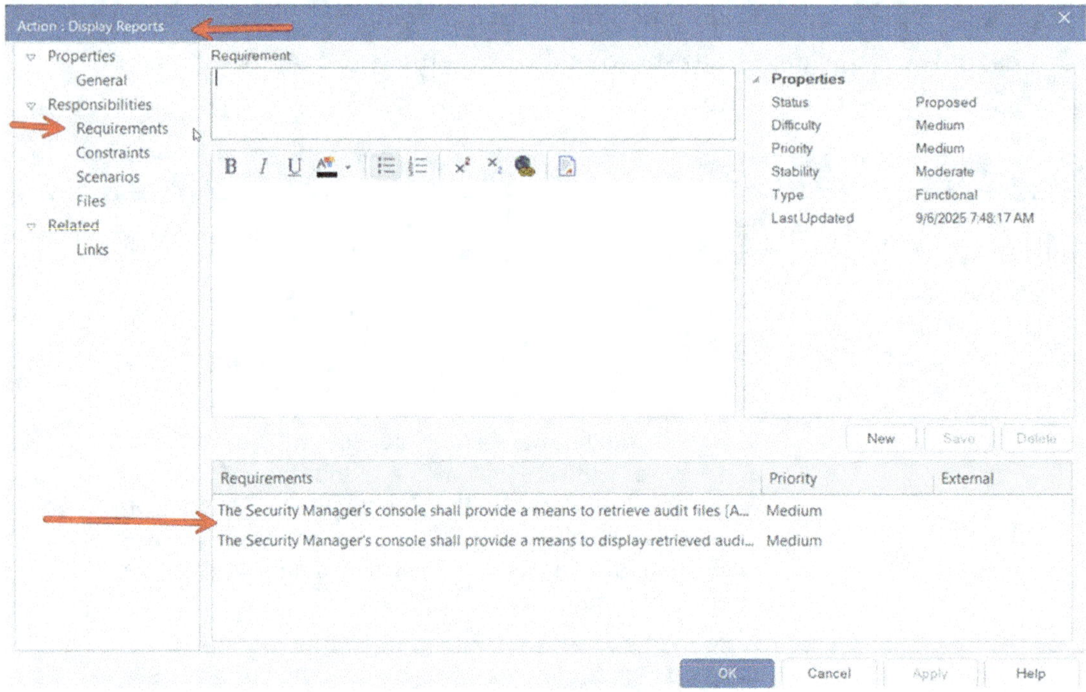

Figure 6-16. *Initial display reports requirements*[16]

At the early stages of development, the requirements may seem very high level and obvious. This is acceptable since they are only a starting point and will be supplemented with additional requirements, or modified, or deleted as the security architecture matures. As with requirements for the rest of the system, the intent is to provide a basis to stimulate thought and act as the starting point for further development. The system engineer and the security engineer/manager should work together during model development to further develop security requirements and modifications to the architecture as necessary. In comparison, the development of the security requirements in a textual fashion alone, in working groups, or by the security engineer alone, can result in missing requirements, extraneous requirements, or incorrectly worded requirements that do not meet the security objectives.

---

[16] Author-created image

Integrating Security Constraints into Design

In the OV-5a Perform Mission taxonomy view Figure 6-17, we show Manage Security as an activity at the same level as other operational activities, all of which form a part of Perform Mission. The placement was deliberate to emphasize that security features are equal in importance and must be incorporated throughout the system. This section will provide examples of how the security features are incorporated into subsystems.

Figure 6-18 shows an example of how the model can change as security requirements are reviewed during the development process. The original view displays the receipt of Security Directives. The directives were defined to include the access list for operator login. After reviewing NIST SP 800-53 AC-2 [1] and NIST SP 800-53 Au-14 [1] Session Audit, it was decided to provide for reporting login actions as an audit report, as shown in the modified audit view in the lower half of the figure. Since Verify User was implemented as a callable action, the additional required activity is shown in Figure 6-19. Note that the process provides for logging both successful and failed logins. This activity covers system start-up AU-14 (1) [1].

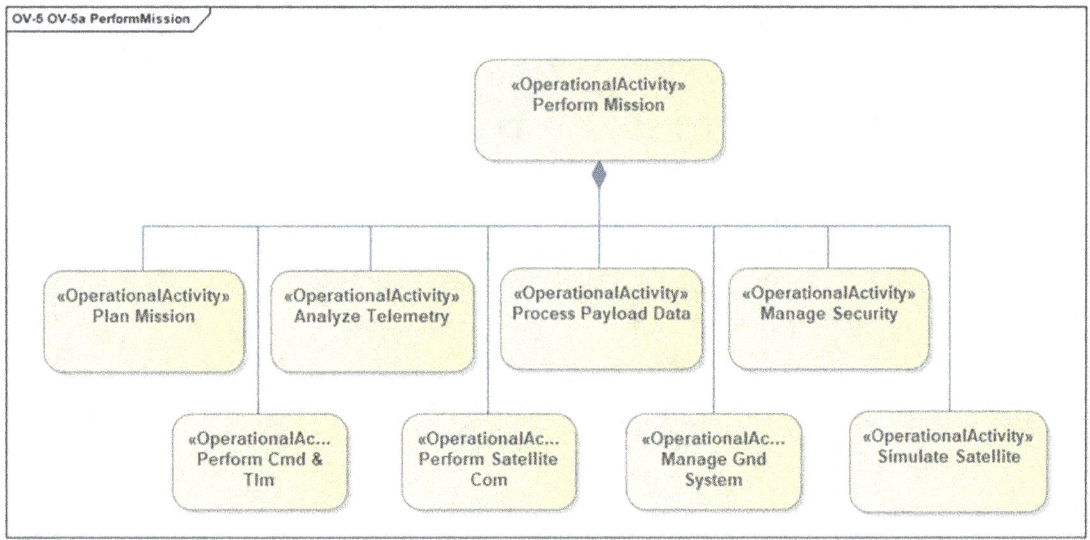

Figure 6-17. *OV-5a perform mission taxonomy view[17]*

---

[17] Author-created image

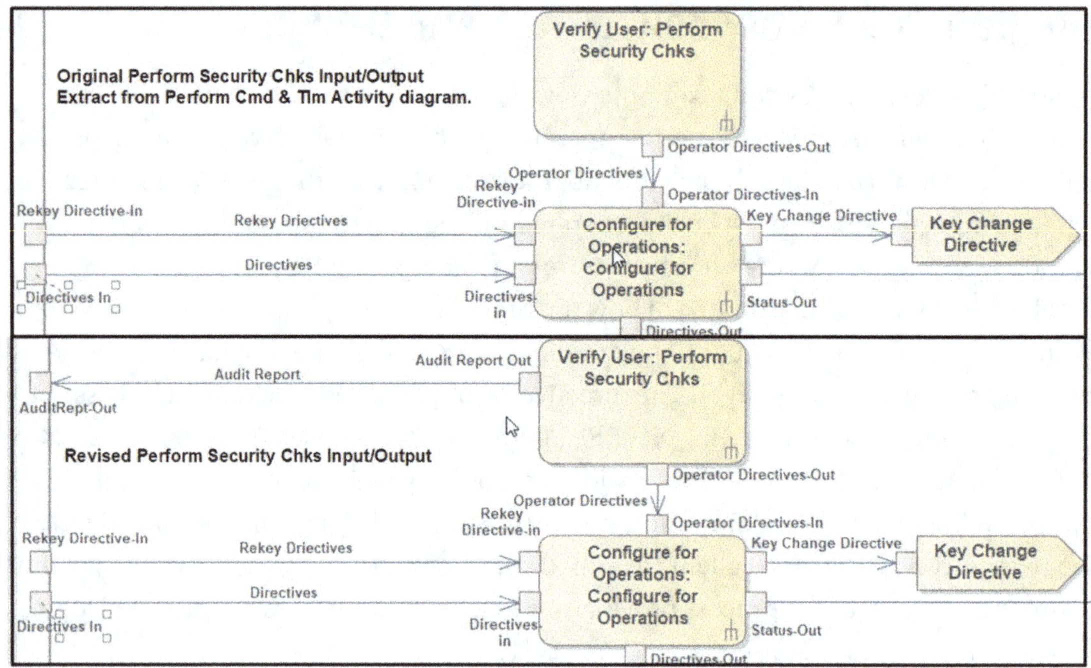

Figure 6-18. *Revision of perform security checks to add audit reporting*[18]

---

[18] Author-created image

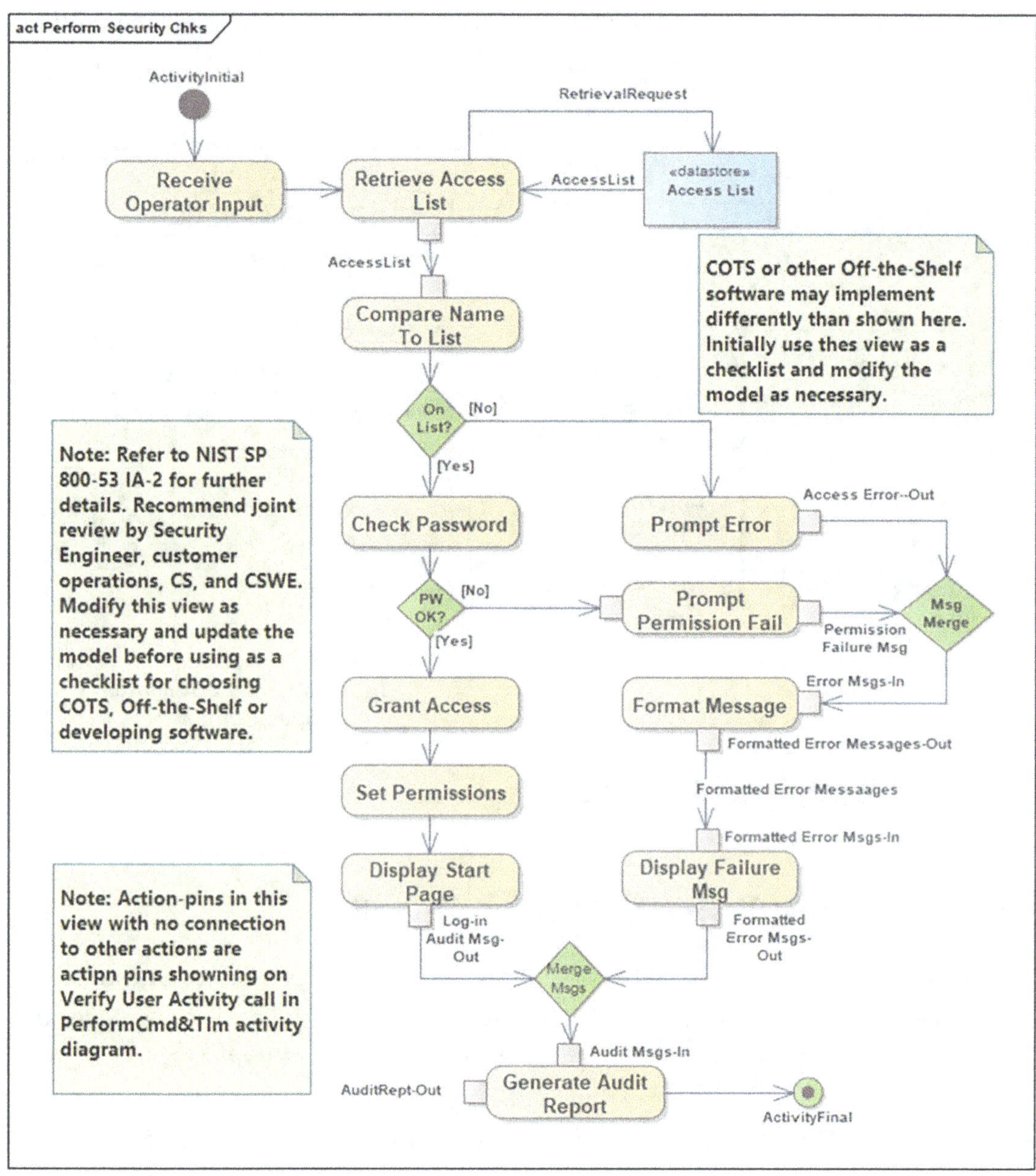

Figure 6-19. *Perform security checks activity diagram*[19]

____

[19] Author-created image

Addressing security updates should be worked into the master schedule and the Agile schedule being used to manage the lower-level design activities, as shown in Figure 6-20.

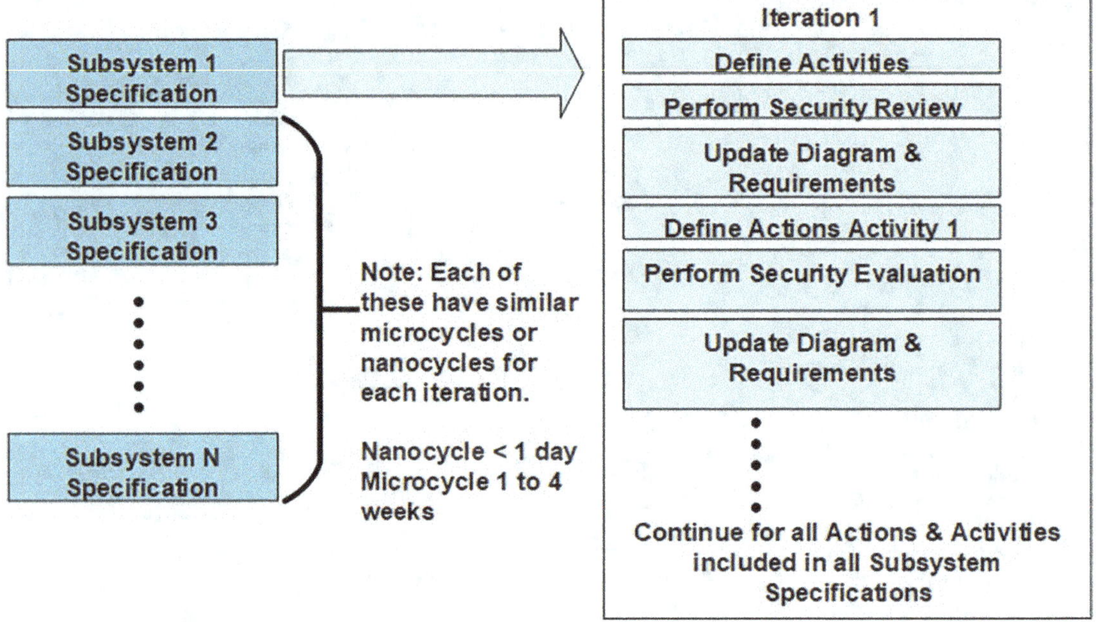

Figure 6-20. *Agile process for addressing security*[20]

Satellite Communications Example

Thus far, we have addressed primarily operations security for the ground. One area of security has unfortunately been viewed as a "drop in" capability. That area is space-to-ground communications. The following discussion addresses the issue at a very high level and does not represent any existing or planned missions. The handling of space-to-ground communications security is dependent on the satellite design approach as well as the overall ground system design. Note that this section is not intended to be a detailed guide to the Consultative Committee for Space Data Systems (CCSDS) or communication security. It is intended as an example of how to deal with system complexity that standards can impose.

---

[20] Author-created image

CCSDS 351.0-M-1) [2] provides a list of security provisions. Specifically, the provisions provide

- Confidentiality—Ensures that only authorized space/ground components can access the data (normally achieved using encryption).

- Authentication—Used to confirm the identity of the sender, i.e., the satellite verifies that the commands and data originated from an authorized ground system, and the ground system verifies that it is communicating with the intended satellite.

- Integrity—Verifies that the data has not been altered during transmission.

- Anti-Replay Protection—Prevents an attacker from replaying a previous transmission to disrupt satellite operations.

- Key Management—Ensures secure generation, distribution, and storage of cryptographic keys used for commanding and telemetry.

- Non-Repudiation—Provides accountability regarding who performed specific operations/activities.

A simplified example of the actions required to provide confidentiality and authentication is shown in Figure 6-21. Note that this is a simplified view and should not be taken as a final design for any satellite system under development. Refer to CCSDS 133.0-B-2 [3] and CCSDS 202.0-B-2 [4] for further information relative to telecommands. Within the graphics, the activities relating to the standards shown above are as follows:

- Confidentiality—Encrypt CCSDS Frame Payload

- Integrity—Generate and Append Message Authentication code

- Anti-Replay Protection—Sequence Number in frame containing the MAC

- Key Management—Performed by Manage Security (refer to Figures 6-7a and 6-7b)

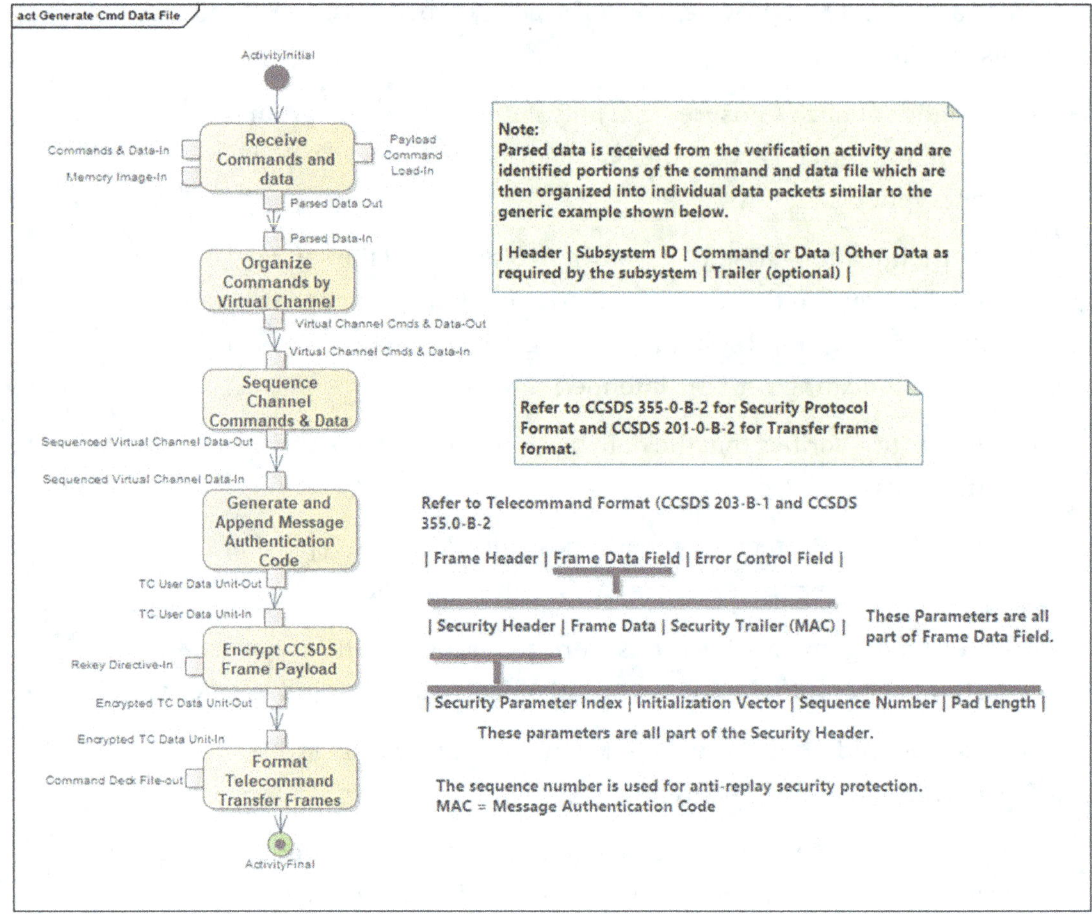

Figure 6-21. *Generate command data file example*

The important point is that the model and specification development should consider the incorporation of security features at all points in the model and system's detailed design. From a practical sense, the engineer should be thinking through the process of what activities are required, what the interfaces between activities should be, and where the security features should be considered at all points in the model and requirements development. From a cost and schedule standpoint, attention to detail at this point will reduce the probability of issues later in the program and especially during final system accreditation and approval for operation.

Schedule Expansion for Activity Details

As discussed in this chapter, the high-level activities defined in the subsystem specification have been further decomposed. From a modeling perspective, this decomposition is achieved by linking high-level activity views to the supporting lower-level activities. These lower-level activities consist of specific actions along with their corresponding requirements and constraints. The resulting detailed requirements can then be incorporated into the subsystem specification, providing a foundation for the definition of component-level requirements. Additionally, these requirements support the development of detailed performance attributes that, collectively, fulfill the subsystem's higher-level performance objectives.

This methodology aligns well with Agile scheduling practices. As illustrated in the schedule extract in Figure 6-22, short-duration tasks are identified, such as those shown in lines 1 and 4. These tasks represent nanocycles within a Sprint cycle, which itself is a segment of the broader project schedule. A critical aspect of this approach is that both modeling and requirements development are structured as short-duration, iterative tasks.

It is essential that both management and development teams understand that the integration of modeling, requirements development, and Agile scheduling enhances project control. This combined approach reduces the risk of overlooked or unnecessary requirements and mitigates the associated schedule delays and overruns later in the project lifecycle.

ID	Task Name	Start	Finish	Duration	Apr 2026					
					30	31	1	2	3	4
1	**Planner Log-In View and Requirements**	3/30/2026	3/31/2026	8h						
2	Planner Input Diagram & Requirments	3/30/2026	3/30/2026	4h						
3	Retrieve Access List Diagram & Requirements	3/30/2026	3/31/2026	4h						
4	**Verify Planner Input Against Retrieved Access List Data**	3/31/2026	4/1/2026	10h						
5	Find Name on Access List Diagram and Requirements	3/31/2026	3/31/2026	4h						
6	Compare Name and Verification Data Against Access List Diagram & Requirements	3/31/2026	4/1/2026	4h						
7	Send Pass/Fail Message Diagram & Requirements	4/1/2026	4/1/2026	2h						

Figure 6-22. *Extract of nanocycle tasks from Agile Log-in sprint cycle*

Chapter Lessons Learned

- SysML was shown to be a better choice of approach for detailed system definition since it is better suited for a drill down in system activities and interfaces than OV-5b or SV-4a.

- Security should be designed in not added on.

- Governing documents such as NIST SP 800-53 should be referenced by activities in the model and cite the specific control reference for each activity/requirement.

- Don't forget to account for security during system initiation—i.e., first use. Don't allow uncleared administrators to do the initial setup and building of the initial access lists.

- NIST SP 800-53 provisions are stated in administrative language for the most part. The development engineer will need to rephrase the requirements in terms of what the system must do to meet the requirements.

- Communications security is handled by other requirements, such as the need to encrypt transmissions (and the type/strength of the encryption algorithm) and provide firewalls, etc.

- Specific attention needs to be paid to the message interchanges necessary for secure communications—i.e., authentication, etc.

- The development schedule needs to ensure time is allotted to security reviews and the development of security features.

References

[1]   NIST SP 800-53 Revision 5, available at `https://doi.org/10.6028/NIST.SP.800-53r5`

[2]   Consultative Committee for Space Data Systems (2012) Security Architecture for Space Data Systems (CCSDS-351.0-M-1 Issue 1), Washington, D.C.: CCSDS Secretariat Space Communications and Navigation Office, 7L70, Space Operations Mission Directorate, NASA (available at `https://ccsds.org`)

[3] Consultative Committee for Space Data Systems (2020) Space Packet Protocol (CCSDS 133.0-B-2 Issue 2), Washington, D.C.: CCSDS Secretariat Space Communications and Navigation Office, 7L70, Space Operations Mission Directorate, NASA (available at `https://ccsds.org`)

[4] Consultative Committee for Space Data Systems (2020) Telecommand Part 2 Data Routing Service (CCSDS 202.0-B-2 Issue 2), Washington, D.C.: CCSDS Secretariat Space Communications and Navigation Office, 7L70, Space Operations Mission Directorate, NASA (available at `https://ccsds.org`)

Acronym List

Acronym	Definition
AU	Audit
CCSDS	Consultative Committee for Space Data Systems
COTS	Commercial off the Shelf
DODAF	Department of Defense Architecture Framework
MAC	Message Authentication Codes
NIST	National Institute of Standards and Technology
OV	Operations View
POAM	Plan of Action and Milestones
SP	Special Publication
SV	System View

CHAPTER 7

Allocation of System Activities

This chapter explores the role of SysML Modeling—particularly block definition diagrams (bdd) and internal block diagrams (ibd)—in defining system structure and allocating activities in support of mission requirements. It discusses the evolution from capabilities and operational activities, as defined in DoDAF views, to the physical and logical decomposition of system elements through Modeling. Emphasis is placed on the disciplined use of Modeling to avoid premature design decisions driven by the adoption of commercial off-the-shelf (COTS) solutions, which can result in incomplete or misaligned requirements. The chapter outlines how the bdd can serve as a foundation for subsystem specification and how linking capabilities, requirements, and activities to system components enhances traceability. Furthermore, it details the transition from operational requirements in a Technical Requirements Document (TRD) to a system specification and demonstrates how SysML views like SV-4 support this process. The chapter underscores the importance of maintaining alignment between modeled requirements and physical system design, particularly as projects advance toward implementation.

Guide for Managers and Engineers

Engineers should evaluate the concepts presented here with particular attention to how the Block Definition Diagram (bdd) and Internal Block Diagram (ibd) relate to system activities. These diagrams are often viewed in isolation, but it's critical to analyze how structural elements (shown in bdd and ibd) support the necessary system behaviors and functions. Overlooking this relationship can lead to incomplete or inconsistent subsystem designs.

© Dennis Hansen 2025
D. Hansen, *Model-Based Systems Engineering and Requirements Definition,*
https://doi.org/10.1007/979-8-8688-2043-4_7

Managers should recognize this analysis as a key step in ensuring that major subsystem components support all required system activities. This process helps validate that both subsystem definitions and any products considered for procurement adequately address operational needs. Investing time in this alignment is crucial as it reduces the risk of missing essential system or subsystem functions.

For example, consider the selection of an antenna system for a polar orbiting satellite. The antenna system consists of several subsystems, such as tracking and control, control center signal routing to the antenna, antenna structure, antenna drive, parabolic dish, and feed subsystem. These can all be blocks in the block definition diagram (bdd) and should contain primary requirements such as "The antenna shall track polar orbiting satellites at an altitude of 833 km."

Examining the components involved, we would create several internal block diagrams (ibd), each with its own requirements and constraints that build from the basic requirement to track a polar satellite at 833 km. For example, the antenna drive subsystem would need requirements to accelerate a mass of XXX in the azimuth and YYY in the elevation directions. This requirement is driven by those associated with the antenna dish and feed subsystems. The mass of the antenna dish and feed subsystem, documented in another ibd, is driven by the signal gain required to perform the mission, which determines the size of the antenna dish required. Finally, the antenna structure requirements are driven by the antenna dish and the required acceleration and velocity.

Ensuring that the subsystems, model bdd, ibd, and parametric diagrams (created in a bdd type diagram) have consistent and mutually supported requirements is essential to ensure that the total antenna subsystem is specified correctly. These specification requirements are then used in the selection of the correct antenna system (if bought as a unit). Using cost as the primary consideration rather than ensuring alignment of these requirements across the system will result in the installation of an antenna system that does not support the mission.

bdd/ibd and Activity Allocation

At first, it may seem strange to consider a bdd or ibd as an allocation of activities. Then again, the bdd provides a means of defining subsystems that support the overall mission (in this case, the ground system that supports the mission). They can typically contain compartments containing: Parts, References, Values, Constraints, Operations (or others as SysML evolves). As mentioned previously, block definition diagrams are not restricted to just the start of the model and can be created during any stage of the model development.

It is crucial to develop the block definition diagram (bdd) and internal block diagram (ibd) views early in the process, continuing from the activity definition phase to the more physical aspects of bdd and ibd. Aligning the modeling views with associated requirements and constraints ensures traceability throughout the system. The relationship between activity requirements and bdd/ibd will reveal design gaps and prevent problems during detailed development.

Remember, this book is dedicated to using modeling to uncover and develop the requirements. We started with the DoDAF concept of "capabilities" and then proceeded to define the activities and functions/actions that serve to provide those capabilities. As a result, we concentrated on what the system needs to do to accomplish the mission using DoDAF. We then proceeded to cover what needs to be done to provide the activities using the DoDAF System View and SysML activity diagrams.

Moving forward, we need to consider the prospective system structure. We should examine where the system activities are performed and determine if there are any lower-level interfaces that need to be addressed. This sequence of actions may seem counterintuitive to many engineers, who have become accustomed to thinking in terms of big block architecture design due to a push to become "integrators" of design reuse and COTS, rather than architects and engineers.

Consider the case of a product designed to control subsystems and networks in a large system. What functionality does the product provide? Based on the structure of the system being developed—that is, activities, bdd, and ibd allocation—will the product directly support the system, or will custom code or scripts be required to modify the product interface to provide the requested functionality? Above all, will product vendor support or labor be required (incurring additional cost and schedule) to make the product work in a defined environment? Failure to use the model to help answer these questions will result in significant problems later in the program and affect cost and schedule.

The availability of COTS and the reuse of previous system designs have served to, in some cases, reduce costs. On the other hand, they have resulted in "lazy engineering." The system developers started to think in terms of the integration of larger components and software. This may seemingly reduce the engineering workload; however, the real result is that there will be a less rigorous definition of the system and the subsystem requirements necessary to support the higher-level system requirements. The term rigorous should be interpreted as incomplete, misleading, misstated, or not applicable (a good idea but lends nothing to the system or mission).

A block definition diagram (bdd) can be used to start hardware and software components definition. Note that the blocks can be structured based on the aggregation of activities. The ground system bdd is shown in Figures 7-1a and 7-1b. Looking at how the view has changed from activities to a physical breakout of the system demonstrates how engineers and management can jump ahead in the process and fall into the trap of trying to reuse or buy COTS for each of the blocks. If we compare the Ground System Management block and the Manage Ground System activity diagram (Figures 7-2a and 7-2b) and in particular the communications paths required for control and status, we start to see that it would be very easy to jump at a COTS product promising extensive functionality and at the same time find that we would potentially miss some functionality and associated requirements if we were to do so. Use the bdd to start identifying subsystem specifications and interface requirements for communications with other subsystems within the system.

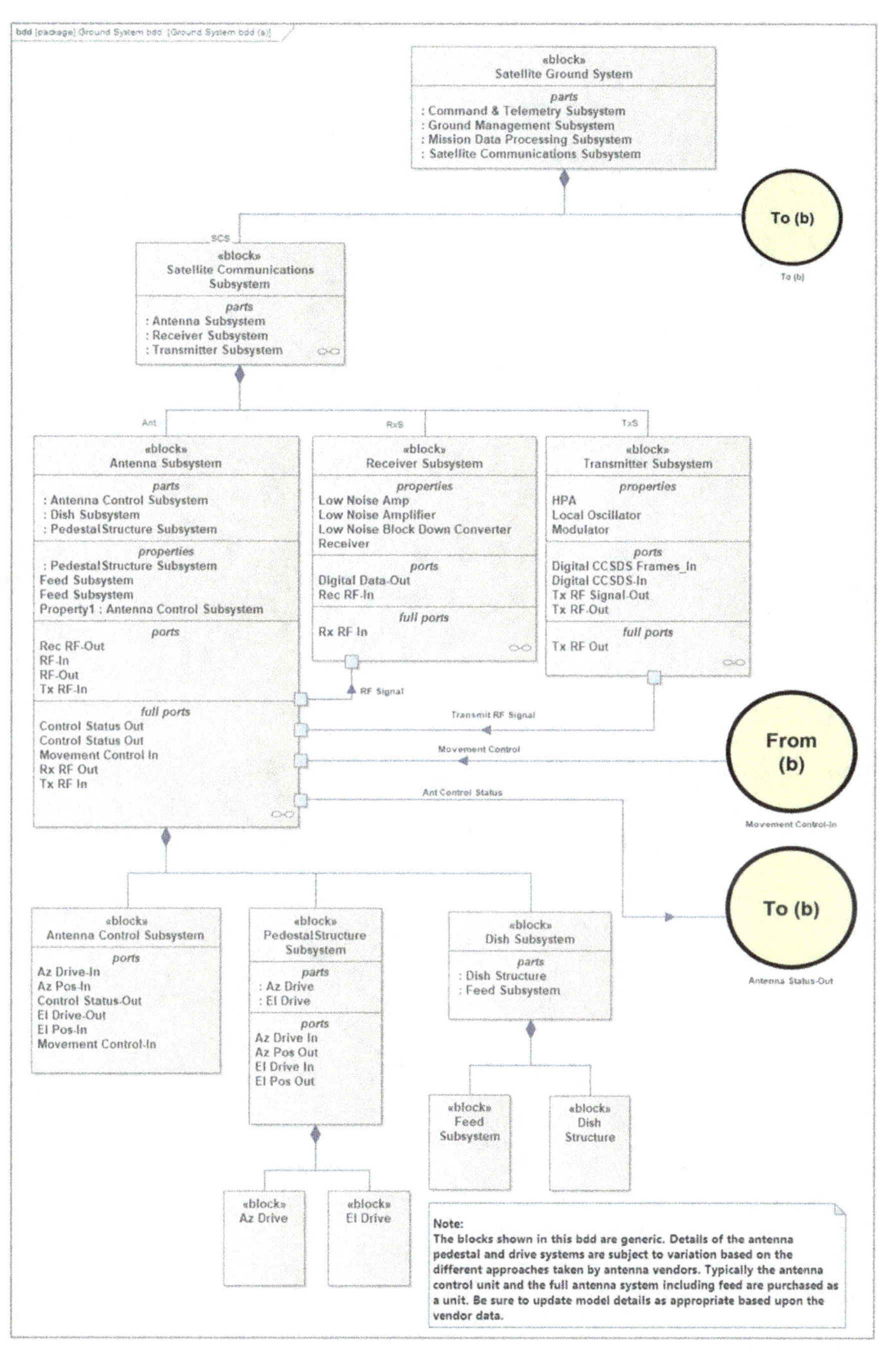

Figure 7-1a. *Satellite ground system bdd*[1]

---

[1] Author-created image

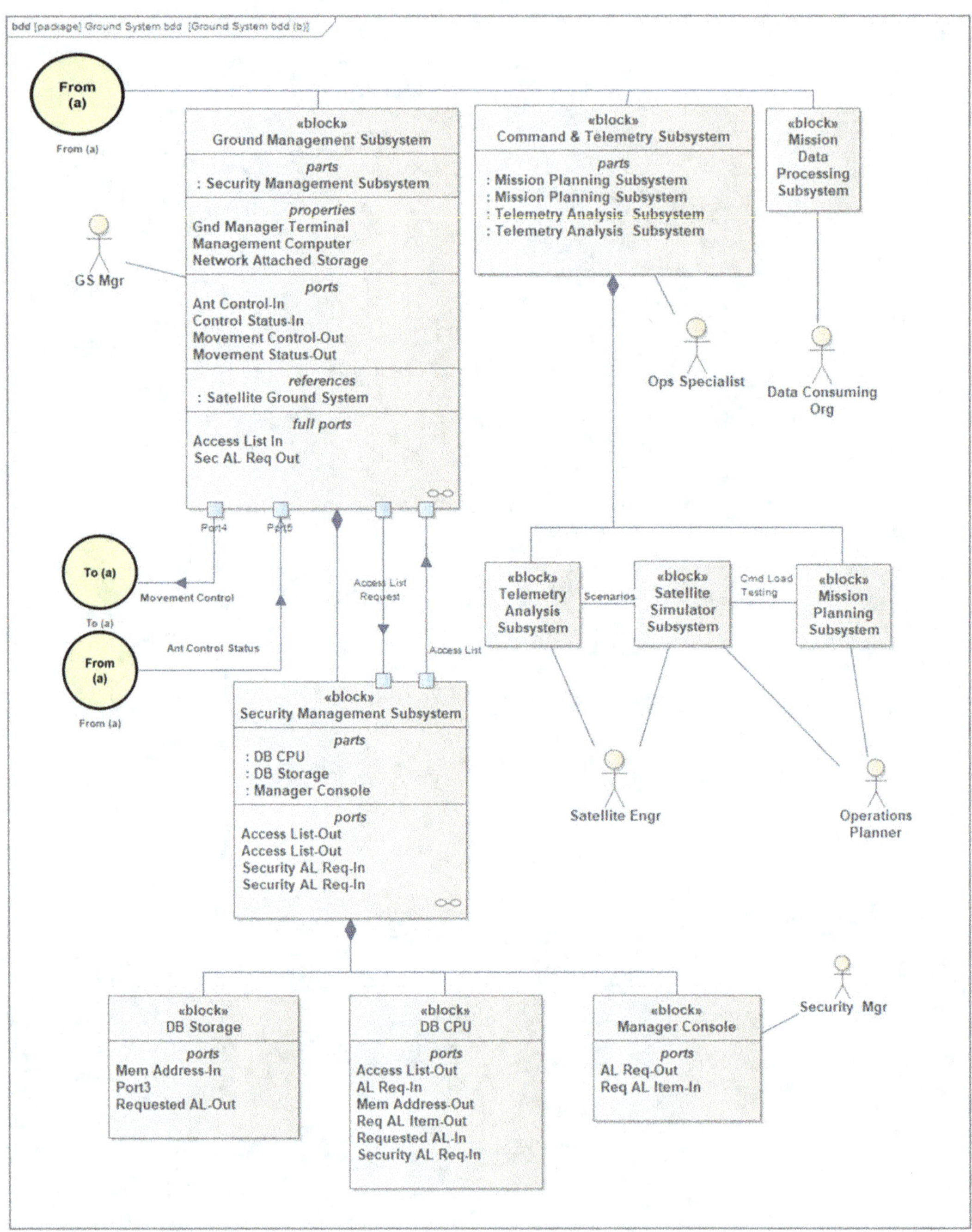

Figure 7-1b. *(continued)*

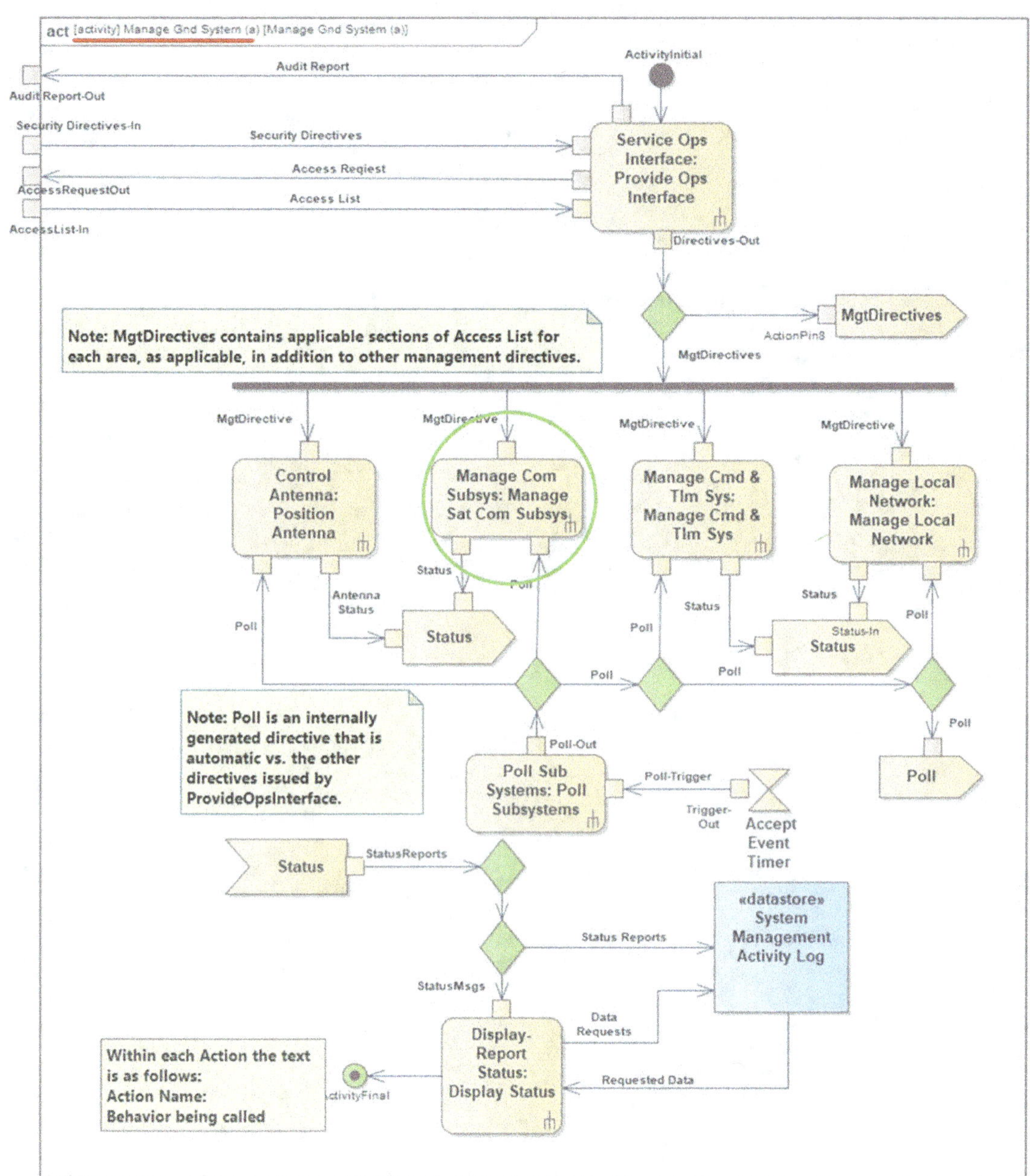

Figure 7-2a. *Ground system management activity diagram*[2]

---

[2] Author-created image

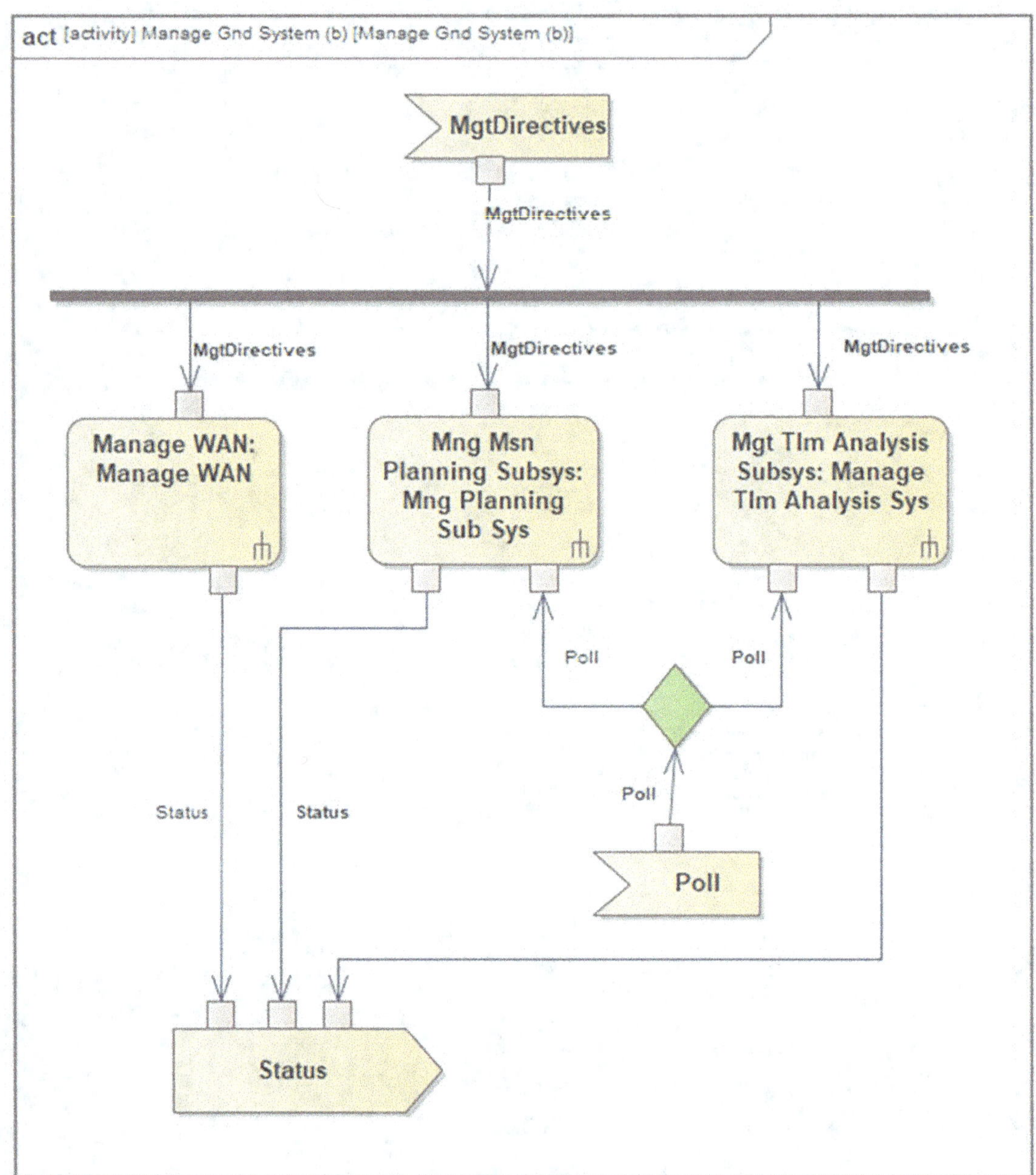

Figure 7-2b. *(continued)*

Note that a connector is used between the Satellite Ground System, Ground Management Subsystem block and the Satellite Communications block in Figures 7-1a and 7-1b. This signifies that the two subsystems are aggregated parts of the Satellite Ground System. If we look further at the call behavior for the Manage Comm Subsystem (circled in Figure 7-2a), we find an activity for Manage Communications Subsystem. If we follow the action call down further to the actions performed by the Manage Communications Subsystem (Figures 7-3a and 7-3b), we start to see the potential for missing functionality. When we consider that each of the actions has one or more requirements or constraints associated with it, it becomes obvious that rushing to a product can result in missing functionality or, in some cases, contain unnecessary functionality that may increase the security attack surface.

Model elements, as shown in the previous figures, do not detail security aspects. Managers and the Chief Systems Engineer should ensure that the system modeling collaborates with the security engineer to incorporate protections at appropriate points. Security directives, a special type of directive issued by the Service Ops Interface at the top of Figure 7-2a, are crucial in this context. For example, in managing the communication subsystem, typical NIST SP 800-53 security controls include AC-3 for access control (i.e., who has privileges for configuration management), AU-2 for audit event logging, and select items from System and Communications Protection (SC) controls. For further guidance on acquiring systems and services that meet requirements for trusted components, refer to NIST SP 800-53 (SA-15).

Within Figure 7-3a note the blue requirement elements that show a trace to individual actions. This is one recognized approach to show detailed traceability of the NIST requirements to the actions. For more complex views a matrix approach is recommended since the view can become too complex for practical purposes.

If the intent is to provide as much capability as possible based upon the capabilities/limitations of prospective COTS or reuse, the independently developed model and associated requirements can be used to identify and document shortcomings. Knowing what is missing or only what is partially implemented will help to document operational procedures, i.e., ensure the procedures match the capabilities. It can also serve as a "wish list" for future modifications.

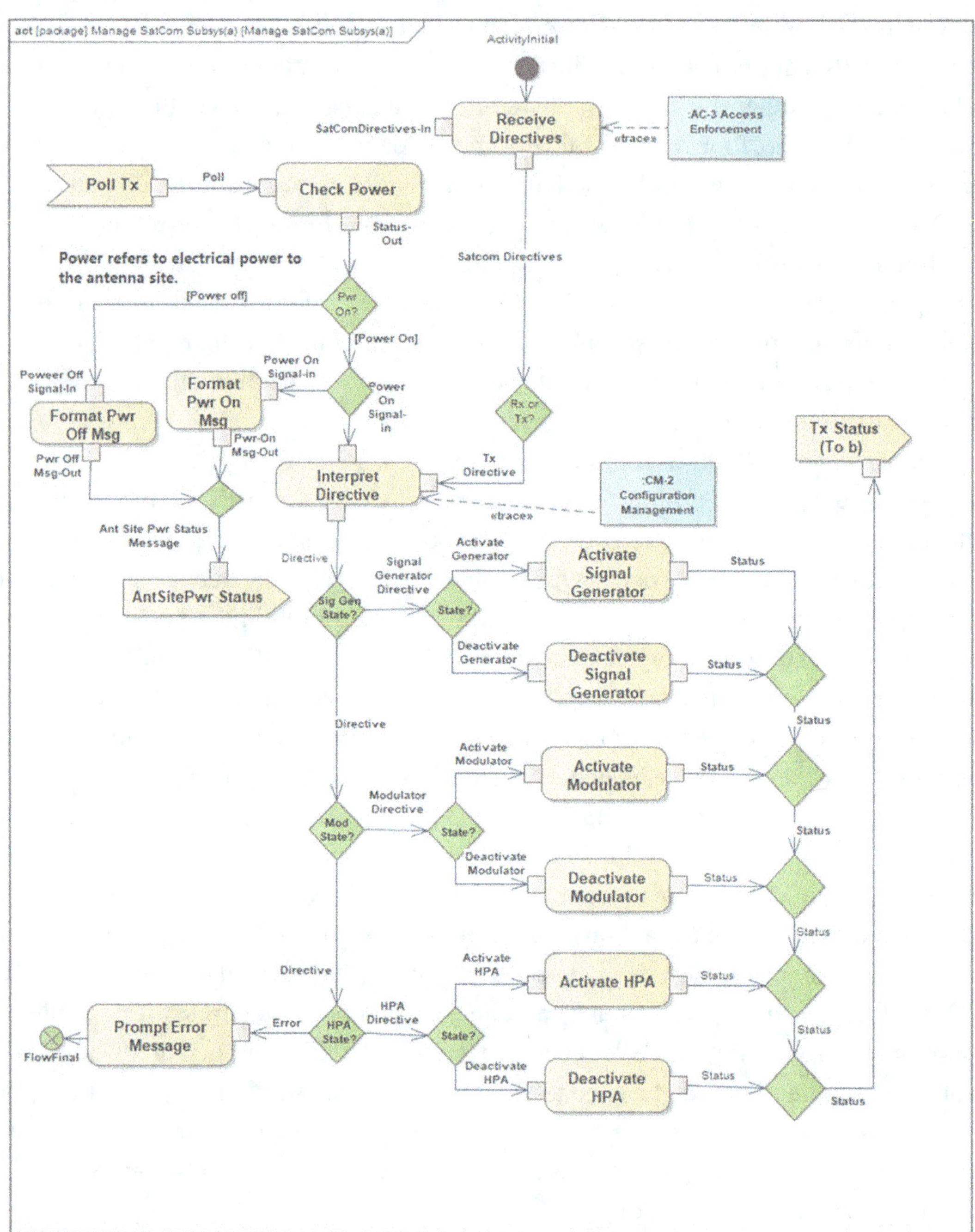

Figure 7-3a. *Manage satellite communications subsystem activity diagram[3]*

[3] Author-created image

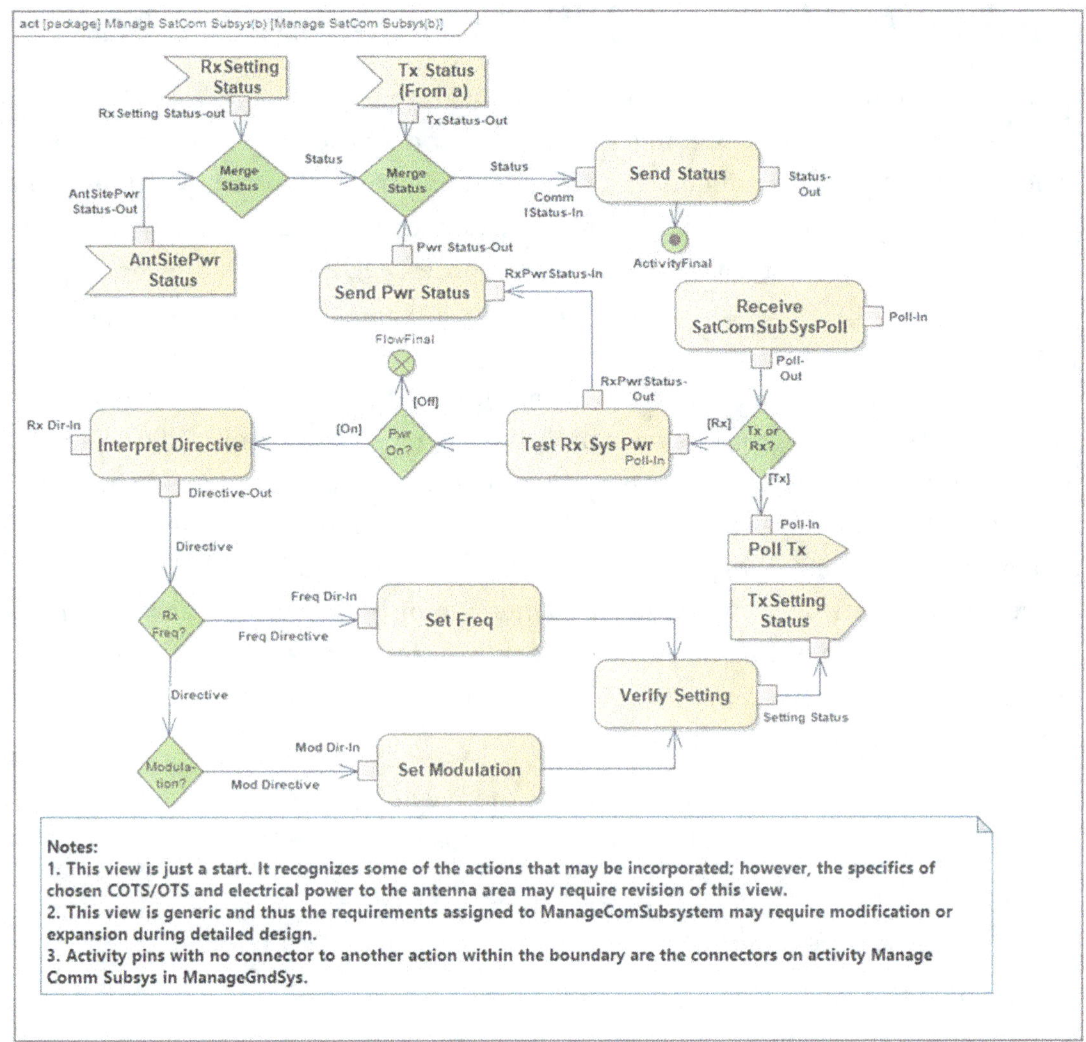

Figure 7-3b. *(continued)*

Capabilities CV-2 and CDD Relationship to a bdd

The previous discussion of capability development and generation of the CV-2 addressed what the system is required to do. It is a good idea to link those capabilities defined for the CV-2 to the Satellite Ground System bdd. The ability to link requirements to multiple model elements may vary depending on the modeling and requirements tools employed. If necessary, use external tools such as DOORS, which provide additional fields within each record. The concept of linking requirements will apply to all the bdd elements.

The defined capabilities relate to the highest level within the bdd hierarchy. In this case, Satellite Ground System, as shown in Figure 7-4, receives the capabilities defined from the CV-2 development. It is a good idea to generate a relationship matrix between the bdd and the capability view. An example is shown in Figure 7-5. Keep in mind that the capabilities are at a very high level and our Ground System bdd contains blocks representing subsystems, including components supporting the subsystems. This may seem to be a useless exercise; however, consider the thought process necessary to assign a relationship between the capabilities and the system operational elements. Common discoveries made during this process involve the following:

1. Discovery of model errors, primarily those where a view has had an item deleted, but the model database did not reflect the deletion.

2. Physical constraints.

3. Potential interactions between blocks are necessary to provide a capability.

The constraints and physical requirements identified through this exercise should be included in the Technical Requirements Document (TRD). Note that the Capability Development Document (CDD) and TRD are typically government documents used to define and justify an acquisition. Commercial organizations are encouraged to create similar documents to provide a foundation for a new system or product.

Additionally, the CDD often contains sections that fall outside the scope of the Model-Based Systems Engineering (MBSE) model. For non-government agencies, the CDD can be streamlined to include only the capabilities and other materials as required by the acquiring organization.

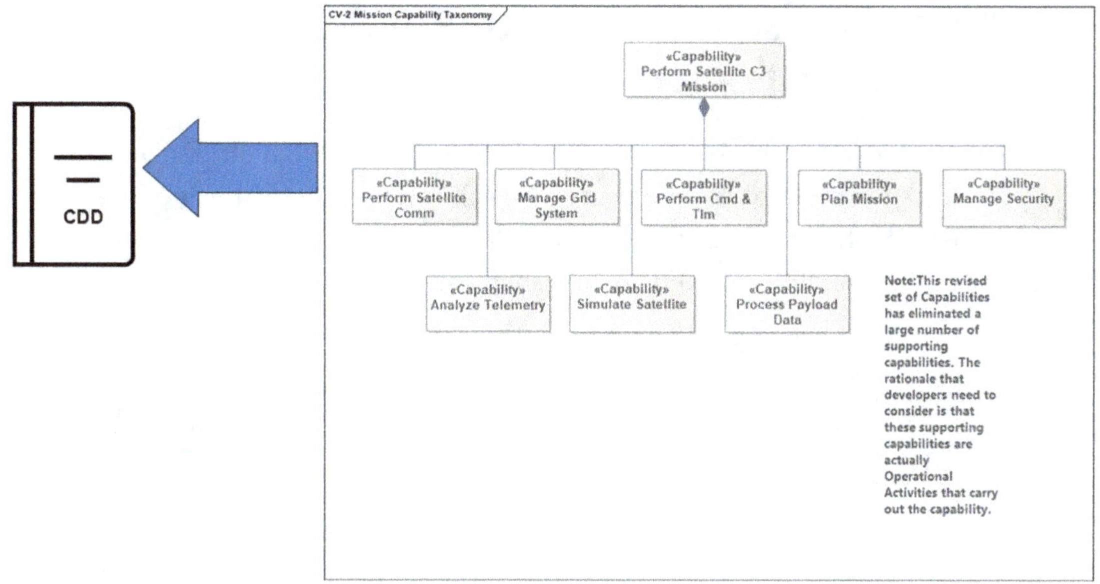

Figure 7-4. Perform mission CV-2 to CDD[4]

Source \ Target	CV-2 Model With Child Capabilities::Analyze Telemetry	CV-2 Model With Child Capabilities::Archive Tlm	CV-2 Model With Child Capabilities::Capability Model	CV-2 Model With Child Capabilities::Display Tlm	CV-2 Model With Child Capabilities::Manage Gnd System	CV-2 Model With Child Capabilities::Manage Security	CV-2 Model With Child Capabilities::Perform Cmd &	CV-2 Model With Child Capabilities::Perform Satellit	CV-2 Model With Child Capabilities::Perform Satellit	CV-2 Model With Child Capabilities::Plan Mission	CV-2 Model With Child Capabilities::Receive Telemetry	CV-2 Model With Child Capabilities::Rx TLM & Data	CV-2 Model With Child Capabilities::Send Cmd Deck	CV-2 Model With Child Capabilities::Send Payload D	CV-2 Model With Child Capabilities::Simulate Satellite	CV-2 Model With Child Capabilities::Stage Command	CV-2 Model With Child Capabilities::Transmit Cmds
Ground System (bdd)::Antenna Control Subsystem									↑								
Ground System (bdd)::Antenna Subsystem									↑								
Ground System (bdd)::Az Drive									↑								
Ground System (bdd)::AzDrive									↑								
Ground System (bdd)::Command & Telemetry Subsystem							↑										
Ground System (bdd)::DB CPU						↑											
Ground System (bdd)::DB Storage						↑											
Ground System (bdd)::Dish Structure									↑								

Figure 7-5. Example bdd to CV-2 relationship matrix[5]

---

[4] Author-created image

[5] Author-created image

Activities and Technical Requirements Document (TRD)

The TRD is developed to express the end user's perspective on what the system needs to do, while the specifications concentrate on how the system should be developed. This relationship is shown in Figure 7-6. All the Operational requirements developed to support the CDD capabilities should be published within the TRD.

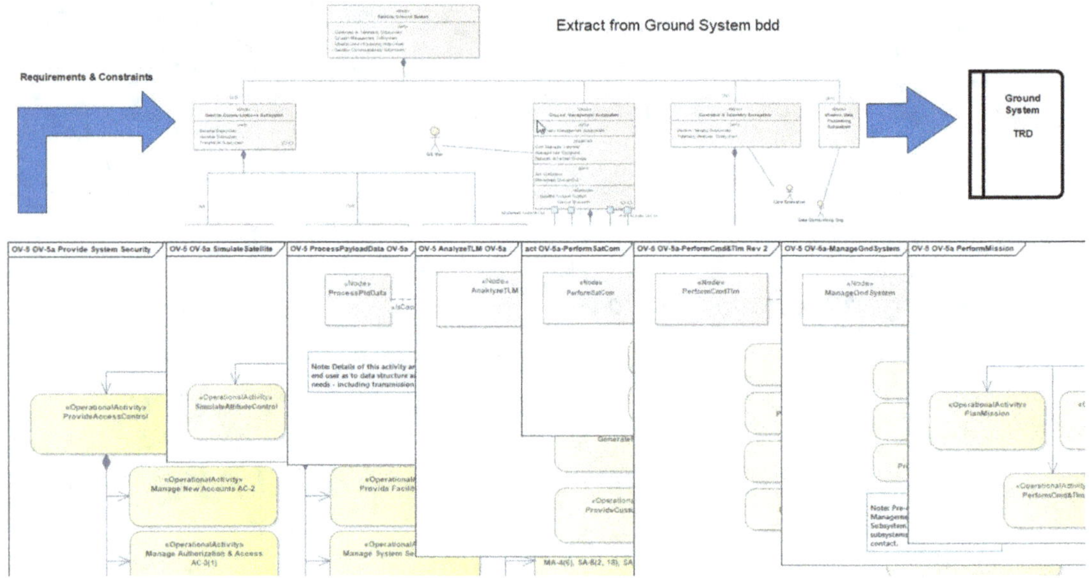

Figure 7-6. *Operations view to bdd and TRD*[6]

System Functionality and the System Specification

The transition from a TRD to the System Specification is often (but shouldn't be) an exercise in restating TRD requirements and potentially adding a few "extra" requirements. Developing the system specification in this manner results in issues downstream especially during the system test phase of the program. As with developing the TRD, the functionality and activity requirements gathered during the Modeling effort should be the basis for the System Specification, as shown in Figure 7-7. Keep in mind

---

[6] Author-created image

the specification of actual components and technologies is re-served for the Subsystem Specifications. Refer to DI-IPSC-81431A [10] for example content for government system/subsystem specifications. As stated earlier, a transition to SysML may occur at the point where the System Functional Views (SV-4) are being developed.

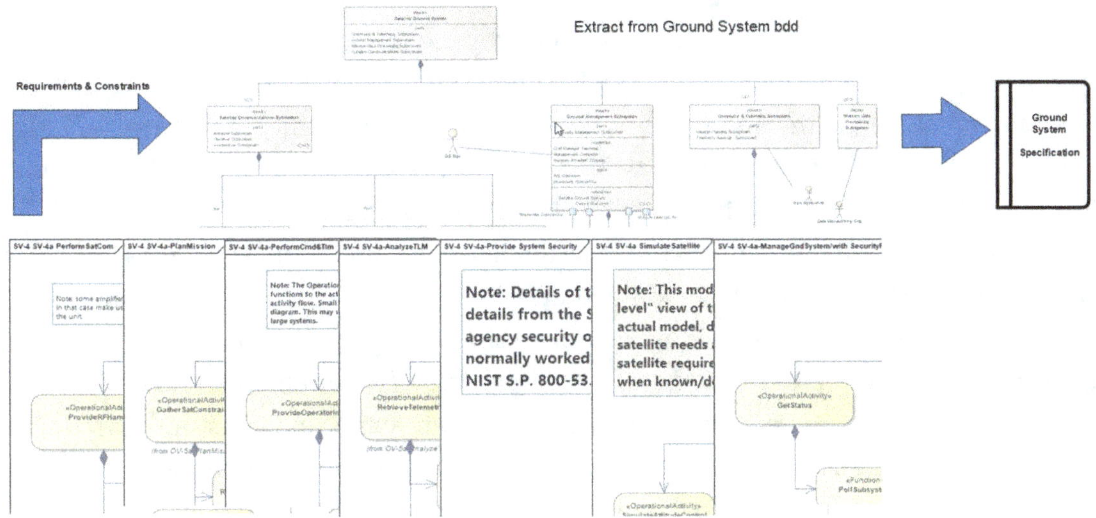

Figure 7-7. *System functionality to system specification*[7]

SV-4 and SysML to System and Subsystem Specification

We have just shown the relation between the SV-4 views and the System Specification. As stated earlier, this is the point at which considerations for a switch to SysML can be evaluated. If the switch is made, a seamless transition between architecture and system design can be achieved. An example of this transition is shown in Figures 7-8a and 7-8b. Notice how we still have not moved toward architectural approach implementation technologies (i.e., Cloud, Service Oriented Architecture (SOA), etc.)

---

[7] Author-created image

In Chapter 6, section "SysML Manage Security Example", we covered a breakout of the ground system management and associated security as an example of how the higher level functionality reflected by the activities can be linked to the implementation of required actions. These activities and implementing actions form the basis for the high-level operational system requirements.

Looking at the high-level activities and the bdd and ibd views we see how the operational activities can start to be allocated to subsystems and supporting components. Note that the bdd may evolve based on the availability of supporting components that meet the operational needs. The breakout of the Ground Management Subsystem is shown as an ibd in Figure 7-9. Notice how we have shifted to a more physical view of the system/subsystem. The details of the operational activities and their supporting actions should not be modified unless it proves that existing technology is unable to meet the needs previously documented. It is important to keep in mind that that some modifications to the bdd and ibd in the form of requirements, constraints and performance parameters may be made. The requirements and constraints section of the block should be updated, and the rationale should be added to the Notes section as pointed to in Figure 7-10. Note that this example is from SPARX EA; however, other modeling tools provide a similar capability.

When progressing to the ibd the relation of lower-level activity views should be considered. These lower levels of activity should be mapped to the applicable ibd element and the associated subsystem specification. By doing this work in the Modeling tool and using linkages within the tool it ensures that there is a flow and relationship between the highest level system elements and the lowest level subsystem.

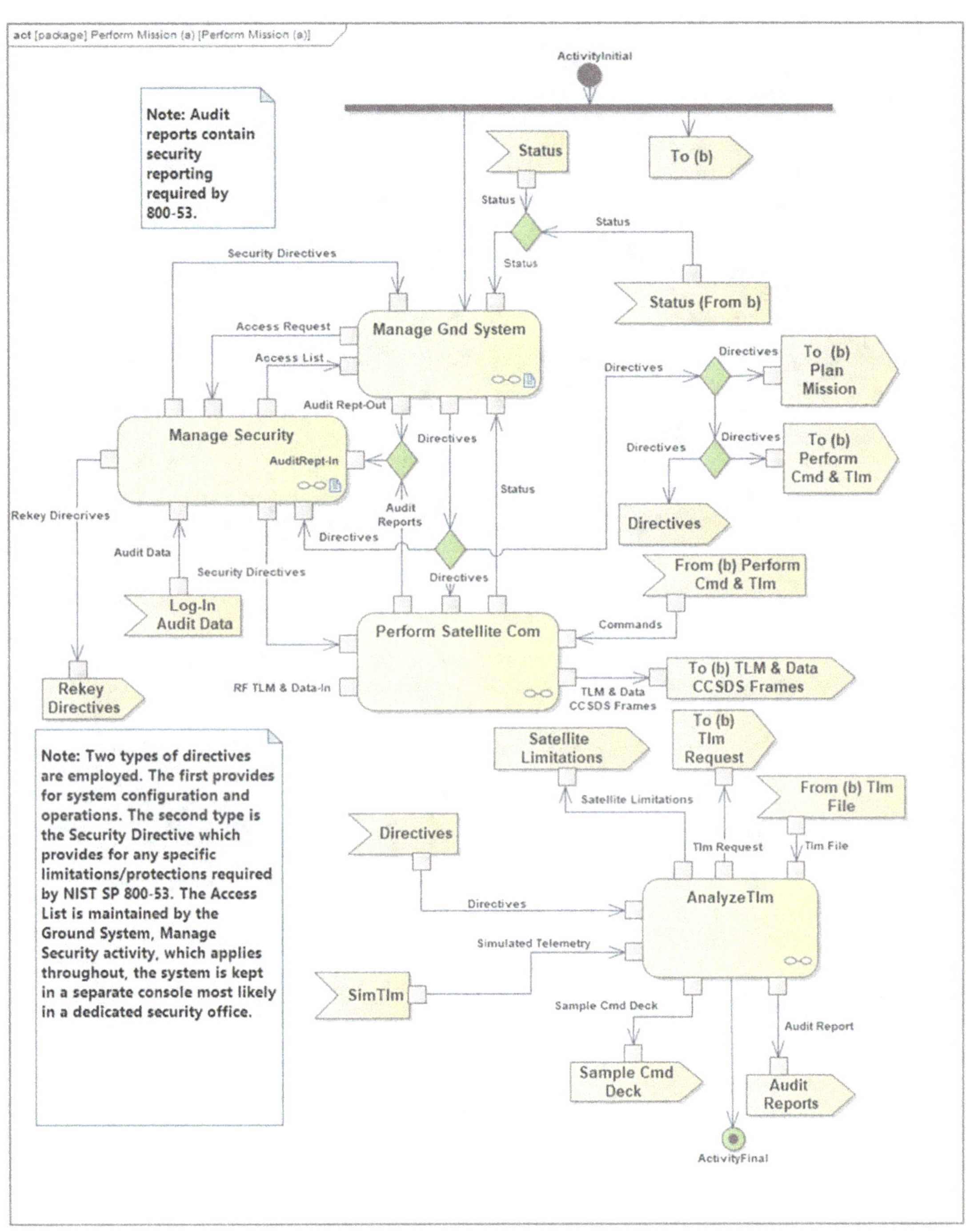

Figure 7-8a. *SysML perform mission activity diagram*[8]

---

[8] Author-created image

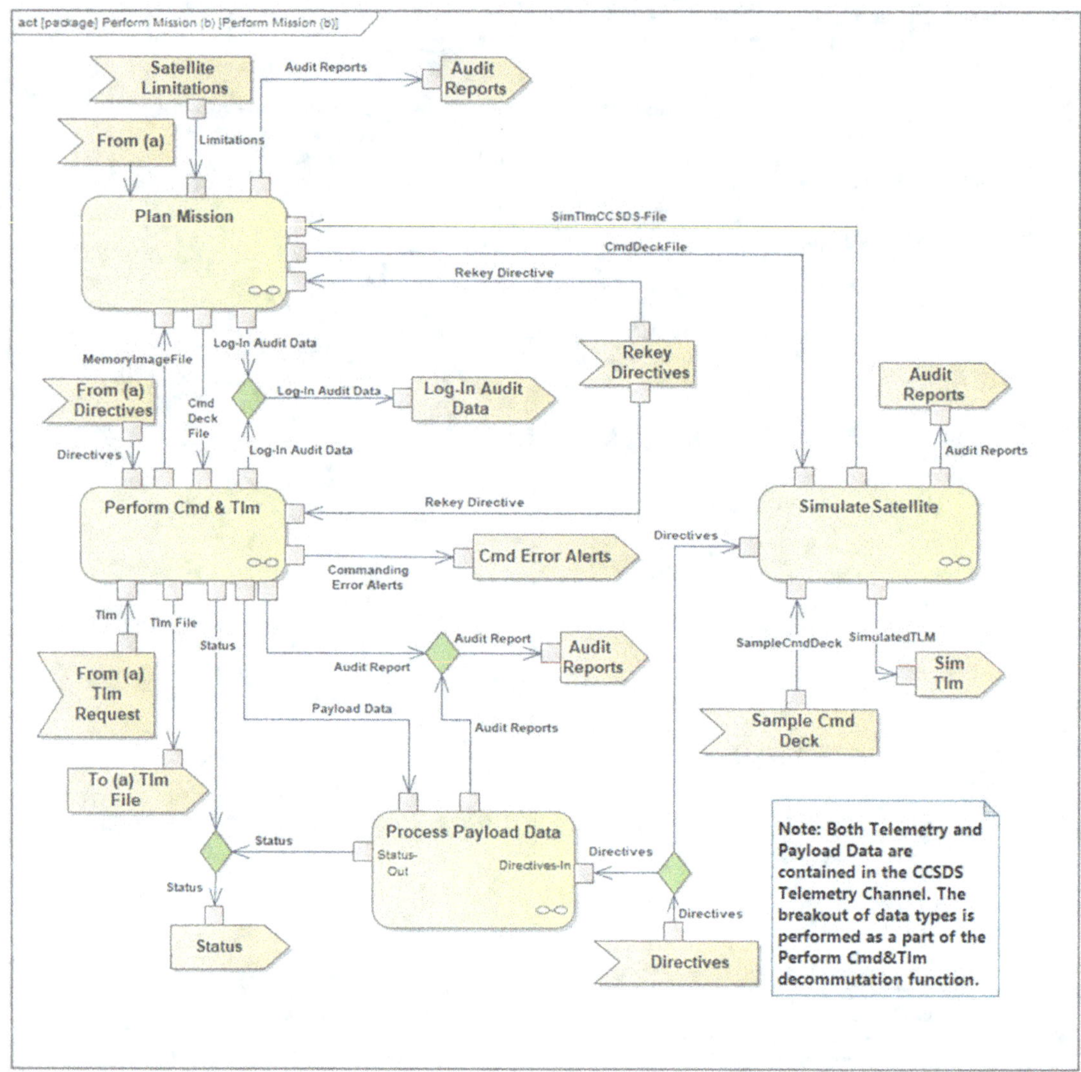

Figure 7-8b. *(continued)*

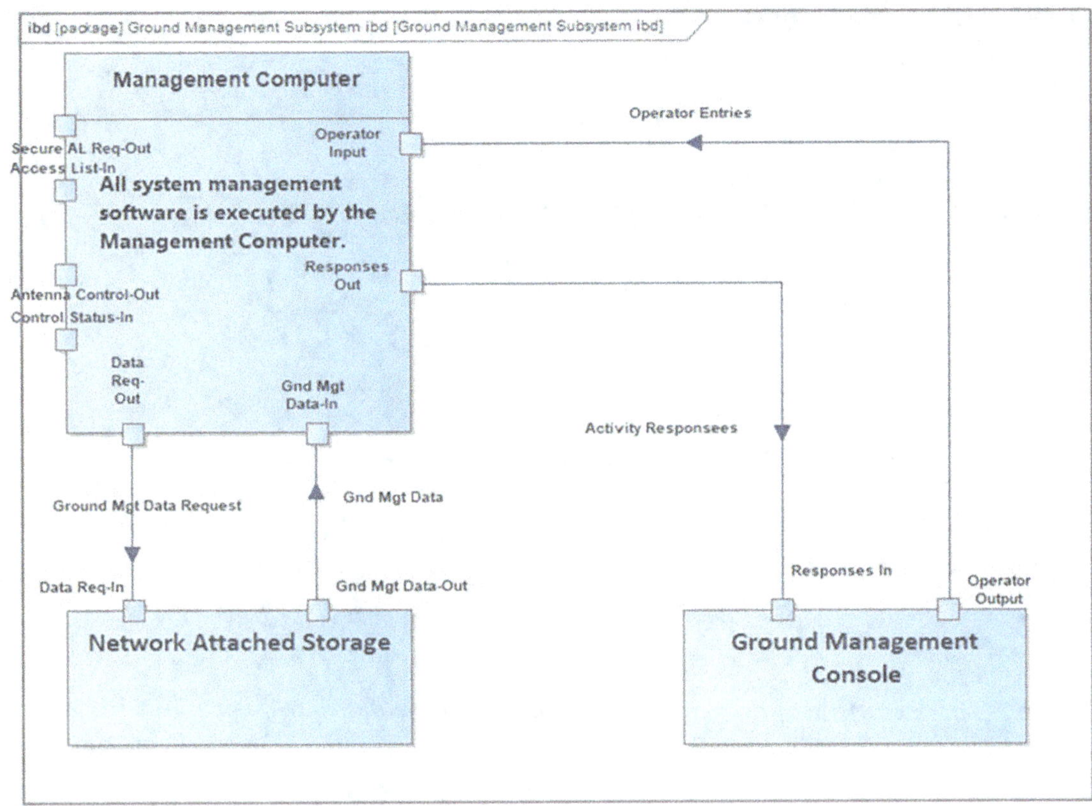

Figure 7-9. Ground management subsystem ibd[9]

---

[9] Author-created image

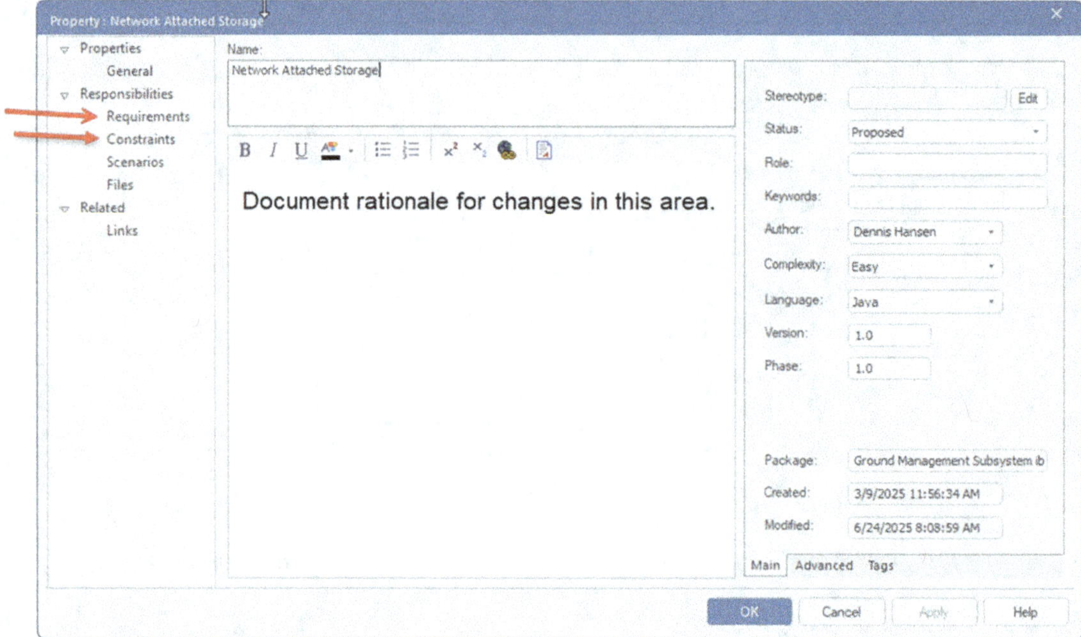

Figure 7-10. *Example of documenting updates in modeling tool*

Chapter Lessons Learned

- Many programs start SysML with a bdd. They are thinking about how to build the system and the large pieces of the system, rather than what activities/functions the system and subsystems need to perform.

- Start the process with the activities and functions before you move on to structure.

- Use the bdd to trace the activities and requirements down to physical subsystems.

- An ibd can be used to begin the definition of the lower-level physical implementation of the subsystems.

- The capabilities (documented in the CV-2) can aid in the allocation of system/subsystem requirements to a bdd. When the capabilities were originally developed, the people developing the CV-2 and / or Capabilities Description Document could not avoid thinking of where the capabilities applied within the physical system. Take advantage of this quirk in the initial definition of the system.

- Remember how the model views and associated requirements map to the TRD/initial systems specification.

- Remember how the SV-4a and SysML views and associated requirements map to the System Specification.

- Model the ibd, lower-level activities, and associated requirements in the Modeling tool to ensure that there is a flow and consistency from the highest system level to the lowest level subsystem.

- When the process is followed, alignment of requirements and models from the TRD to the final specifications is assured.

References

[1]   NIST SP 800-53 (SA-15) Revision 5 available at
      `https://doi.org/10.6028/NIST.SP.800-53r5`

[2]   DI-IPSC-81431A US Department of Defense available at
      `https://assist.dla.mil`

Acronym List

Acronym	Definition
bdd	Block Definition Diagram
CDD	Capability Development Document
COTS	Commercial off the Shelf
CV	Capability View

(continued)

Acronym	Definition
DODAF	Department of Defense Architecture Framework
ibd	Internal Block Diagram
IPSC	Information Processing Standards and Criteria
MBSE	Model-Based Systems Engineering
NIST	National Institute of Standards and Technology
OV	Operations View
POAM	Plan of Action and Milestones
SA	System and Services Acquisition
SOA	Service-Oriented Architecture
SP	Special Publication
SV	System View
SysML	Systems Modeling Language

CHAPTER 8

Modeling and Performance Requirements Specification

Performance specification is often a source of challenges during system development. While high-level performance requirements are relatively straightforward to define, for instance, a mission may require that an observation made by a satellite be reported to an operations specialist within five seconds, difficulties arise in translating such requirements into specific performance expectations for all related activities and system elements.

This chapter explores the use of parametric modeling and analysis tools to refine and allocate performance requirements across all system components and activities. It also addresses nonfunctional requirements, particularly as they relate to specification within block definition diagrams. The process demonstrates how the requirements defined during modeling can be directly applied to the system specification.

Additionally, the chapter emphasizes the importance of integrating system test planning early in the development process. Engaging test engineers from the outset—rather than waiting until design completion—helps ensure that performance requirements are verifiable. Finally, the chapter discusses system implementation in the context of selecting appropriate technologies and products to meet defined requirements. In total, the chapter emphasizes that early integration of parametric modeling with test planning ensures performance requirements are realistic, traceable, and verifiable across system components.

195

© Dennis Hansen 2025
D. Hansen, *Model-Based Systems Engineering and Requirements Definition*,
https://doi.org/10.1007/979-8-8688-2043-4_8

Guide for Managers and Engineers

This chapter provides managers with a concise overview of the work required to effectively document system performance. Understanding this scope is critical for defining task schedules and estimating durations. For both engineers and managers, the chapter demonstrates how parametric modeling supports the documentation of results from detailed analyses using tools like MATLAB. The model offers a visual representation of system element activities, serving as a framework for analysis. Conversely, insights gained from the analysis may inform updates to the model and its associated requirements.

Incorporation of Performance

Now that the activities have been developed, we can start looking at performance details. Note that at the start of the project, some high-level analysis and specifications may be developed. For systems, such as a fighter jet, performance in terms of top speed, rate of climb, etc., can be determined based upon performance analysis of an adversary aircraft. For a satellite ground system, the performance of the parabolic dish antenna pointing may be determined by analysis of the satellite orbits. Parameters such as antenna rotational and elevation acceleration required can be determined based on satellite altitude and the orbital velocity and inclination required to maintain the required orbit.

In both cases, it is necessary to perform the analysis required to determine these high-level performance requirements in advance of the detailed development of activity diagrams and other DoDAF and SysML products. The performance of subsystems will combine to provide the required system performance.

A key element of the system's performance is the time required for each interaction between activities and actions. Too often, most of the attention is paid to the performance of individual actions while passing over the timing required. Sequence Diagrams should be developed to detail the sequencing of messages between actions. From there, the timing relative to the interactions (i.e., sequence, message transmission time, etc.) should be determined. A performance requirement should be developed for each message exchange.

From a ground system perspective, the command and telemetry functionality and supporting activities present a good example for performance breakdown. Let's look at the sequence diagram for command and telemetry in Figures 8-1a and 8-1b.

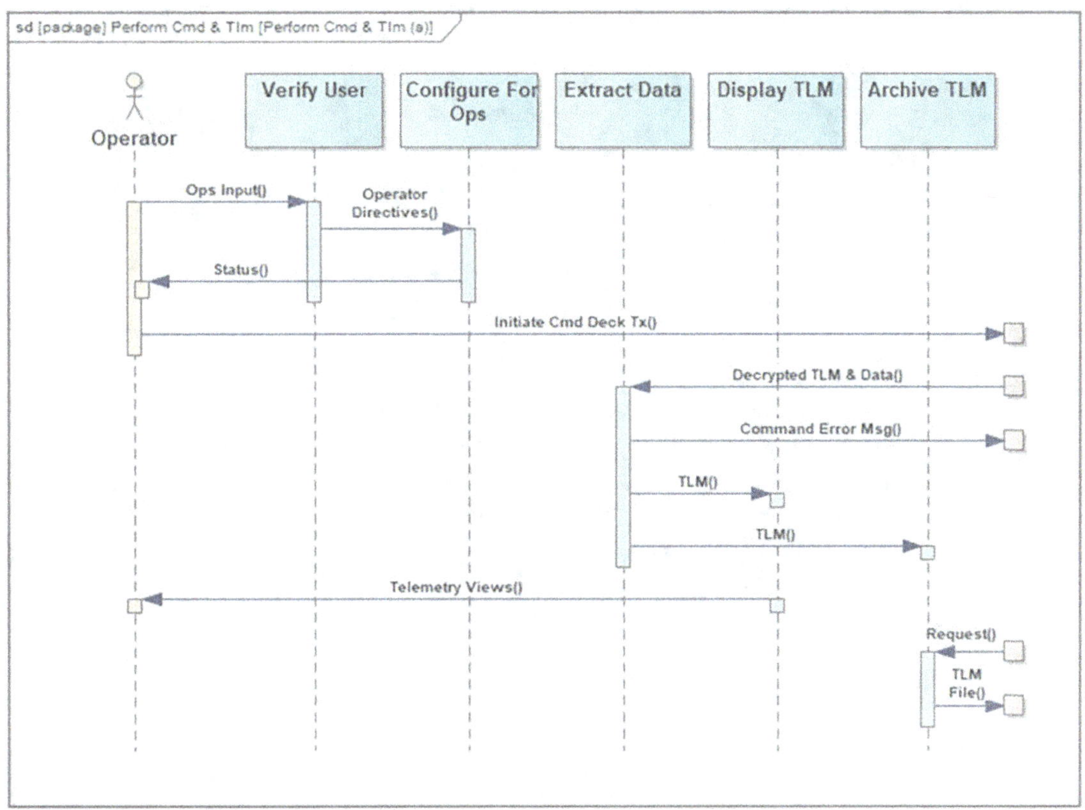

Figure 8-1a. *Command and telemetry sequence diagram*[1]

---

[1] Author-created image

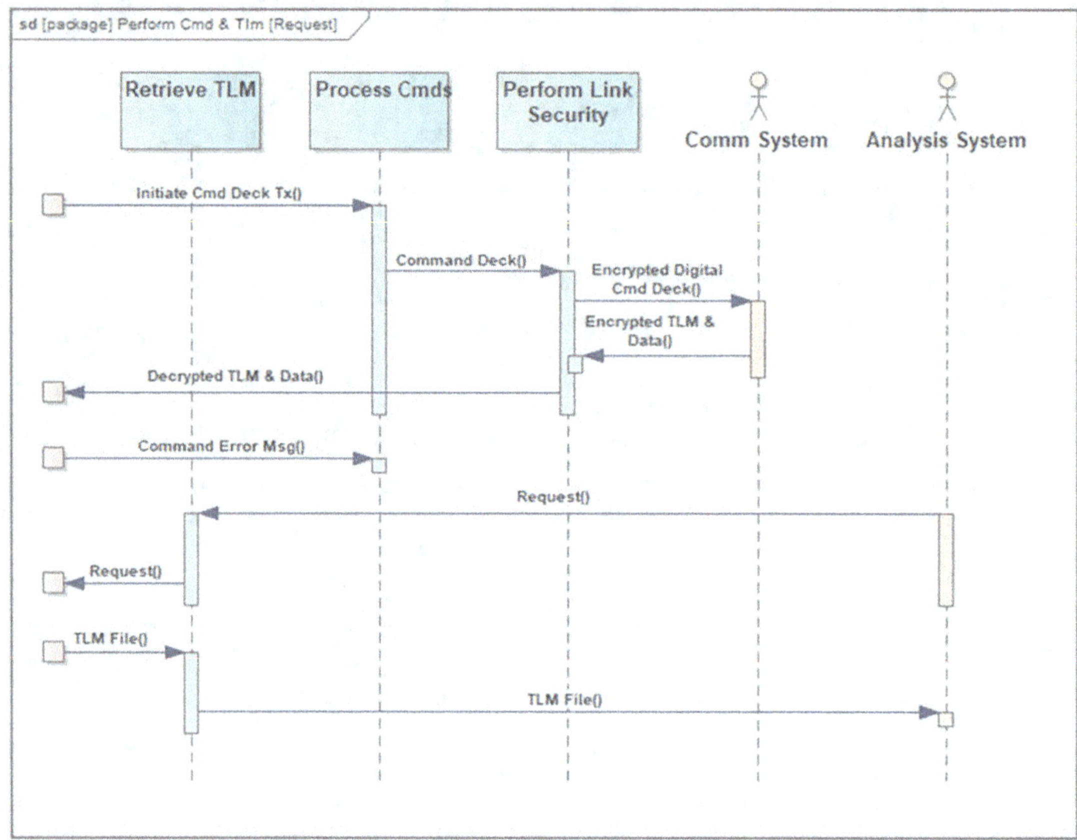

Figure 8-1b. *(continued)*

On the surface, it appears that all we have are interactions that do not possess a need to express performance. Note that we need to consider performance in terms of specific interaction flows that, in this case, deal with one of the real-time aspects of the system's operation. We need to start with satellite and ground communications. In many cases the data rates may be predetermined. If not, we need to determine what data rates are required. To do this we should look at the entire flow of telemetry and data from the satellite and consider operational factors. For the ground system example, consider the following factors:

Orbit and contact duration

- Geostationary—potentially always in view of a ground station.

    - If the satellite is geostationary, determine if the ground station is dedicated to that one satellite or shared amongst several satellites.

- Potential impact to time available to downlink data and telemetry.

- Low Earth Orbit—limited contact time based upon time in view.

  - If the orbit is sun synchronous, there will be a limited number of orbital contacts available. The contact time available will vary since all orbits will not go directly overhead. As a rule, data downlink and commanding are limited to when antenna elevation is 10 degrees or greater. Actual available time may be limited to as little as two minutes.

Data quantity

- Geostationary—potentially always in view of a ground station.

  - If the satellite is geostationary, determine if the ground station is dedicated to that one satellite or shared amongst several satellites.

  - Potential impact to time available to downlink data and telemetry.

- Low Earth Orbit—limited contact time based upon time in view.

  - If the orbit is sun synchronous, there will be a limited number of orbital contacts available. The contact time available will vary since all orbits will not go directly overhead. As a rule, data downlink and commanding are limited to when antenna elevation is 10 degrees or greater. Actual available time may be limited to as little as two minutes.

Aggregate Performance

- The aggregate performance (data rate) of the uplink and downlink is a function of the quantity of data relative to the contact time available.

This is one instance of a set of interactions that require specification of performance. Note that there may be constraints that need to be addressed as well. These may involve technological limits or, in this case, potential regulatory limitations covering power limitations and frequency use, which both affect the data rate limits. Regardless of the system type, in this case, the satellite ground system, a set of performance factors will be required. For example, a bridge can be considered a "system." The performance factors would involve items such as the strength of materials (materials used in the beams), required wind loading, maximum span between supports, vibration damping parameters, etc.

Parametric Model

Before we start, it is important to distinguish the parametric model from the bdd. Essentially, the parametric model is a model of performance requirements and the mathematics associated with system/subsystem operation. In many cases, a model can represent a single interchange. In combination, the results of several of these parametric models are combined to calculate an overall system level performance attribute. For our example, we will look at determining the downlink data rate that will be supported. The parametric modeling should start with a constraint block diagram to document items such as measurable limits on the operation, as shown in Figure 8-2. Note that a bdd is used for the constraint block diagram.

Using the example of calculating the required link budget, notice that the bdd block shown in Figure 8-2 shows a simplified view of the calculations required for determining the receive rate. The parametrics view in Figure 8-3 shows how the problem is solved. The results of the calculation expressed in the parametrics view are translated into a requirement for the Receive Tlm action as shown in Figure 8-4. Overall, the use of the model activity, bdd, and parametric diagram will document the approach taken to calculate the required link budget, thus providing traceability for the link budget calculations. This will be of great use in the future if a new satellite is to be added to the constellation.

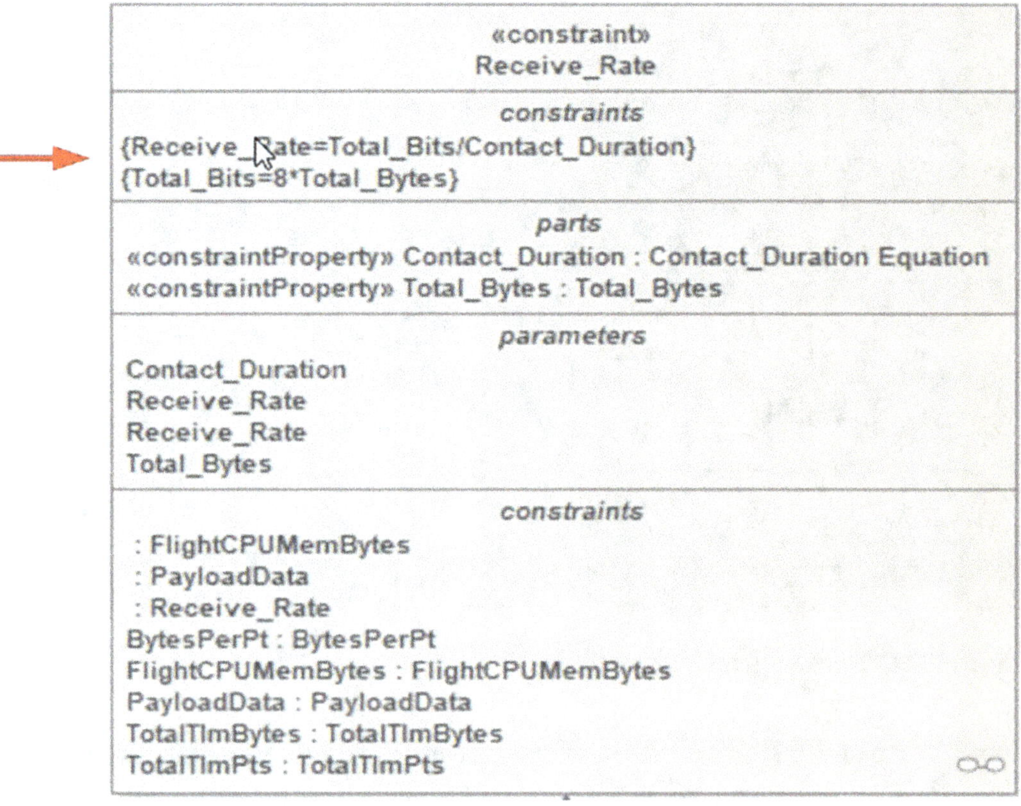

Figure 8-2. Constraint block diagram[2]

____

[2] Author-created image

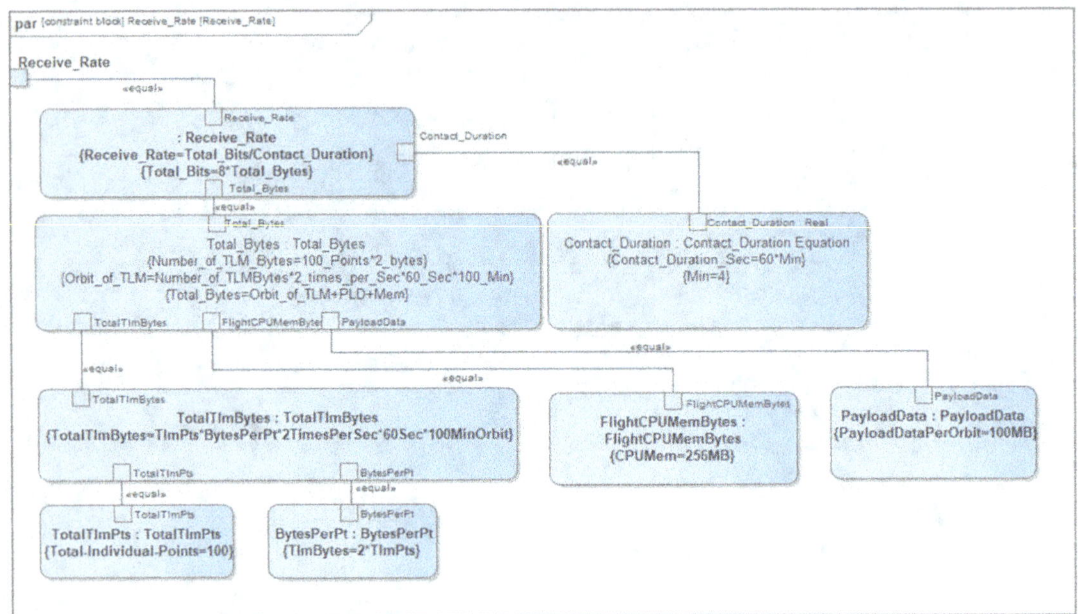

Figure 8-3. *Parametrics diagram*[3]

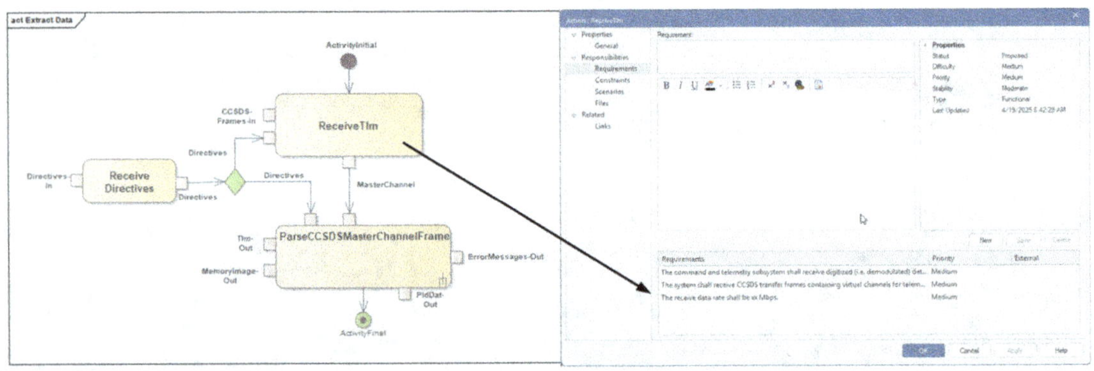

Figure 8-4. *Performance requirement added to SysML activity*[4]

---

[3] Author-created image

[4] Author-created image

This process should be performed for all activities and interfaces that have a direct effect on subsystem and system performance. In some cases, an external tool such as MATLAB might be used to perform the analysis reflected in the constraint(s). In this case, annotations can be made in the diagrams as shown in Figure 8-5. Some modeling tools such as SPARX EA provide add-ons that provide direct interface with tools such as MATLAB. Refer to the documentation for the modeling tool in use within your organization to see if support is provided for tools such as MATLAB.

Using modeling tools provides a means to maintain linkages between views and parametric diagrams. Furthermore, results from tools such as MATLAB can be incorporated into the model's parametric constraint views, creating a single repository for all data. This approach ensures consistency across the system design and establishes a connection to performance validation in the test procedures developed alongside the model.

The use of external tools such as MATLAB provides a means of doing complex mathematical calculations to be included in the parameter constraints. As highlighted above this is valuable for maintaining a consistent view of the system. Caution must be taken to ensure that updates in one tool, such as MATLAB, are reflected in the modeling tool. This can present a challenge during a project that is being developed on a tight schedule since there is a tendency to setaside these synchonization activities in a "to do" list that may not be completed before the project moves to the next stage. The key is team discipline and collaboration to ensure synchronization between the tools.

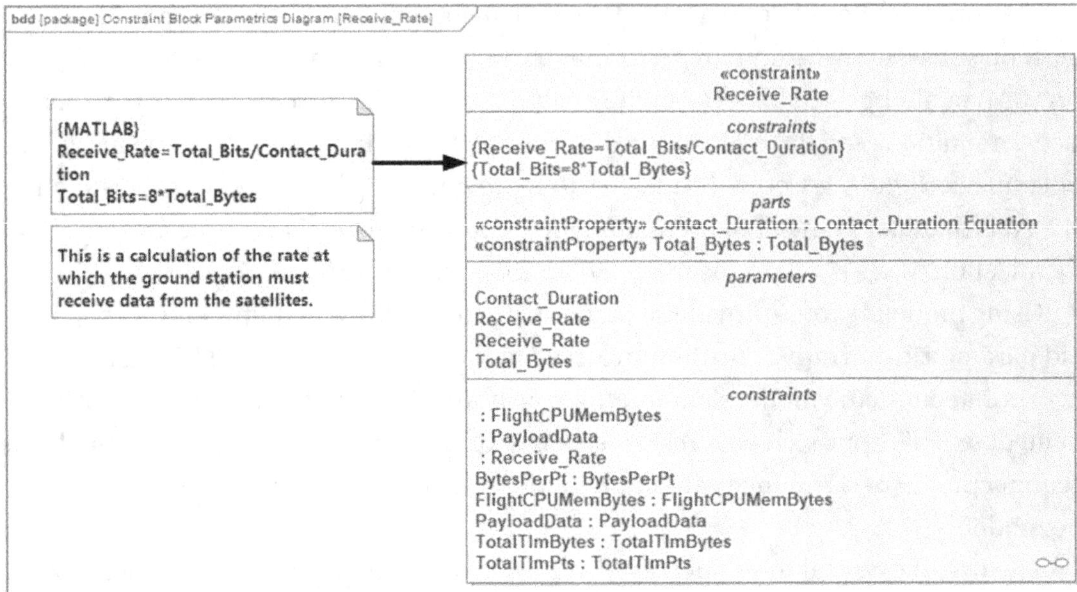

Figure 8-5. *Example of analysis tool incorporation*[5]

Performance Requirements

For this example, we will refer to the Figures 8-1a and 8-1b sequence diagram and a partial list of the activities in Table 8-1. The table provides an example of specification coverage relative to the Perform Link Security, Extract Data activities, and Comm System actor. Note that Comm System is shown as an actor in Figures 8-1a and 8-1b since it is external to the Perform Cmd & Tlm activity. When viewed by itself, the Comm System would be shown as an activity diagram that covers just that subsystem.

---

[5] Author-created image

Table 8-1. *Partial listing of activities and specified performance*

Activity	Specification
Perform Link Security	Crypto hardware specifications and network performance specifications. • Example specification requirements: The crypto shall accept data at a rate of XXX Mbps. The network link shall provide a throughput of ZZZ Mbps for the data stream—i.e., the data field exclusive of protocol overhead.
Extract Data	Command and Telemetry Subsystem • Example Specification requirement: Data shall be extracted from the transport frame at a rate of XXX bytes per second. Note this is required to keep up with the input rate.

Perform Satellite Comm	System Specification
	
	• Example specification requirement: The satellite link shall support the telemetry downlink with an error rate of 10^{-3} or better.
	
	Communications Subsystem Specification
	
	• Example specification requirements: The antenna shall have a transmit gain of XXX dB. The antenna shall have a receive gain of YYY dB.
	• Note: it is often the case that the frequencies involved may be significantly different, which relates to the potential gain of the antenna, for example, an L-Band uplink and an S-Band downlink with Space Ground Link Subsystem.
	
	Component Specifications
	
	• Active components (Example: bit synchronization)
	   o Example specification requirement: The receive bit synchronization shall maintain synchronization down to 100mVpp with performance down to −3 dB E_b/N_o.
	• Passive components such as the antenna dish and feed subsystem (affects gain and ability to handle specified data rate)
	   o Example specification text: The parabolic dish shall have a surface accuracy such that the root mean square (RMS) surface deviation from the ideal parabolic shape does not exceed **0.5 mm RMS** across the reflecting aperture.
	• Note: the specification requirements may be in terms of other parameters used to calculate/determine the bit rate handling capability.

Non-functional Requirements

One approach to developing "text based" non-functional requirements is to capture them as requirements for each applicable activity and block definition diagram element. If the modeling tool in use does not provide for documenting the requirements or constraints, use the notes section that is normally provided by modeling tools. The advantage of this approach is that the non-functional requirement is always directly related to the model element and system areas that they apply to. As before, the data added to the requirement/constraint should be entered into the requirements database in the section applicable to the system item that hosted the constraint/non-functional requirement. Note that SysML standards, for bdd or ibd compartments as well as for activities, do not directly address non-functional requirements such as colors, finishes, human factors, etc. Because of this, the engineer should physically address the non-functional requirements within a requirements management tool (such as IBM DOORS or Visure) and/or manually prepared specifications.

In terms of adding non-functional requirements for capabilities and activities, be cautious. When using the constraint feature in the modeling tool (Figure 8-6), recall that constraints are most frequently used for the capture of equations or other mathematical functions. This does not mean that a constraint can't be a general restriction, such as constraining communications to a frequency band, as shown in the figure below, or even limitations for non-functional items. From a practical perspective, the non-functional requirements are easier to spot when working with the bdd and ibd views since the blocks can normally be viewed as physical parts of the system. Documenting the nonfunctional requirements in the bdd and ibd can help to ensure a linkage between the modeling and the requirements tool. This helps to maintain consistency from initial modeling through system specifications and following on to component development/procurement specifications. In most cases, these specifications provide the basis for test requirements and inspection of physical components; thus, consistency is essential.

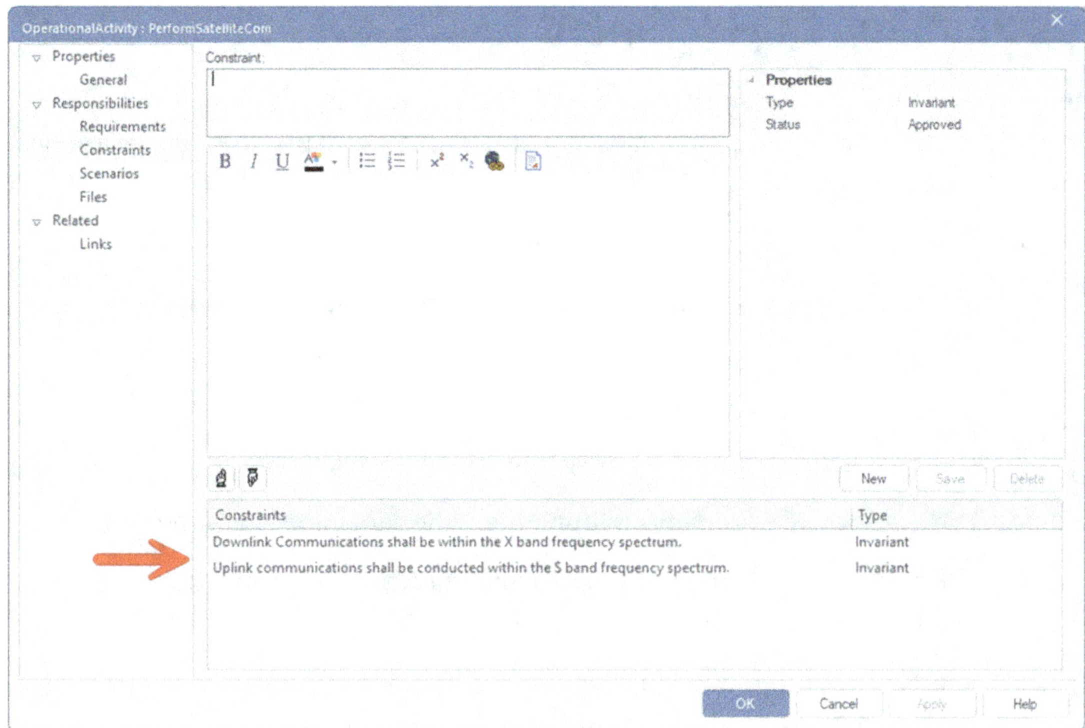

Figure 8-6. *Constraint capture in the modeling tool[6]*

During model development the nonfunctional requirements are easier to spot when working with the bdd and ibd views; however, this does not mean that nonfunctional requirements cannot be found when working on the capabilities and activities.

It is recommended that the nonfunctional requirements in the model be treated in the same way as the functional requirements when using the modeling tool. Develop the requirements in the tool with each element as applicable and export with the rest of the requirements to a requirements tool such as IBM DOORS. By using this approach, requirement and constraint consistency and traceability are maintained between the tools being used.

---

[6] Author-created image

Specification Development

The key to the development and delivery of effective systems is to have complete, consistent, and accurate development documentation. All systems should have a series of mutually supportive development documents to describe

- The need for a system that consists of

  - Purpose of the system (if generated by end using organization)

  - Market being addressed (if the system is a commercial item being placed on the company product list)

- The capabilities required to satisfy the end user's needs

- The technical requirements to implement the capabilities required

- The high-level system requirements that implement the technical requirements

- Interface documentation to describe the interface of the system to other systems (internal to the organization and external)

- The subsystem requirements that are necessary to implement the high-level system requirements

- Interface documentation describing the interfaces between subsystems

- Hardware requirements covering items making up the system

  - It can be for an item that supports performing a function, such as a computer, disk drive, etc.

  - It can be for structural components.

  - Non-functional items such as form, fit, color, etc.

Note how there is a flow to the documents (i.e., Statement of Need and Capability Development Document) and specifications. Each item supports the development of the next item. Keep in mind that developing the capabilities and requirements while developing the model will enforce the accuracy and completeness of the documentation and help ensure that each document supports the next document in the flow.

A typical specification tree example is shown in Figures 8-7a and 8-7b. The responsibility for developing each specification is included in each specification block. These responsibility assignments are only suggestions; however, they are based on observations over many years of system development. For government programs, the Statement of Need and Capability Development Document are often held as internal documents since they contain data that is competition sensitive. For example, budgets, internal schedules, program administration details, etc. It is strongly recommended that government organizations create a releasable version of these documents. These releasable documents can be used by the development organizations to develop the system architecture and design.

As covered earlier in this book, it is imperative that all details of the system architecture and design development relate and link to each other. Performing the modeling as part of the requirements development and aligning model artifacts with specific specifications aids the thought and reasoning process essential for both the acquisition organization and development organization in developing specifications and a design that fulfills the operational needs. An earlier example included the evaluation of modeled capabilities vs. system requirements (the initial requirements contained in the technical requirements document). The thought process can determine that an activity and supporting requirement are a capability supporting a need. It can also reveal that a capability is an activity that supports a capability.

This evaluation during model development can ensure that capability development documents and technical requirement documents are mutually supportive. Thus far, we have observed the development of requirements and constraints from initial capabilities through to the system and subsystem specifications. This is only one half of the effort. If changes are made at the lowest levels of specifications, there is potential for these changes to affect the higher-level specifications.

This is where modeling tools can aid the process. If design changes are proposed for the detailed design, the model and associated requirements should be updated to reflect these changes. Since most modeling tools allow a switch to UML, the lower-level models can be part of the original system model. This provides a means to trace the effects of a change in a lower-level design and specification back through the model and specifications to the original system specification. This is a more reliable method for ensuring that the specifications maintain consistency and traceability up and down the specification tree.

If the system development and acquisition process is treated as the development of independent documents and elements of design to meet contractual deliveries, there is a good chance that problems will occur later in the development process. Typical problems deal with interfaces, missing or incorrectly implemented capabilities, operational features, and performance issues.

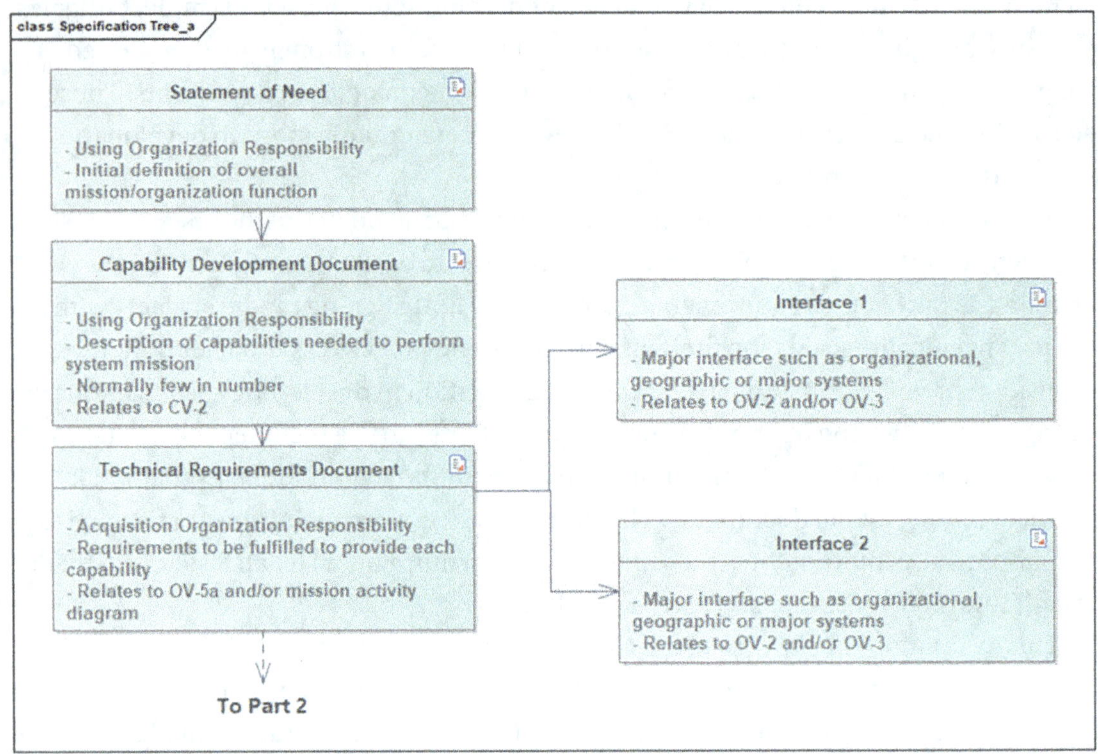

Figure 8-7a. *Specification tree*[7]

---

[7] Author-created image

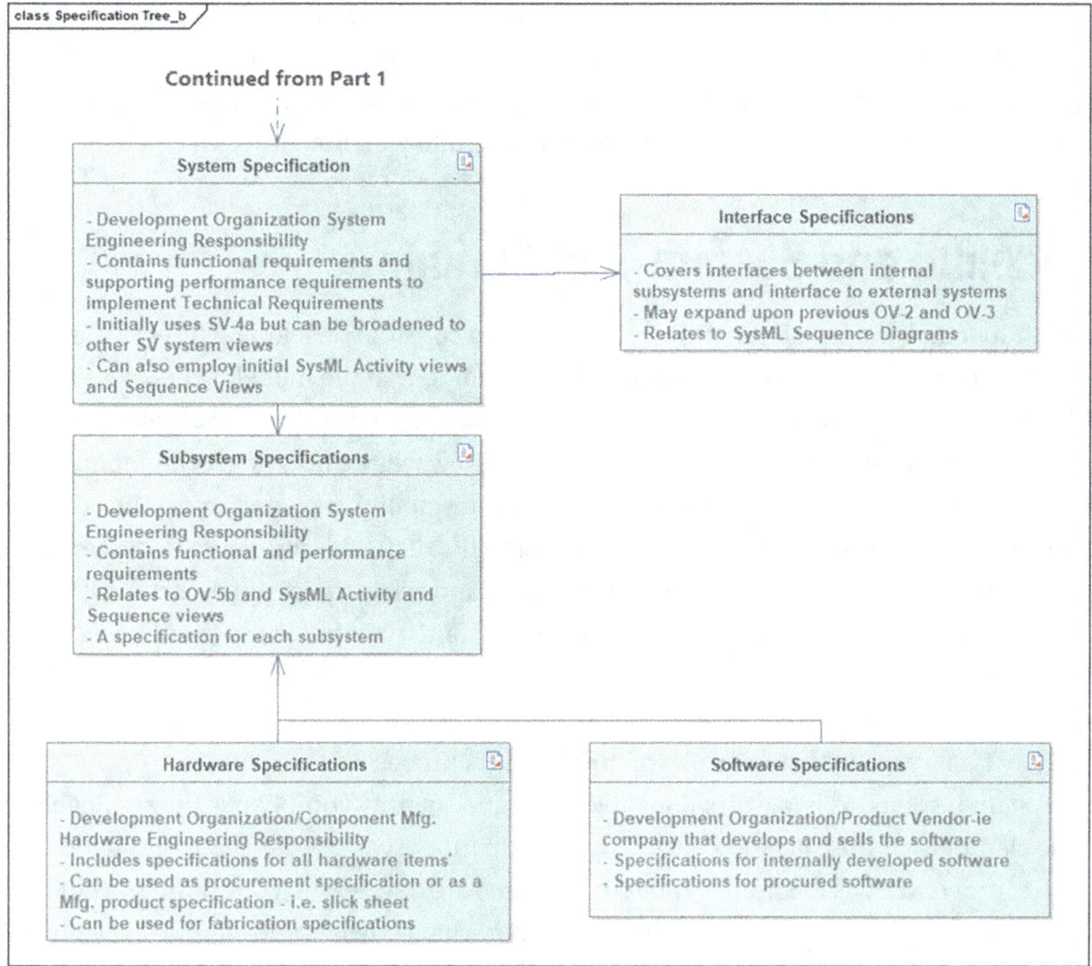

Figure 8-7b. *(continued)*

Producing the Specification

As covered earlier, some modeling tools currently have built-in capabilities to publish documents. This includes generation of templates for various documents and import of compatible templates developed outside of the tool. Templates provided with the tools may be very generic and may not (if this is not for internal use) meet contractual requirements. Custom templates may be produced using customer directions, referred to as Data Item Descriptions for government contracts.

Some organizations make use of tools such as DOORS or Visure for requirements management. In those cases, the requirements generated during development of model activities and other objects are copied from the modeling tool and pasted into the requirements management tool. The specifications are most often produced from the requirements tools rather than the model. As with publishing from a model, a custom template must be developed based on customer or internal directions.

Modeling and System Test Planning

As with specification development, it is important to consider developing test cases and test procedures as you develop the model. Keep in mind that the modeling effort is an aid to the "thought process" for system development. A key test for validating each model element and associated requirement is to think of "how will we test the requirement." Most books covering requirement development call out "testability" as a key factor. They don't, however, cover how to critically examine the testability of the requirement. Also, keep in mind we are developing the activities, interactions, and related performance during the modeling effort. The individual assigned to perform and manage testing should be a key member of model peer reviews at each step of development. This will help to enforce the "thought process" associated with each activity, interaction, and requirement. The test engineer is key to refining the results of this "thought process."

System testing involves the overall operation and security compliance (as applicable) of the elements comprising the system. The system model can assist in generating the tests and test procedures as the model and requirements are developed. For example, as the model is developed, the engineer is thinking about what activities and supporting actions are required and how they relate. At this point, the testing of these activities/actions and their relationship should be documented. This initial test documentation can be just a description of what needs to be accomplished. As the model development continues, the initial detailed test procedures should be developed at the completion activity and action element modeling. When the subsystem model is completed, the test data should be combined and expanded into the detailed plan and procedures covering this portion of the system. Upon completion of the total system model, these sections of test data should be combined and reviewed/edited to form the overall system test plan and procedures.

Note that this approach should also be used for the UML modeling of the lower-level elements by the software/hardware engineer. These test step details cover the operations and interactions at the lowest level of element operation. For example, the software operation during an operator login or the hardware amplifier operational characteristics across the amplification range.

Modeling tools often provide capabilities for testing; however, it is important to distinguish between testing/simulating the model and generating the tests performed for System acceptance. For our purposes, we will concentrate on the tests necessary for system acceptance.

Depending on the modeling tool being used, the difficulty in accommodating the system and subsystem test procedures may vary. Each tool has its own advantages and disadvantages. For example, the SPARX EA tool provides the means of attaching a linked document to each element. This linked document, which is retained within the model in RTF format, can contain the test planning and test procedures for each requirement. The RTF format used for these documents should be based upon a standard RTF template generated for the team at the beginning of a project. This template should contain all of the sections called for by organization standards, or if a government program, standards such as DI-NDTI-80566A Test Plan and DI-NDTI-80603A Test Procedure. For SPARX EA applications, the availability of a linked document is shown by a document symbol in the bottom right portion of the element in the activity document, as shown in Figure 8-8. Note that the RTF document should be created from within the modeling tool as shown in Figure 8-9. For the Sparx EA case, if the document exists, it will open the document. If it has not been created, it will provide for creating the document.

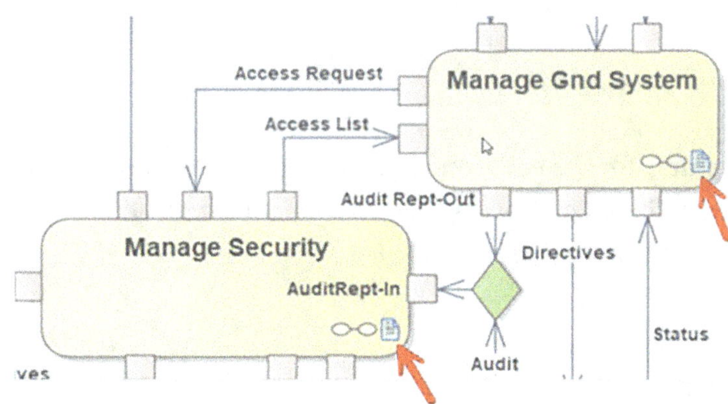

Figure 8-8. *Example of linked test document*[8]

---

[8] Author-created image

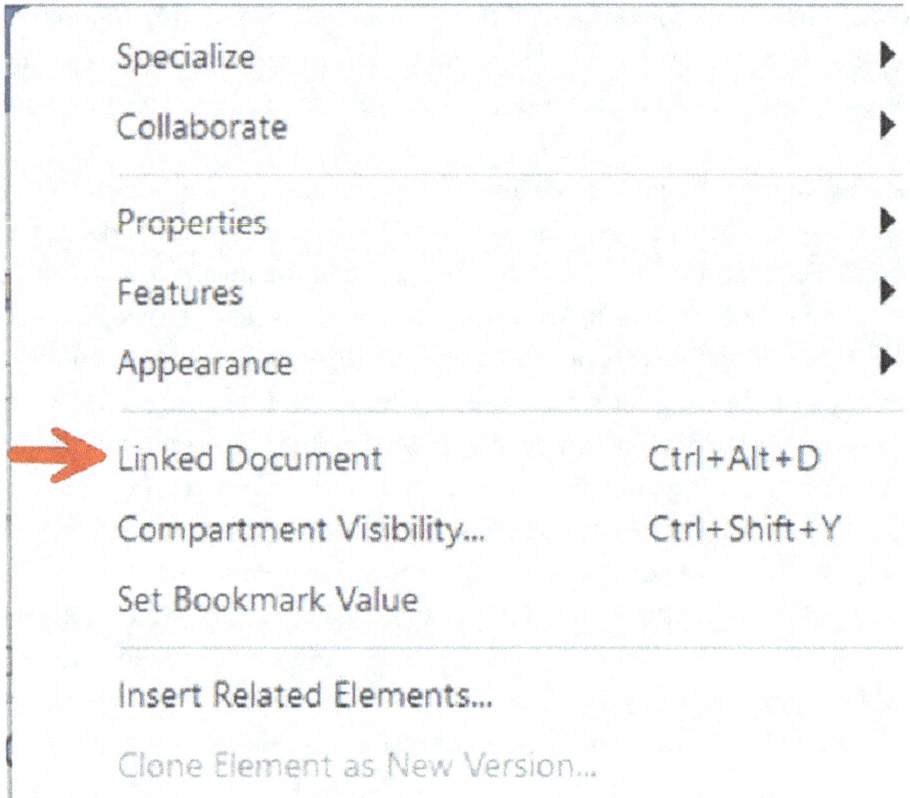

Figure 8-9. *SPARX EA example of linking test document*[9]

As with the example for the creation of the Capability Development Document, the Systems Requirement Specification can be developed in conjunction with the modeling using an agile approach, as shown in Figure 8-10.

---

[9] Author-created image

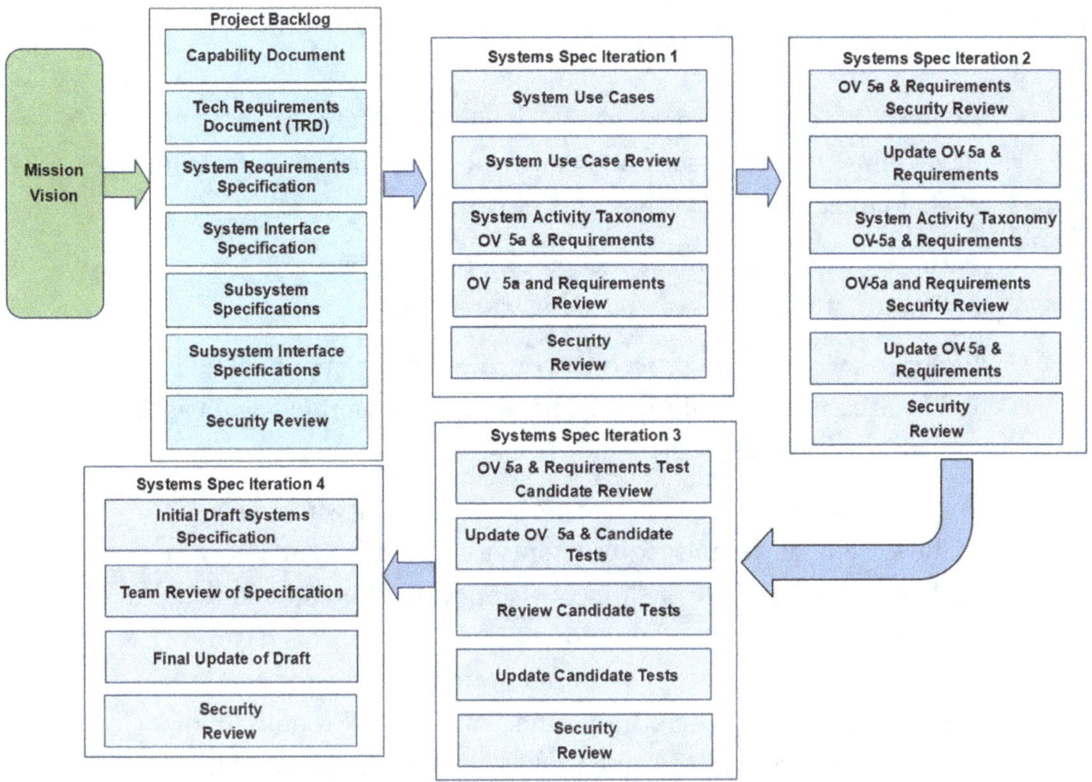

Figure 8-10. *Agile requirements and test development*[10]

Regardless of the tool employed, the key is to begin developing test plans and procedures as the modeling definition is being developed. This does not mean that the team must begin the total top-down set of procedures during the modeling. The intent is to gather the procedures for each system element and then gather and organize them as significant portions of the system architecture and design are completed. These procedures can be used for subsystem testing and refined based upon lessons learned during the tests. The final organization of the system test procedures, consisting of all previously developed model derived and subsystem refined procedures, should be accomplished in one or more months before scheduled system/acceptance testing.

---

[10] Adaptation—Dr. Bruce Powell Douglass, Agile Model-Based Systems Engineering Cookbook, Packt, 2022, Figure 1-3

Here are some key recommendations for the development organization regarding system testing:

- Assign a test engineer starting at the beginning of OV-5a development. This person can begin evaluating methods of test for each architecture area as they are defined.

- Perform reviews of testing concepts and procedures during peer review of completed elements of the system model.

- Perform reviews of test procedures during subsystem model reviews. Recognize that the results of the review can be examined again as the modeling progresses.

- Perform a review of the final test procedures along with a review of the system model and requirements for each element. Perform updates as necessary to ensure consistency between the model, requirements, design, and test procedures. This approach can help avoid late breaking "requirements creep" where the end user witnessing the testing determines that a supporting requirement is missing or incorrectly implemented. When this happens, final system acceptance will be delayed.

- Consider updating the model if issues are encountered during the subsystem testing. Don't just modify the procedures. There could be related problems with the model logic and hence the subsystem design implementation. Rember, the system test aggregates all or portions of the subsystem tests.

- Ensure that the following team members are retained, if possible, from program start through completion:

  - Chief System Engineer (technical lead for the program)

  - Chief Software Engineer

  - Test Engineer

  - Modeling Engineer (lead)

  - Logistics Specialist

  - Security Engineer

These individuals are the *"corporate knowledge bank"* for the program. They are familiar with all the issues and why the system is structured and tested as shown during final acceptance testing. Dropping the Chief System Engineer, Chief Software Engineer, and modeling engineer early in the program (e.g., upon completion of Critical Design Review) will not cut program costs, especially if difficulties arise during preparation for or performance of acceptance testing. The model and the corporate knowledge are the key to keeping the testing on track. In addition, the late assignment of a test engineer will result in rushed development of the test procedures during test preparation and most likely will result in considerable rework of test procedures and/or addition of staff to assist in refining procedures. Review of requirements and constraints attached to each model artifact by the Test Engineer as they are developed will ensure that test steps have a direct relation to both the system model artifact as well as the development of test steps that directly address testing of the system as modeled and developed.

System Implementation Approach

Thus far, we have concentrated on what the system needs to do and not how it is to be built. Specifications have been limited to the capabilities, activities, and actions to be performed. Implementation items should now be added as necessary to complete the system definition. The implementation approach should not impact the system capabilities and activities. If an implementation approach being evaluated does impact either a capability or activity, it should be discarded in favor of a different approach. If another approach is not available, then the capability or activity involved should be evaluated to determine if it is beyond the current state of the art. If there is a state-of-the-art issue, the mission should be evaluated to determine if there is another way to obtain the same or similar results with another implementation approach that will achieve the same objectives.

Situations such as this point to the advantage of performing the modeling and system analysis early in the project. It avoids the cost impacts and serious delays that can occur if the issue is discovered late in the project due to rework. An even more serious outcome could be the decision to drop a mission capability to meet cost constraints. If dropping a mission capability or activity occurs, the probability of mission success should be evaluated, and the mission definition should be analyzed to determine if an alternate approach will work.

This book uses the development of a satellite ground system as a case study. In such systems, the consequences of mission failure are often less severe than in contexts like aerial combat, missile interception, or other performance- and capability-critical missions. The modeling introduced earlier in the book is intended to assess the applicability of various technologies to the system design and to support trade-offs between competing options. However, teams frequently commit to specific technologies before performing this analysis, which can lead to future issues and increased development costs. Examples of technology implementation approaches are provided in the following subsections.

Use of Cloud Computing

Cloud computing from a Modeling standpoint is limited to activities and actions necessary for the interface between the application and the operating environment. Cloud computing environments have become popular in recent years. There are many reasons for this popularity. Here are a few:

- On-demand usage

- Ubiquitous access (i.e., service is widely accessible)

- Multitenancy (and resource pooling)

- Elasticity

- Measured usage

- Resiliency

First, consider that these reasons do not and should not affect the required mission capabilities or the activities. They can affect how we accomplish the design (in particular the interfaces between the application and the operating environment) and the mission. For example:

1. Some or all the system can be accomplished within the same physical building or campus.

2. Some or all the system supporting elements can be distributed to other sites using communications systems (network, satellite, etc.).

3. Some or all the system capabilities can be performed by a commercial or cooperative organization.

4. Reduced up-front investment costs.

Other than the first and last items, these items all impact security concerns. Questions relating to the trust boundary and the administration of security need to be addressed upfront as part of the "design requirements" and, in the case of using a commercial approach, implementation contracts. For the case of using commercial cloud services, there are potential issues with overlapping trust boundaries. The organizations may have different security controls in place. Altering the controls within the boundaries can be a challenge.

If the cloud is based within the end-user facilities, there is a good chance that commercial cloud software will be used. Keep in mind that commercial products can introduce an increased surface for attack, especially if the operating environment has any point where an interface to an outside network is possible.

The use of a cloud solution (private or commercial/public) should be modeled as part of the initial effort and updated as necessary as the model and design progress. A block definition diagram (bdd) can be used to show the geographical distribution of activities. The security controls employed should be evaluated and updated/enhanced as necessary. Activity diagrams and lower-level supporting actions should be updated to show the controls and how they work relative to the geographic distribution. In general, the activity updates may not be required if the original modeling of controls is complete and accurate. The key activities that may be impacted would involve the communications between sites and any changes negotiated as part of a Service Level Agreement (SLA).

Remember, modeling, including that required for security between the third-party cloud provider facilities and the customer facilities, is part of the design "thought process" (not just a documentation deliverable to be developed after the fact or separate from the design process). It forces consideration of other issues, including security.

Docker Platform as a Service (PaaS)

Container approaches and the use of virtual machines have become popular in recent years. With a cloud implementation, the fundamental capabilities, activities, and supporting actions will not change. The changes will come at the software design level (modeled with UML or SysML). Note that the modeling will relate to the implementation of applications within containers and potentially the interactions between the applications and the Docker engine. As before, the capabilities and requirements developed via the model for the CDD and System Specification have not changed. However, there may be model and subsystem specification changes.

Service Oriented Architecture (SOA)

The use of SOA will not affect the basic capabilities and activities modeled and documented in the CDD and System Specifications. It *can* affect the subsystem specifications and supporting modeling (in UML or SysML).

Let's look at what the SOA components are:

- The business (mission) process instances (i.e., the overall mission will consist of multiple processes). These are normally covered by the CDD and System Specification.

- Services, which are the functions being performed to perform/ support the processes. These are normally covered by the Subsystem/ Component specifications and associated UML/SysML models.

- Operations, grouped with services, that perform the details of the processing. These are normally contained in Detailed Design Documents. Lower-level breakouts of the previously developed models are used.

- Messages that perform communication between the operations (encapsulated by the services).

Security controls should be included in the modeling to ensure that no gaps will exist in security coverage based upon the distribution of services and operations. Keep in mind that software/hardware products used for SOA can substantially increase the attack surface. Detailed modeling analysis can help determine where security safeguards should be incorporated.

Performance issues should be examined before finally committing to SOA or any of the other technologies. Remember, when messaging is involved, or processes are layered to a high degree that performance can be an issue if the system being developed is intended for real-time operation. This is where performance modeling can be employed. SysML can be used to model performance attributes relative to multiple parts of the system. It does not do the calculations necessary to determine the performance. Typically, a tool such as MATLAB is used to perform detailed performance analysis.

System Sustainability and Security

Successful completion of acceptance testing is not the end of the story for modeling and maintaining the model. It is highly recommended that the acquisition organization and the organization responsible for the maintenance of the system retain and use the model. This is especially true when

- It is intended that the system remain operational for five years or more. This is due to the rapid obsolescence and product changes associated with modern components such as computers. Changes associated with repair actions could change system performance or functionality. Commercial software updates can also drive computer and other component obsolescence and difficulties with support.

- System problems are recurring, i.e., either a function malfunction or problems in one subsystem/portion of a subsystem.

- Planning for and initiating corrective actions.

- Evaluating excessively high component or software-implemented function failure rates.

- Considering substitution of hardware items during repair (original component not made or has been modified by the original manufacturer. For hardware items, this is relatively straightforward.

- Considering substitution with new or upgraded software products. For software items, consider your own experience (if you have worked on other programs/projects) where the miracle "one line of code" fix resulted in problems in one or more additional parts of the system.

Incorporation of the Model for Sustainment

As stated earlier in this book, the model should be maintained throughout the system life cycle. The model relates to overall system portfolio management as shown in Figure 8-11. Maintaining the model ensures continuity between design intent, evolving requirements, and operational realities, reducing the risk of ad hoc fixes or undocumented changes. The interactions shown in this view are generalized to show typical usage. The following sections discuss various usages of this sustainability approach. Note that a Business Process Modeling and Notation (BPMN) approach is used to illustrate the process in each case.

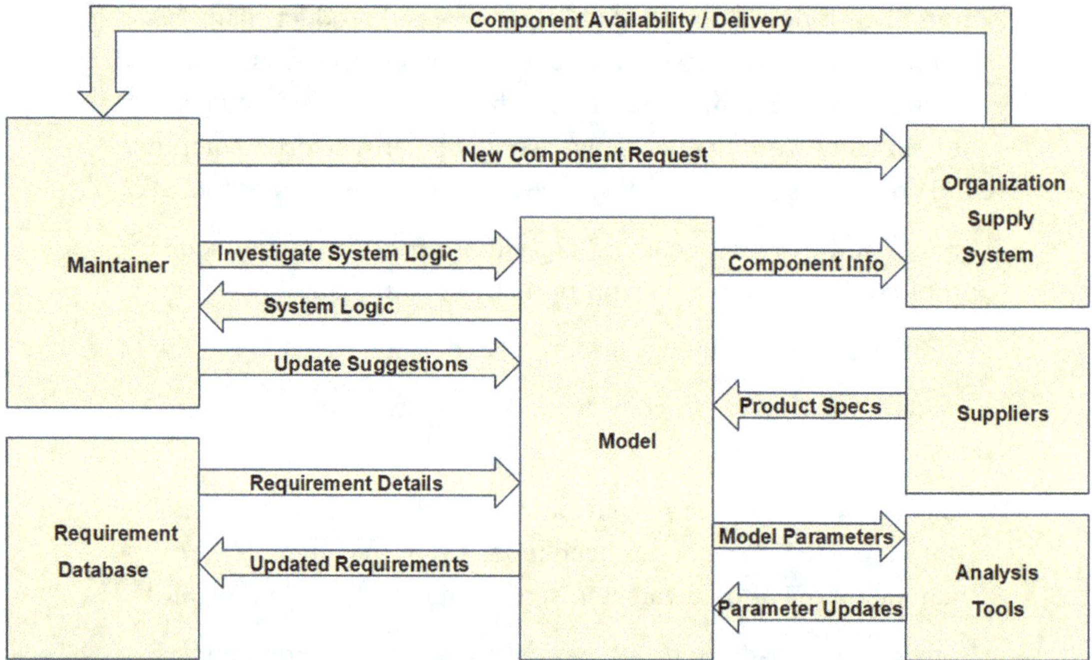

Figure 8-11. *General sustainment view[11]*

---

[11] Author-created image

Let's take this example and break it down into the details of the processes and interactions. Figure 8-12 shows a process interaction view. For our purposes, the view starts with a maintenance process and ends with an update of the model if required. The model also shows four intermediate events. The events shown (i.e., the annotated circles) reflect the completion of some action. These events recognize that there are results that need to be retained either for future use or to resolve a current issue.

As with the system modeling, we can break down each of these processes into a sequence of activities. For our example, we will break down the Maintain System process as shown in Figure 8-13. Keep in mind that this view is just an example and that individual organizations may develop a different view based on their own governing directives and required processes.

Looking at Figures 8-11 and 8-12, questions may also arise as to the need for continued ability to perform performance analysis since the system design is complete and the system is operational. Note that over the life of the system performance characteristics may have been altered based on failures within various parts of the system or replacement of hardware/software components with new or similar components. As a supplement to the model views, it is recommended that lessons learned be documented as faults are discovered and changes are made, If the lessons learned are grouped in the model with the views that are applicable we create a feedback loop that will help future programs. Note that popular tools such as Sparx EA and Magic Draw provide for publishing a model report that can be published outside of the model for use by other programs. This report will place the lessons learned in context and will be of great use to future development teams.

A generalized sequence diagram of the overall sustainment process is shown in Figure 8-14.

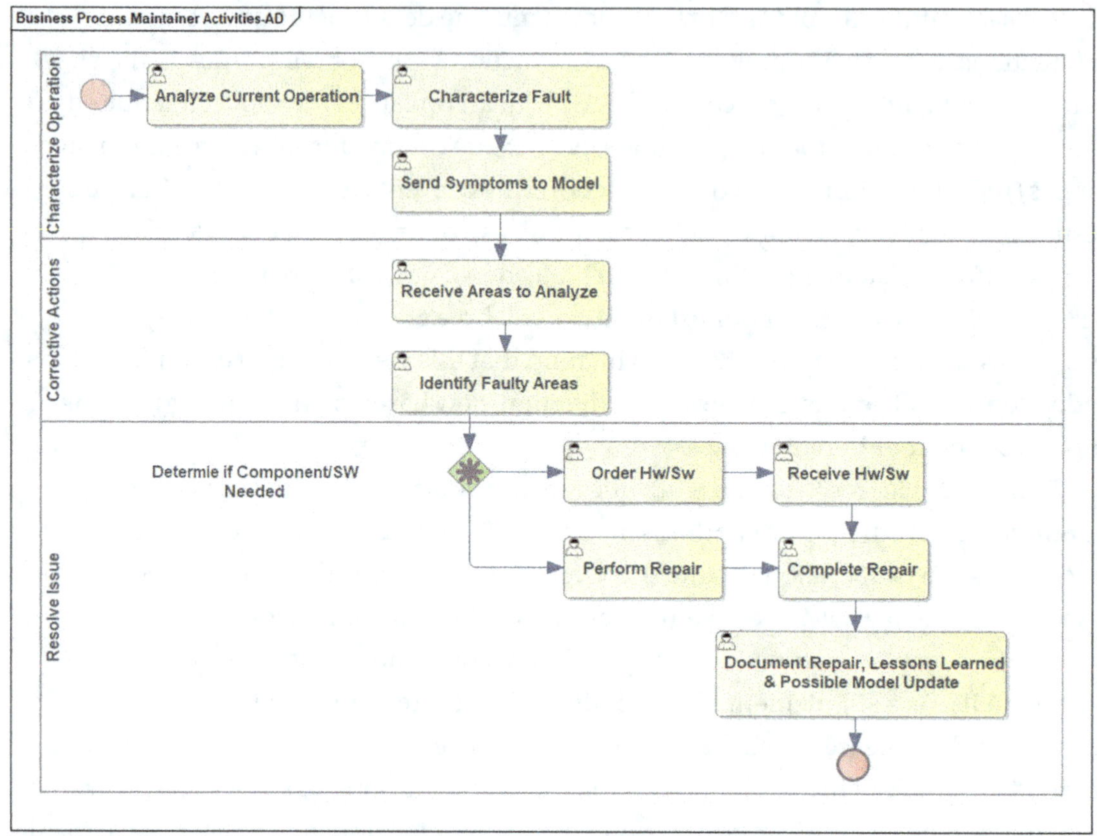

Figure 8-12. *System sustainment process*[12]

---

[12] Author-created image

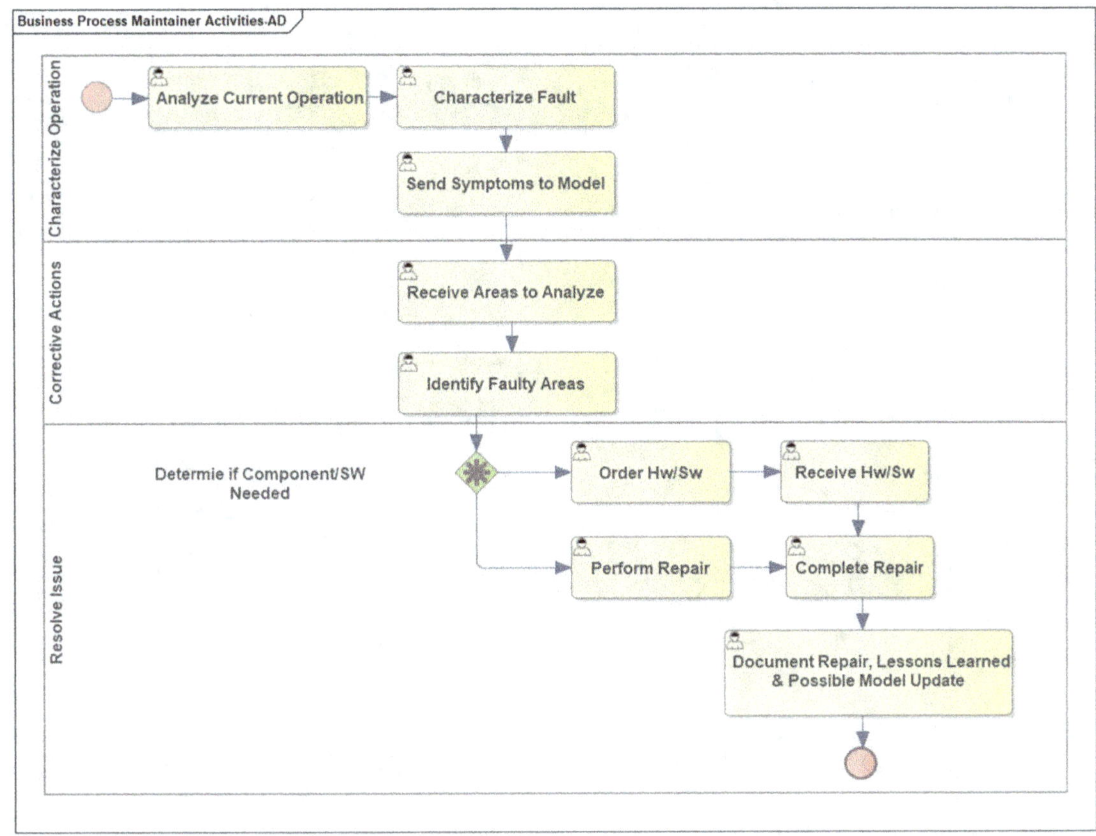

Figure 8-13. *Maintainer activities*[13]

---

[13] Author-created image

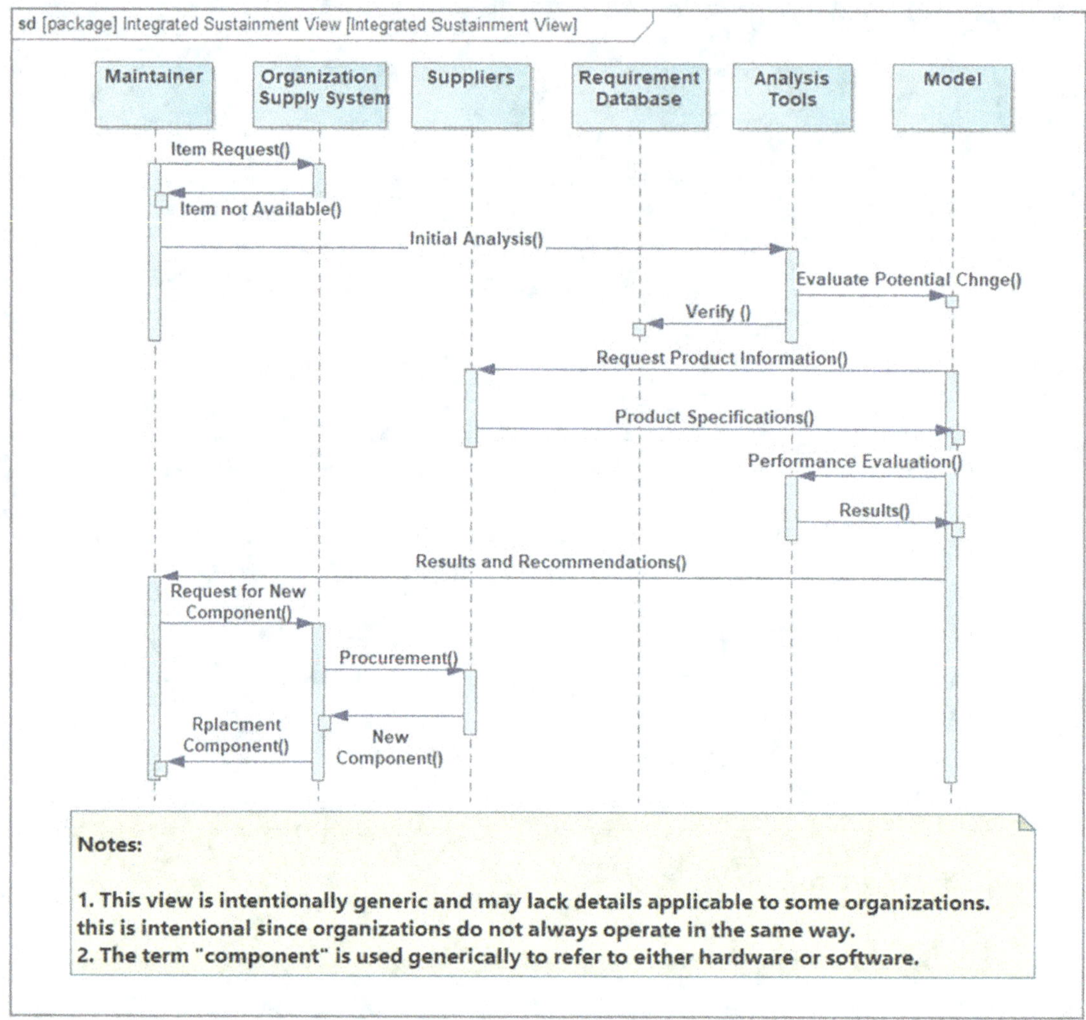

Figure 8-14. *Generalized sustainment sequence diagram*[14]

Sustainment and Security

We earlier addressed the concept of including security in the system modeling in Chapter 3. Throughout the life of the system, security notices will be promulgated throughout the industry and government agencies. These notices often require changes to hardware and software components that may have been used.

---

[14] Author-created image

The biggest security mistake would be to just keep adding software and hardware patches without doing some analysis first. The model, if properly maintained, will aid in this analysis. The model can be used as a guide to evaluating the "updated" software for "*unadvertised*" features. This includes vulnerability analysis and patch evaluation in the context of the model. When the model is not used and maintained, patching can become reactive and risk-prone. In contrast, linking security advisories and patches to the model enables proactive, traceable security risk mitigation. Taking the analysis further, the evaluation person/team can determine if the changes will create potential security risks. Since the source code is normally not available, this evaluation would be a combination of test and comparison against the model.

In the days when software was produced "in house" rather than using several integrated commercial/open-source software modules it was relatively straightforward to analyze the logic of the software to determine if a security flaw exists. Over the last several decades, there has been a tendency to use massive software packages or reuse commercial or open-source software containers in software development. The intent has been to reduce development costs. The result has been just the opposite in terms of excessive licensing costs and the cost to resolve continual security issues.

The trends in commercial software have been to keep adding "features" and combine software from various sources (vendor mergers allowing incorporation of software from both companies and other existing products). The new *"improved"* software package, often containing features not needed by the end user, draws higher license costs, and increases the software "bloat." This software bloat also has the unintended consequences of an increased "attack surface" for adversaries to exploit. The increased attack surface increases sustainment costs to keep up with the resultant threats.

For end user organizations, the best approach is requiring maintenance of the system model as a part of the overall sustainment effort. As security notices are published, the system sustainers can use the model to trace through the system and software logic looking for places that may be vulnerable to the threat contained in the security notice. Relating the model to the installed system is relatively easy when the software is developed in-house. The incorporation of commercial packages will make this easier in terms of isolating to a large software package or complex hardware item and more difficult at the detailed level. In these cases, the end user is reliant on the software and hardware vendor to find the flaw that enabled the successful cyber-attack.

Planning and Scheduling for Performance and Non-functional Requirements

In earlier chapters the schedule primarily involved the functional activities and interactions. From a practical perspective the performance modeling will be accomplished at the same time. In fact, some activity diagrams and requirements may be altered based on performance analysis. In other words, there may be some degree of iteration to optimize performance. Performance analysis and parametric models should be inserted into the Agile Sprint cycles as necessary to reflect the necessary performance analysis.

Nonfunctional requirements should also be accounted for as necessary within each Sprint cycle. Though not associated with the MBSE theme of this book it is important to point out that they must be documented within each subsystem and component section within the model as well as in the specification under development. Examples of nonfunctional requirements include corrosion coatings, color chips for racks and equipment, etc. The organization of this book has been focused on determining what the system is required to accomplish, which can be a complex process. The performance and specification nonperformance aspects have been addressed separately since they can lend considerable complexity to the overall discussion of modeling a system. This organization should not imply that the performance analysis and specification should be put off until the end of the project. The analysis and specification should be accomplished as the model progresses.

The Devlopment team should consider the functional and non-functional requirements in terms of separate parallel workflows in terms of Agile scheduling rather than considering the non-functional requirements as an afterthought. This helps to avoid late-stage redesigns and ensures that the subsystem specifications evolve with both functional and non-functional considerations in balance.

Chapter Lessons Learned

- Both performance and non-functional requirements must evolve iteratively with the model.

- Addressing both the performance and non-functional requirements in the model and supporting requirements tool ensures that parametric models, the requirements hierarchy, and sustainment are integrated practices. They are not sequential add-ons that could result in issues during the development, testing, and sustainment of the system.

- Performance is often specified at the highest level – i.e. capability level. Consider that the requirement may be to accomplish a task before a related task starts and that the overall time from start to finish must be less than or equal to a specific time. Do not specify an exact performance for the system / subsystem at this point. You could create a conflict of requirements later in the process.

- Use the interactions developed for a sequence diagram to establish lower-level performance parameters.

- Develop the performance parameters manually or with a tool such as MATLAB for the interfaces and the activities.

- Use parametric Modeling to document the results of analysis and performance calculations in the Modeling tool.

- Non-functional requirements should be added to the physical requirements within the specification being developed at this time. For example, equipment racks shall be painted using color chip Federal Standard 595 chip number 36231 (avionics panels).

- Requirements and requirement documents are hierarchical, and it is imperative that model views and requirements supporting each level of the hierarchy are consistent and supportive. Use of a Specification Tree, maintained in the Modeling tool aids in maintaining the system specifications.

- Documents for test planning can be included as links within the SysML views. This will help to keep the test procedures documented with the model activities that will be tested.

- Implementation approaches shown are not an endorsement of any specific software product. Performance as it relates to the system operation will need to be measured in a test environment to determine the effect on required operational performance. The results of the tests should be documented in the applicable parametric model.

- The model should be maintained for the system life cycle. An example of how the model fits into the sustainment process and how it can be used for evaluation of operational problems was shown.

- The planning and scheduling of the parametric Modeling should be incorporated into the applicable sections of the schedule addressing those subsystems (Modeling and design). Use of Agile approaches should incorporate specific analysis, etc., as a micro cycle in the schedule.

Acronym List

Acronym	Definition
BPMN	Business Process Modeling and Notation
CDD	Capability Development Document
Cmd	Command
DODAF	Department of Defense Architecture Framework
MATLAB	MATrix LABoratory (MathWorks programming language)
RTF	Rich Text Format
SOA	Service Oriented Architecture
SP	Special Publication
SV	System View

Epilogue

Summary

The development example in this book is generic and doesn't represent any existing satellite ground system currently in development or in existence. Note that the modeling and requirement generation steps presented in this book are high-level generalizations. The assembly line example is also generic and should not be used directly to design a specific assembly line. Some parts of the assembly line, such as the design of the facility housing the assembly line and details of the assembly line, are omitted.

The concepts and processes described in this book are not limited to satellite or other systems as we know them today. Emerging technologies such as artificial intelligence, self-driving cars, and cyber-resilient data systems can also benefit from simultaneous modeling and requirements generation. Regardless of the technology, we always start with a mission, the capabilities needed to fulfill that mission, and the activities and actions required to perform it. For example, an AI system is a pipeline that collects data, learns patterns from it, and applies those patterns to make predictions, decisions, or generate new content. Each of these steps is an activity that can be modeled, and requirements can be generated to support each activity. In other words, the modeling-requirements paradigm remains valid. The implementation may involve new languages and structures but the underlying concept of doing the modeling and requirements development remains intact.

Leverage the requirements and models produced during your project development. Use them to produce or update training materials, repair protocols, and troubleshooting manuals. This guarantees long-term sustainability, especially when the original developers are no longer available. It provides continuity for maintenance teams and future enhancements.

Finally, remember that the key to good design and sustainable systems that meet mission needs is the thought process. Simultaneous modeling and requirement development aid the thought process and are essential to maintain consistency throughout any project.

© Dennis Hansen 2025
D. Hansen, *Model-Based Systems Engineering and Requirements Definition,*
https://doi.org/10.1007/979-8-8688-2043-4

APPENDIX A

CCSDS Background Information

This book is intended to support the definition of system models and requirements for systems of any size. To illustrate key concepts, a satellite ground system example is used throughout. In this context, references are made to standards and recommendations from the Consultative Committee for Space Data Systems (CCSDS). These documents, while extensive and highly specific to space systems, help clarify the examples presented in this appendix.

To assist the reader in understanding these examples, a brief overview of CCSDS protocols and formatting is provided. The goal is to convey the purpose and outcomes of system modeling activities at a high level of abstraction.

This appendix also highlights an important point for both managers and engineers: developing detailed levels of a system model involves significantly more work than merely creating graphics. Project schedules and cost estimates are often underestimated by focusing only on visual components. The CCSDS example demonstrates that in complex systems, such as satellite command and control, substantial research is required during model development. For effective planning, modeling and research should be conducted in parallel whenever possible.

Satellite Commanding Subsystem Protocol Operations

For this example, we will walk through the assembly of the uplink received from Mission Planning. The protocol stack for telecommand is shown in Figure A-1a, Figure A-1b, and Figure A-1c. Note that at the top of the stack, we have Data Management Services. The data from mission planning was originally received by the Applications Process Layer.

© Dennis Hansen 2025
D. Hansen, *Model-Based Systems Engineering and Requirements Definition*,
https://doi.org/10.1007/979-8-8688-2043-4

In this example, the Command Directive is a file containing all command directives required for uplink. The System Management Layer translates the received data file to match the required format and syntax of the satellite. The Packetization layer forms the final data packets that will be forwarded to the data routing service. At the Coding Layer, encryption occurs in the Perform Cmd & Tlm activities and the RF signal, and the physical layer is handled by Perform Satellite Com.

Note that this CCSDS example has similarity to normal communications in that the CCSDS protocol stack is similar to the Open Systems Interconnection (OSI) protocol stack, as shown in Figure A-2. For those not familiar with data communication, software using the OSI protocol stack is used for your e-mail, web browser, and other programs needing network access on your desktop and laptop computer.

In our satellite ground system example, note that we create the command deck in mission planning. The command deck creation in our system provides for initial packetization of the command data in the data field and covers the protocol formatting tasks for the top three layers of the CCSDS stack, which is analogous to the top three levels of the OSI stack as seen in Figure A-2. The model inclusion of the transfer of the command deck from Plan Mission to Perform Cmd & Tlm is shown in Figure A-3.

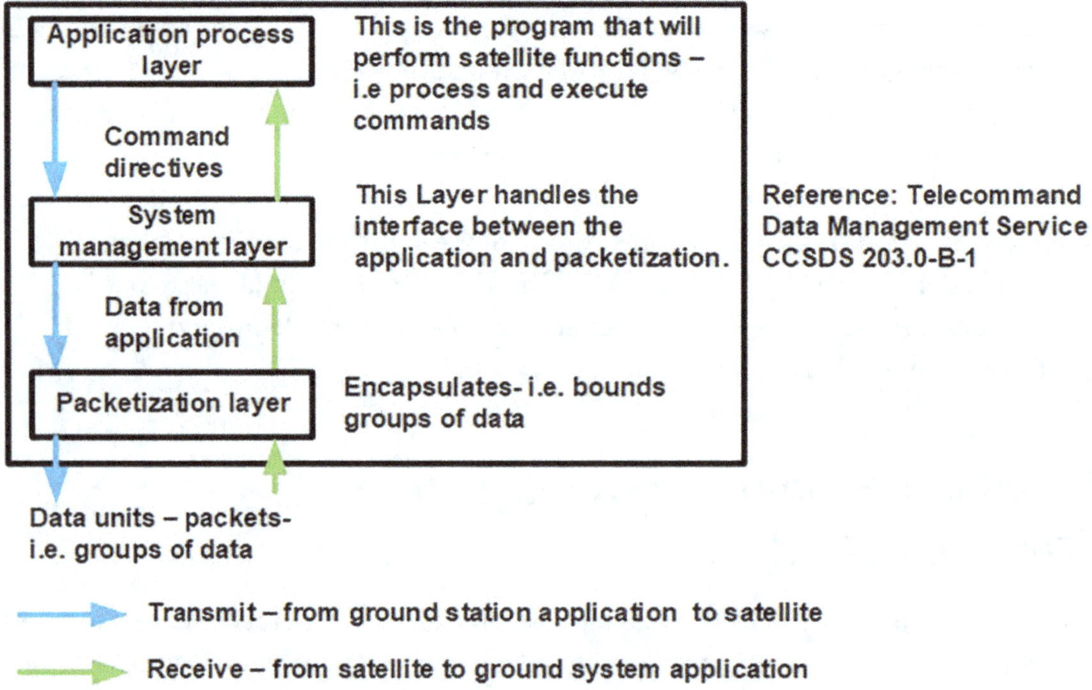

Figure A-1a. *CCSDS data management stack*

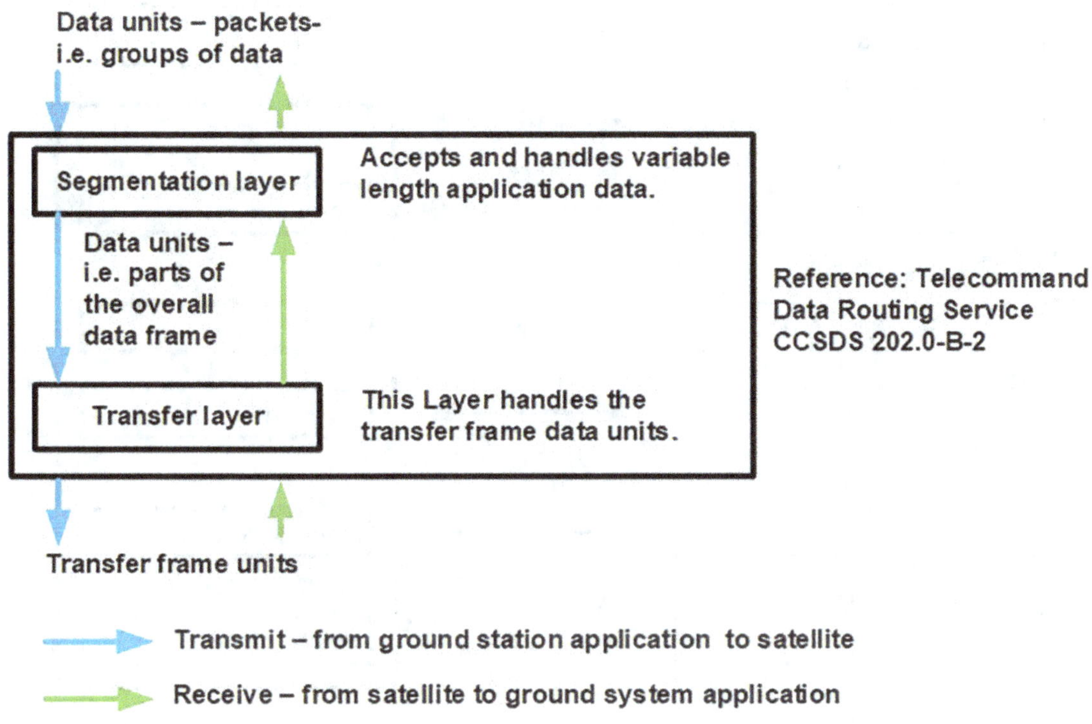

Figure A-1b. *Data routing service*

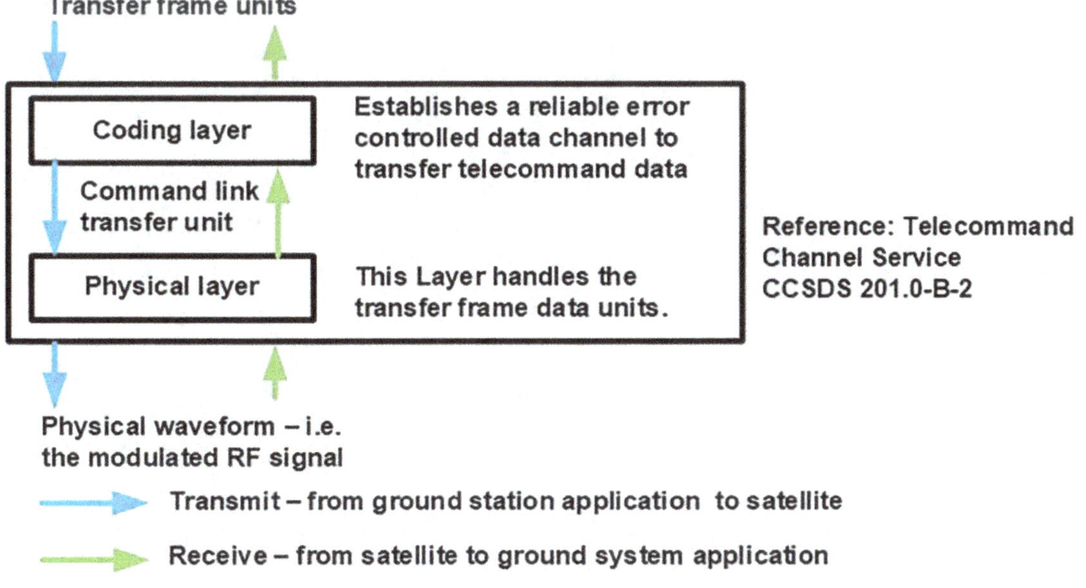

Figure A-1c. *Channel service*

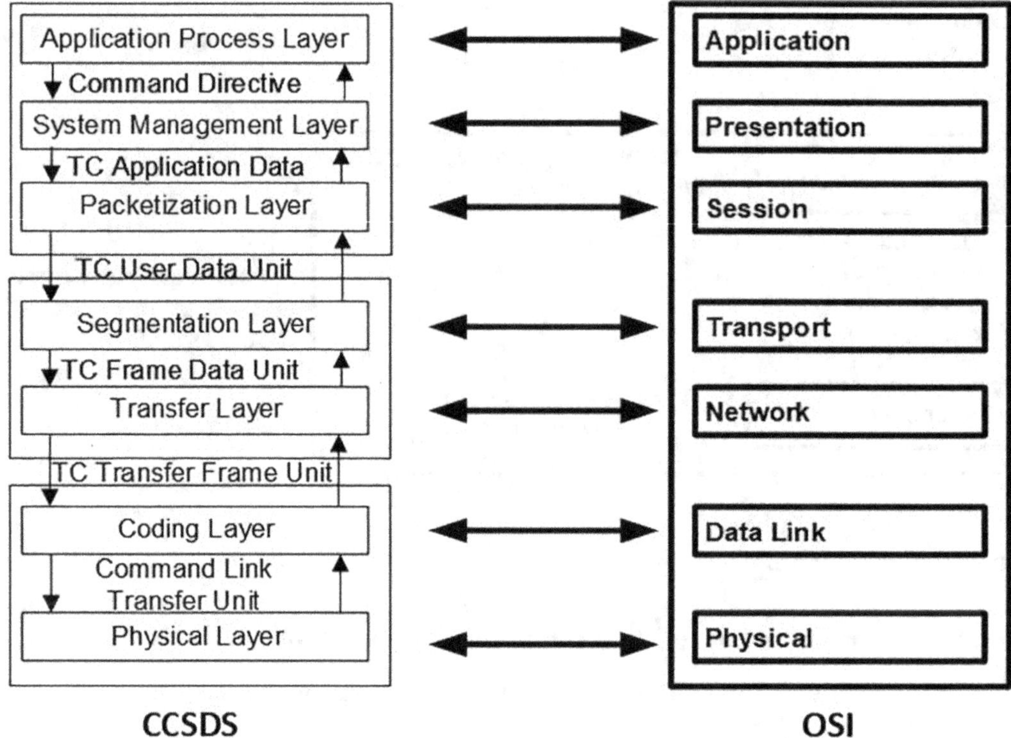

Figure A-2. *CCSDS to OSI protocol stack comparison*

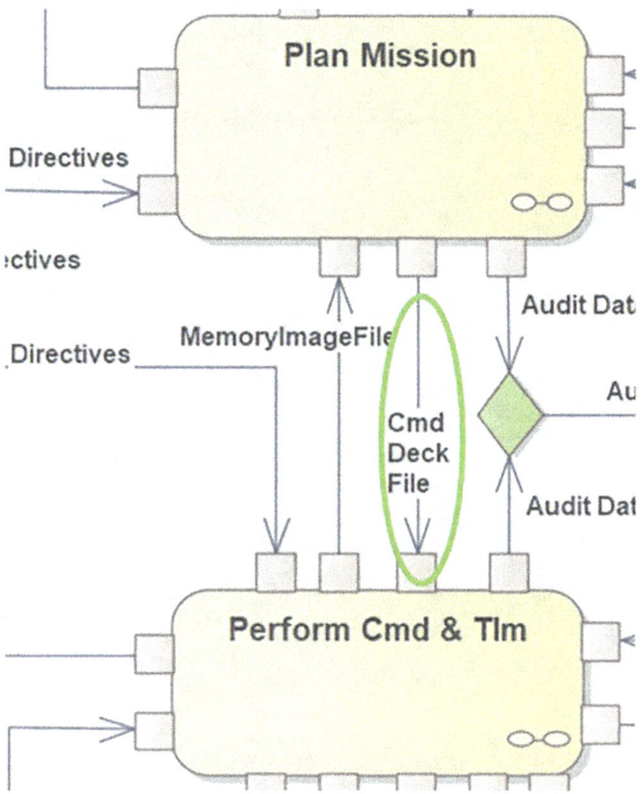

Figure A-3. *Transfer of command decl from plan mission to perform Cmd & Tlm*[1]

---

[1] Author-created image

Modeling Approach Relative to Different Types of System

Management and Engineering Applicability

Managers: This appendix explains how the Modeling and requirements development as covered in this book apply to any type of system. Not just a satellite ground system. skim the lower-level engineering detail and concentrate on the general process and how Modeling helps to define and keep projects on track. An example of a fictitious product, called Product X, has been used in this section to illustrate that the modeling and requirements generation process is the same for the satellite ground system and Product X. The main difference between the two would be the number of model views and number of requirements since the two systems are different.

Engineers: This appendix shows how to relate the concepts in this book to other types of systems. It employs a combination of DoDAF and SysML modeling views to align with the approach used in the satellite ground system. DoDAF was originally developed by the Department of Defense (DoD) to support system acquisition processes in compliance with the Clinger-Cohen Act (Public Law No. 104-106, February 10, 1996; Division E, Subtitle C, Section 5125). Since then, the Unified Architecture Framework (UAF) has been introduced as a more modern alternative, offering improved integration with SysML and system design practices. Consequently, UAF modeling elements can be used in place of their DoDAF counterparts. A comparative overview of DoDAF and UAF is presented in Appendix C.

Framework for Developing a Manufacturing System for Product X

While this methodology draws inspiration from the book's focus on satellite ground systems, it's broadly applicable to the development of a manufacturing system - illustrated here with the fictional Product X. The steps outlined below are intentionally high-level; depending on the complexity and requirements of a real-world system, these may vary in depth.

Phase 1: Define and Frame the Factory Scope

Step 1: Define the Product

Outline the product's functional scope—identify the number of distinct functions and their complexity, as these will drive subsystem definitions. Also, establish the expected production rate based on demand forecasts.

Step 2: Formulate a Need Statement

Based on your product definition, draft a concise statement articulating the mission objective and constraints.

Phase 2: Model System Capabilities

Step 3: Develop a Capability Model

Diagram the system's overarching capabilities - e.g., transferring a product from one production phase to the next - without detailing the implementation.

Step 4: Document Capabilities

Capture the modelled capabilities in a structured document for reference and traceability.

Step 5: Create a High-Level Operational View (OV-1)

Use a visual representation to summarize operations, helping stakeholders understand the system with just a glance.

Phase 3: Subsystems and Requirements

Step 6: Decompose Capabilities into Subsystems

Identify distinct subsystems based on capabilities, then represent them as interconnected nodes in a flow diagram, similar to an OV-2.

Step 7: Generate a Requirements Taxonomy (OV-5a)

Map capabilities to subsystems, then develop specific requirements for each node. Performing this step within the Modeling environment ensures visual and textual coherence.

Step 8: Create Initial Block Definition Diagrams (bdd)

Assign activities to system components. For example, map "move component" to a conveyor. Label blocks with meaningful names and document their performance and physical specifications.

Phase 4: System Specification and Validation

Step 9: Draft Requirements and System Specification Documents

Aggregate requirements into a comprehensive specification. In government projects, this might split into a Technical Requirements Document and a System Specification; commercial projects often consolidate them into one.

Step 10: Align Requirements with Models and Develop Test Plans

Validate requirements across all model views and design test procedures to confirm system functionality.

Phase 5: Functional and Subsystem Design

Step 11: Build a Functional View

Create diagrams showing how each station or node operates. Document corresponding functional requirements.

Step 12: Compile Subsystem Specifications

Consolidate functional requirements gathered above into subsystem-specific specifications.

Step 13: Transition to SysML-Based Modeling

Shift to a set of SysML diagrams to align with engineering conventions. Start with a top-level Activity View that illustrates subsystem interactions and drill down into detailed tasks as needed.

Step 14: Expand Requirements and Test Plans

Incorporate additional requirements developed during SysML modeling into subsystem specs. Refine test steps to validate subsystem-level behaviors.

Phase 6: Managing Conditional Paths and Maintenance

Step 15: Model Sequences for Alternate Production Paths

For operations involving potential deviations (e.g., defect detection and rework), use sequence diagrams to visualize alternative workflows and reintegration into the main production line.

Step 16: Detail Action-Level Activities

Using the developed activity diagrams, expand each node to specify task-level actions.

Step 17: Develop Support Documentation

Summary

Keep in mind that these steps are high-level generalizations of what is required. Do not attempt to use these steps directly to design an assembly line. For example, we have omitted the design of the facility housing the assembly line if a new facility is needed or the modification details for an existing facility.

Leverage the requirements and models to produce or update training materials, repair protocols, and troubleshooting manuals. This ensures long-term sustainability, especially when the original developers are no longer available, providing continuity for maintenance teams and future enhancements.

APPENDIX C

Comparison of Modeling Languages

This comparison does not provide comprehensive coverage of the Unified Architecture Framework (UAF) in relation to DoDAF and SysML. For more detailed information, please refer to the references listed at the end of this appendix.

The following table (Table C-1) summarizes a comparison of UAF with DoDAF and SysML [1]. The approach presented for the satellite ground system example earlier in this book did not address all possible DoDAF views shown in the table, as the intent was to demonstrate the development of requirements using modeling as the basis for the process. In particular, the Project View (PV-2 and PV-3) was not shown in the satellite ground system example. The PV-2 graphical view was replaced with a Gantt chart, which is authorized by the DoD Deputy Chief Information Officer [2]. The PV-3 capability mapping to activity elements was accomplished by using a matrix view. PV-3 mapping to programs and projects was not covered in the example since the intent of the example was to show how to use the model to derive requirements and not the larger acquisition issues addressed by the PV-3.

The UAF is most likely to be used by non-government organizations. However, the use of UAF does not preclude the use of SysML or UML for detailed design, as UAF is an architecture and constraint-based framework rather than a detailed design modeling language [3]. Note that UPDM mentioned earlier in this book has been replaced by UAF; however, there are representations in the operations and services views that are used. For example, the OV-5a and OV-5b views are sometimes used. UAF and SysML have broader differences than UAF and DoDAF/UPDM. Consider the example dealing with Provide Ops Interface in Figure C-1 and Figure C-2 that show how the UAF view focuses on the operational architecture and associated processes, while the SysML view is more explicit in how the system needs to function.

© Dennis Hansen 2025
D. Hansen, *Model-Based Systems Engineering and Requirements Definition*,
https://doi.org/10.1007/979-8-8688-2043-4

Table C-1. *Comparison summary of modeling languages*

Aspect	UAF	DoDAF	SysML
Gather stakeholder needs	Architecture Management (AM) views address stakeholder concerns and drivers.	Not a view per se; inputs like Statements of Need feed into Capability or Operational views.	Captured in Use Cases and stakeholder requirements derived from external statements.
Details of each need	Strategic and Capability domains: Strategies, Objectives, Capabilities, MOEs.	CV-2 (Capability Taxonomy); also, CV-1 and CV-6 provide strategic and capability context.	Use Case and Activity diagrams to describe needs; additional details captured in model notes.
Operational Details	Operational domain: MoPs, operational taxonomy, activity flows, sequences, state transitions, exchanges.	OV-1 to OV-6 describe operational concepts, nodes, activities, and exchanges.	Use Case, Activity, and Sequence diagrams to capture behavior; State Machine diagrams show states.
Services	Service domain: service functions, dependencies, agreements, protocols.	SvcV-1 (Service Context), CV-7 (Capability to Services Mapping), SvcV-2.	Not formally represented; can be modelled via stereotypes or in notes.
Resources	Resources domain: includes physical assets, functions, states, sequences, and exchanges.	SV-1 to SV-5, SvcV-2, and some OV views model resources and interactions.	Captured using Block Definition, Internal Block, and Activity diagrams.
Standards	Standards domain: profiles and standards forecast modeled explicitly.	Standards typically documented as constraints in views or metadata annotations.	Standards treated as constraints; modelled via Requirements or Constraint Blocks.

(continued)

Table C-1. (*continued*)

Aspect	UAF	DoDAF	SysML
Personnel	Personnel domain: roles, responsibilities, skills, organization.	Represented in OV-4 (Organizational Relationships), sometimes included in notes or views.	Modelled manually using stereotype extensions or captured in notes/ requirements.
Security	Security domain: policies, risk assessment, mitigations, enclaves.	Typically modelled via custom extensions or represented in activities/functions.	Represented through Modeling of security-related functions; not natively addressed.
Projects	Projects domain: schedules, milestones, dependencies, and performers.	PV-2 (Project Timelines) and PV-3 (Project to Capability Mapping) support projects.	Schedule data can be included externally; not directly modeled in the SysML core.
Actual Resources	Tracked via the Actual Resources concept in the Resource domain (e.g., Actual Person, Actual Asset).	Not explicitly defined in core views but may be documented in SVs or through metadata.	Must be modelled via custom elements or external data; not part of core SysML semantics.

Comparison of SysML and UML

Feature	SysML	UML
Focus	Systems – hardware, software, data, people	Software systems.
Requirements Modeling	Native support in the language	Not supported as part of the language. Supported by external means.
Parametric Modeling	Parametric diagrams for performance and constraint Modeling	Not supported.

(continued)

Feature	SysML	UML
Structural Modeling	Blocks, ports, and connectors for system components	Classes and objects for software structure.
Behavioral Modeling	Activity, Sequence, State Machine	Activity, Sequence, State Machine, Use Case (note some tools, such as SPARX EA, provide for inclusion of Use Case in the SysML toolbox).
Modeling of Physical Systems	Direct support for hardware, sensors, actuators, etc.	Not included. Must be accomplished separately.
Complexity Management	Provides for hierarchical decomposition—e.g., Internal block diagrams	Supports modularity through the use of packages. Lacks detailed tailoring for systems.
Requirement Traceability	Built into the language and most SysML modeling tools	Not integrated into the language. Traceability handled outside of the language.

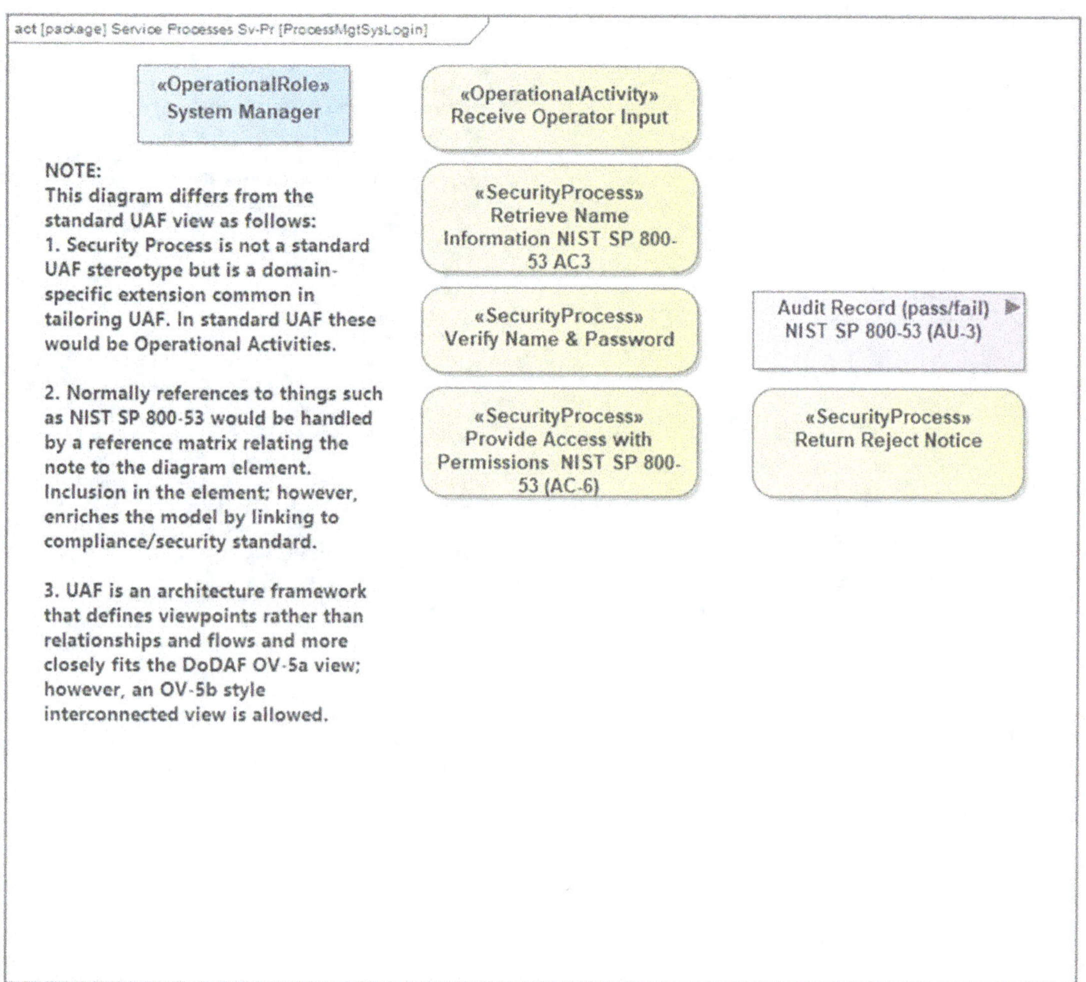

Figure C-1. UAF log-in service process

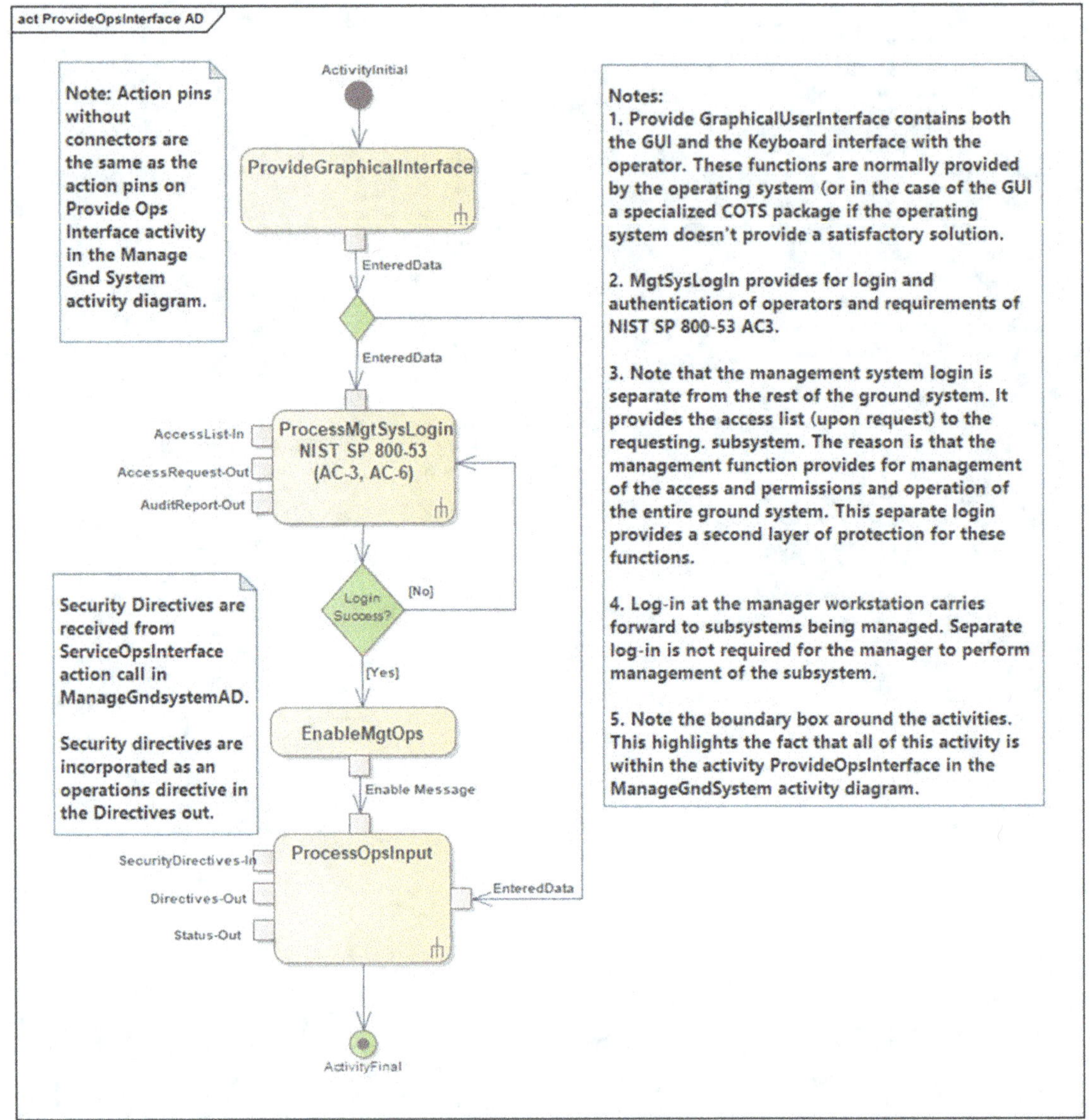

Figure C-2. *SysML log-in activity diagram*

References

[1]   Object Management Group Unified Architecture Framework
      Modeling Language (UAFML), Version 1.3, Normative
      dtc/2024-11-01 November 8, 2024 (`https://www.omg.org/spec/`
      `UAF/1.3/Beta1/UAFML/PDF`)

[2]   DoDAF Viewpoints and Models, Chief Information Officer
      U.S. Department of Defense, (`https://dodcio.defense.gov/`
      `Library/DoD-Architecture-Framework/dodaf20_pv2/`)

[3]   Object management Group Unified Architecture Framework
      (UAF) Domain Metamodel, Version 1.3, Normative
      dtc/2024-11-03 (`https://www.omg.org/spec/UAF/1.3/Beta1/`
      `DMM/PDF`)

Models As a Testing Aid

Guide for Managers and Engineers

After the development and design of a system are completed, the focus shifts to acceptance testing. After system acceptance, testing is used as a part of troubleshooting problems. In both cases, the model provides a guide to the logic of the system interactions and operation. If the incorporation of test planning was accomplished when the model was being developed, the model provides an accurate means of tracing through the system operation and identification of where the source of the problem may be. Keep in mind that discoveries during fault isolation and resolution may show the need for model updates to serve as a basis for system upgrades. Keeping the model current as upgrades are made will close the loop for system sustainment and provide an accurate reflection of the system's design and configuration when used for considering updating the system—that is, security patches, new features, etc.

For analog systems, testing and troubleshooting involved checking the result of an action, and if performance is not as expected, a tracing of the signal through the system was performed to find the problem area. The advent of digital systems shifted the process to examining the results at points along the digital process chain. For modern complex systems, the incorporation of software has increased the issues with employing older techniques. The isolation of a problem now involves evaluation of the logic behind the software in addition to isolating hardware problems.

Problem isolation and repair during sustainment now becomes a cost and system up-time (when revenue depends on providing service to a customer) issue for management. For engineers and technicians, complexity has become a greater challenge than for older systems.

© Dennis Hansen 2025

D. Hansen, *Model-Based Systems Engineering and Requirements Definition*,
https://doi.org/10.1007/979-8-8688-2043-4

Employing the Model for Fault Isolation

When first encountering a system fault, there are a few initial steps to take to begin the analysis. In this example, the system erroneously reconfigures when new functionality is required.

Step 1: Examine the fault encountered.

Step 2: Check the model management views to see

- If the requested configuration is provided for in the design.

- If the configuration is active, check the flow of activities to issue the requested configuration.

- Verify that the configuration directive is properly formatted using information contained in the model.

- Ensure that the directives reach the applicable subsystems.

- Examine the logic of the activities/actions shown in the model relative to the directive received by the subsystem.

- Verify that the data and control flows shown in the model view are active and performing as required.

- Isolate the problem with the subsystem using the model and the included information.

The sequence of actions described above can also be used as a guide in preparing an "In Case of Problems" section of a system manual. When used in a manual, additional details such as expected performance, voltages, frequencies, etc., should be added to the steps outlined above.

Automated System Test

Systems often include a pre-operation test series to ensure proper functionality. These tests are essential for human-rated systems or those performing critical operations that could cause damage to themselves, other systems, or produce misleading results when evaluating performance. The previously outlined test steps, based on the model, requirements, and supporting information, can be integrated into the system to be executed during startup or other critical operations.

- Aircraft preflight

- Factory assembly line activation pretest

- Satellite ground system (system Modeling examples used in this book)

  - Satellite communications subsystems status.

  - Commanding subsystem availability and configuration after initially activating the subsystem. That is, are the supporting subsystems active and are their configurations correct and clear of previous operations?

  - Verify that the telemetry system is configured correctly for use with the intended satellite. Specifically, are the appropriate control files prepared for use?

  - Ensure the correct files are in use for planning the mission of a specific spacecraft.

  - Ensure that interfaces with WAN (wide area network) are configured as required for the mission operations.

These examples are very generic. In practice, for the systems being developed, there will be very specific items to be checked during automated system testing.

Index

I, J

K, L

M

N

O

S

GPSR Compliance
The European Union's (EU) General Product Safety Regulation (GPSR) is a set
of rules that requires consumer products to be safe and our obligations to
ensure this.

If you have any concerns about our products, you can contact us on

ProductSafety@springernature.com

In case Publisher is established outside the EU, the EU authorized
representative is:

Springer Nature Customer Service Center GmbH
Europaplatz 3
69115 Heidelberg, Germany